Transitioning
NAVSEA
to the Future
STRATEGY · BUSINESS · ORGANIZATION

Michael V. Hynes, Harry J. Thie, John E. Peters, Elwyn D. Harris, Robert M. Emmerichs,

Brian Nichiporuk, Malcolm MacKinnon, Denis Rushworth, Maurice Eisenstein,

Jennifer Sloan, Charles Lindenblatt, Charles Cannon

Prepared for the United States Navy

Approved for public release: distribution unlimited

RAND

National Defense Research Institute

The research described in this report was conducted for the U.S. Navy within the Acquisition and Technology Policy Center of RAND's National Defense Research Institute, a federally funded research and development center supported by the Office of the Secretary of Defense, the Joint Staff, the unified commands, and the defense agencies under Contract DASW01-01-C-0004.

Library of Congress Cataloging-in-Publication Data

Transitioning NAVSEA to the future: strategy, business, and organization / Michael Hynes ... [et al.].
    p. cm.
    MR-1303
    Includes bibliographical references.
    ISBN 0-8330-2991-6
    1. United States. Navy. 2. Sea-power—United States. 3. United States. Naval Sea Systems Command. I. Hynes, Michael V., 1950–

VA50 .K44 2002
359'.03'0973—dc21

    2001019633

RAND is a nonprofit institution that helps improve policy and decisionmaking through research and analysis. RAND® is a registered trademark. RAND's publications do not necessarily reflect the opinions or policies of its research sponsors.

Cover design by Maritta Tapanainen

Published 2002 by RAND
1700 Main Street, P.O. Box 2138, Santa Monica, CA 90407-2138
1200 South Hayes Street, Arlington, VA 22202-5050
201 North Craig Street, Suite 202, Pittsburgh, PA 15213-1516
RAND URL: http://www.rand.org/
To order RAND documents or to obtain additional information, contact
Distribution Services: Telephone: (310) 451-7002;
Fax: (310) 451-6915; Email: order@rand.org

The Naval Sea Systems Command (NAVSEA) is the largest of the Navy's Systems Commands. Its responsibilities span all aspects of the life cycle of ships, submarines, and their components—from acquisition through support to the Navy Program Executive Officers (PEOs), to in-service engineering and maintenance, to retirement/disposal. To assist NAVSEA in providing this full spectrum of services in the twenty-first century in an environment of continuing downsizing, declining Research, Development, Test, and Evaluation (RDT&E) infrastructure and resources, and increasing competition from the private sector for scientific, engineering, and management resources, this report presents a three-phase planning methodology to identify the implications for NAVSEA's products, services, and organizational alignments within a decade in the future, in 2007.

The planning methodology captures three aspects of the Navy and NAVSEA in 2007: (1) NAVSEA's implementation of Navy strategy, (2) NAVSEA's product emphasis, and (3) NAVSEA's organization. NAVSEA must align its products and services to support Navy strategy. NAVSEA must allocate its resources to best realize Navy strategy. And NAVSEA must organize to best accomplish Navy strategy. The information considered in this report is current as of September 2000.

The planning methodology documented in this report should be of use to other government organizations and to commercial organizations that are engaged in business-planning decisions involving markets, products, activities, technologies, people, facilities, and organizational realignment.

This research was sponsored by Vice Admiral (VADM) G. P. Nanos, Commander of NAVSEA, and was conducted in the Acquisition and Technology and Forces and Resources policy centers of RAND's National Defense Research Institute (NDRI). NDRI is a federally funded research and development center sponsored by the Office of the Secretary of Defense, the Joint Staff, the unified commands, and the defense agencies.

CONTENTS

TABLES

As with any business, the Naval Sea Systems Command (NAVSEA) must evaluate itself in relation to the uncertainty of the future and its current environment. As part of the Department of Defense (DoD), NAVSEA is confronted with pressures to continue downsizing; with declining Research, Development, Test, and Evaluation (RDT&E) infrastructure and resources; and with strong competition from the private sector for scientific, engineering, and management resources. At the same time that it must meet its responsibilities, which span all aspects of the life cycle of ships, submarines, and their components—from acquisition through support to the Navy Program Executive Officers (PEOs), to in-service maintenance and engineering, to retirement/disposal—it must recognize and accommodate both force modernization and sustainment of vital long-term capabilities in the face of declining resources. These tensions require that NAVSEA explore those innovative best practices experimented with and exercised by contemporary organizations, both public and private, in order to avoid trying to do everything well itself while becoming increasingly constrained.

The work of RAND researchers was to formulate a methodology for making business-planning decisions involving the activities, products, markets, technologies, people, and facilities of NAVSEA, initially with a view toward organizational realignment. The time horizon for those plans was 2007, so that the analysis results would be far enough in the future that simple extrapolations of the current status quo would not be appropriate, yet not so far in the future that forecasts of future geopolitical, technological, and business environments would be totally unreliable, and so that a possible implementation of results could influence recommendations for budget cycles before 2007.

Our work supporting NAVSEA organizational decisionmaking involved a three-phase methodology: analysis of the strategic environment in 2007 to identify products, technologies, and activities that are central to the success of current and future naval strategy; a quantitative analysis of those products, technologies, and activities, as well as markets, to further determine which products would have the highest importance and widest breadth for the NAVSEA of 2007;

analysis of potential organizational designs/structures to capitalize on commonalities—*centrality*—among products/personnel/technologies to achieve goals for least cost or high differentiation (i.e., superior value in product quality, special features, or in-service maintenance—*niche specialization*) for NAVSEA customers.

Each analysis began with a review of documents pertinent to the subject, site visits to Navy or NAVSEA organizations to gather additional information or participation in presentations, and team discussions; then selection of a methodology most appropriate for achieving the desired goal; and finally iterations of the methodology to complete a framework for planning. Many times, the methodology for the framework was a RAND-developed tool. The research team was the same for each phase of the analysis and participated in the gathering and analysis of data on NAVSEA. The main methodologies underpinning the three analyses are presented in Table S.1.

Table S.1

Methodological Underpinnings of Study

Strategic Environment and Implications	
Assumption-Based Planning	Identifies the assumptions within planning documents, looks for vulnerabilities in those assumptions, identifies indicators that an assumption is failing, and enables shaping and hedging actions to be taken to add robustness to a plan
Strategy-to-tasks framework	Links national security strategy to NAVSEA mission
Markets and Products and Activities to Fulfill Them	
Market analysis	Identifies forces that will drive growth in emphasis on specific markets
Priority setting/portfolio analysis	Ranks products, markets, activities according to specific measures, then arranges those ranked elements against two of the measures, with different management actions assigned to different ranks
Organization	
Organizational design approach	
Industry structure	Provides context in which the future NAVSEA corporation is intended to operate
Focus	Segments NAVSEA's activities into conceptual business units
Shape	Identifies the horizontal and vertical integration of business units
Size	Develops a methodology to assess NAVSEA's size, given focus and shape, and to determine boundaries for what is inside NAVSEA and what is outside it

STRATEGIC ENVIRONMENT AND IMPLICATIONS

The strategic analysis began with a survey of the policies, directives and mandates, and similar documents that determine the shape of naval strategy, such as the historical record for the range of naval strategies; the President's security strategy, such as Clinton's *A National Security Strategy of Engagement and Enlargement* (The White House, 1995); National Military Strategy, the current one of which organizes around the terms "deter, shape, prepare, respond" (Joint Chiefs of Staff, 1997); *Joint Vision 2020* (Joint Chiefs of Staff, 2000) and the current Navy vision of its operations, *Forward . . . from the Sea* (Department of the Navy, 1994) and tomorrow's vision in *Operational Maneuver from the Sea* (U.S. Marine Corps, 1997).

We then considered forces and influences in the international security environment and organic to the U.S. military that might plausibly bring pressure on the current strategy by confronting it with more-able adversaries, opposing it with innovative approaches that render critical aspects of it less effective, or that deprive the Navy and Marine Corps of essential resources, ships, and other assets. For example, for the 2000–2010 decade, we concluded that fears and suspicions of Washington's plans and motives might cause Russia to compete with the United States through limited modernization of its strategic nuclear force and that the People's Republic of China's procurement patterns reveal a fairly ambitious effort at power-projection modernization.

Next, using Assumption-Based Planning (ABP), we reviewed the available evidence to determine whether there are indications that any threatening developments just posited seem to be taking shape. We concluded that major concerns about the advent of a Revolution in Military Affairs in a potentially hostile force seems very unlikely in the near-term future under consideration. The emergence of a peer competitor likewise seems improbable.

Nevertheless, we identified forces at work—creative foes who contrive means of attack that leave their identities unknown—that could bring pressure on the current strategy, even in the absence of heavy defense investments and major arms transfers, undermining the quality of deterrence. Likewise, we judged that the Navy and Marine Corps role in forward presence for shaping and preparing the theater against dangerous contingencies and unforeseen developments could be undercut if regional adversaries succeed in intimidating local U.S. allies into withdrawing overflight and basing rights.

Finally, we identified the strategic imperatives that must be strengthened and revitalized to maintain the current naval strategy: to deter aggression by maintaining information dominance and potent forces; to shape attitudes and events in key regions through forward presence and the ability to protect the United States' partners; to prepare for all contingencies by maintaining a full complement of scalable capabilities and, again, through forward presence and information dominance; and to respond to near-term regional threats through network-centric warfare (i.e., integrated and networked combat systems) and, again, scalable capabilities and protection of partners. We presented NAVSEA's specific functions, products, and outputs essential to each endeavor toward the bottom of a framework, such as that for Deter in Figure S.1.

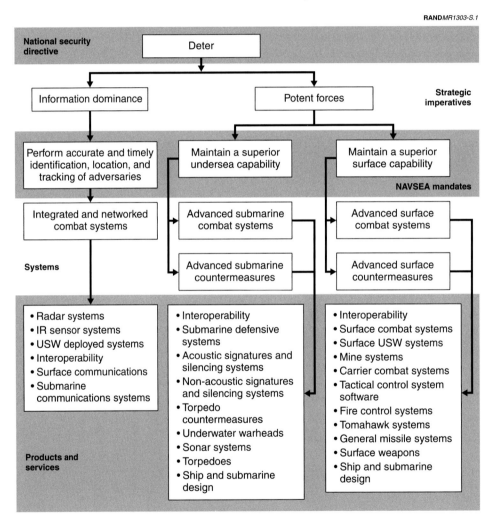

RAND*MR1303-S.1*

Figure S.1—A Strategy-to-Tasks Framework for Deterrence

FROM STRATEGIC IMPERATIVES TO STRATEGIC INTENT FOR COMPETITIVE ADVANTAGE: MARKETS AND THE PRODUCTS AND ACTIVITIES THAT FULFILL THEM

Simply knowing which of various products and activities enjoy high strategic priority is insufficient. For NAVSEA to optimize them, it must first understand the needs and preferences of the Navy markets that will consume the command's products. These factors will influence the specific characteristics of individual products, the way they operate, and the way they are maintained. Our next analysis was directed at understanding the markets, products, and activities for which NAVSEA should be configured in 2007, and the interrelationships (interactions and linkages between and among them) for which NAVSEA should be configured in 2007.

Market Analysis

This required, first, identifying and defining *markets* (the sum of transactions and opportunities for transaction defined by products, customer needs and preferences, and credible competitors) for NAVSEA. The mandates used in the final frameworks in the strategy analysis provided a bridge to this business analysis. We used them as the definitions of individual markets, rearranging and combining some, as well as creating a new market, Acquisition Support. We then performed an analysis of strategic, technology, and business drivers that would be forcing the *emphasis* on certain markets (how the needs and preferences of the customer in a given market are changing and what those needs will be in the future) to grow more than that on others in 2007 (a market analysis) and to develop measures of the relationship between products, markets, and activities and a rating system for those measures so that an iterative portfolio analysis could be performed to distinguish the most important products in the most markets (*central products*) from superior-value, highly differentiated products (*niche products*) having one or two markets.

Portfolio Analysis

To perform such an analysis, it was necessary to gather as much information about NAVSEA and its components as possible to form comprehensive databases, or lists, that could be related to each other. We began with a review of documents on NAVSEA's holdings, or core equities—*Core Equities—Red Team Review* (NAVSEA, 1999a)—which inventoried elements within individual NAVSEA centers or units, the functions and services they provide, type of knowledge, personnel required, facilities within the unit, educational background, etc., with a view to determining which equities should be retained in-house and which could be outsourced.

Our intent was to assist NAVSEA managers in making such determinations across NAVSEA, rather than unit by unit, and to identify commonalities, or linkages, that could optimize the *activities* (processes carried out by a set of organized resources—technologies, personnel, and facilities) to create products offered in markets throughout NAVSEA. For this reason, we also reviewed reports on and inventories of technology and educational needs for the Navy/Marine Corps/shipbuilding industry in the early twenty-first century: Naval Studies Board–National Research Council (NSB–NRC, 1997a), National Research Council (NRC, 1996), ONI (1998), and Gaffney and Saalfeld (1999); interviewed Navy personnel; brought our subject-matter expertise to bear; and made qualitative assessments.

By relating products to markets and to NAVSEA's activities, we were able to arrive at measures having important implications for NAVSEA business planning and organization. Two such measures are relative product importance and market breadth. *Relative product importance* expresses the extent to which a product having a specific importance from 6 to 0 (see The RAND Product-Rating System section of Appendix C for a complete discussion) satisfies customer needs and preferences in a given market, summed across all markets to which the product contributes. The 6, 3, 1, and 0 scores represent the importance specific to each product for each of the 15 markets identified for NAVSEA. A product with a specific importance of 6 defines a market; a product with a score of 3 is important to that market. A product with a score of 1 supports that market. And a product with a score of 0 is not important to that market. This scale is different from the scale used for the different measures, such as the 3, 2, 1, 0 scale for the market-emphasis-growth factor, shown in Table S.2. The table is a spreadsheet of products against markets and shows scores derived by adding or multiplying specific-product-importance scores and market-emphasis-growth factors. *Market breadth* indicates the total number of markets to which the product contributes. The two measures are plotted for all 108 NAVSEA products, in Figure S.2.

The first number in parentheses in each cell in Figure S.2 corresponds to the scoring bin into which the product falls for market breadth in Figure 3.9; the second number in the parentheses corresponds to the scoring bin into which the product falls for relative product importance inFigure 3.8. The products in the High bin are given a 3; the products in the Very Low bin are given a 0. Figure S.2 (Figure 3.10 in the main text) is a cross plot, or grid, showing the interaction of market breadth with relative product importance. The products in cell (3, 3) are the only ones that were in the High bin in both Figures 3.8 and 3.9—i.e., they have both High relative importance and High market breadth. The products in cell (0, 0) in the lower left-hand corner were in the Very Low bin

Table S.2

Section of Product–Market Observables Rating Sheet

Major Product Groups and Products, with Specific Product-Importance Score by Market	NAVSEA Market (and Market-Emphasis-Growth Factor)[a]															Relative Product Importance	Market Breadth	Market-Breadth Growth	Relative Product-Importance Growth
	AAW (0)	AMW (2)	ASU (1)	ASW (2)	CCC (1)	IW (1)	INT (3)	OPA (2)	OMW (0)	MOB (0)	MOS-NCO (0)	ACQ (3)	NSW (0)	STW (2)	DEF (3)				
Test, evaluate, assess																			
USW Operational Range Assessment Systems	0	0	3	3	0	0	0	0	0	0	0	0	0	0	1	7	3	6	12
USW Analysis	0	0	3	3	0	0	0	0	0	0	1	1	3	0	3	14	6	6	21
Missile Simulators, Trainers, and Test/Diagnostic Equipment	3	1	0	0	0	0	0	3	0	0	0	0	0	0	3	10	4	7	17
Weapon and Combat System Assessment Systems	3	3	3	3	0	0	0	0	3	0	1	0	3	3	3	25	9	10	30
Readiness Analysis	3	3	3	3	0	0	0	0	3	3	1	1	3	3	3	29	11	13	33
Navy Metrology Systems	1	1	1	1	1	0	0	3	1	1	1	0	1	1	1	15	12	13	17
MIW Simulation Software	0	1	0	1	0	0	0	0	6	0	1	1	1	0	3	14	7	10	16
Coastal Warfare Analysis	1	3	1	1	0	0	0	0	3	3	1	1	6	1	3	24	11	13	23
Aircraft Modeling and Simulation	0	0	0	0	0	0	0	0	0	0	0	0	0	0	0	0	0	0	0
Theater Warfare Analysis	3	3	3	3	0	0	0	0	3	3	1	1	3	3	3	29	11	13	30
Bullets																			

(Continues to include all product groups and products)

[a] See Figure 3.5 for market-emphasis-growth scores.

RAND*MR1303-TS.2*

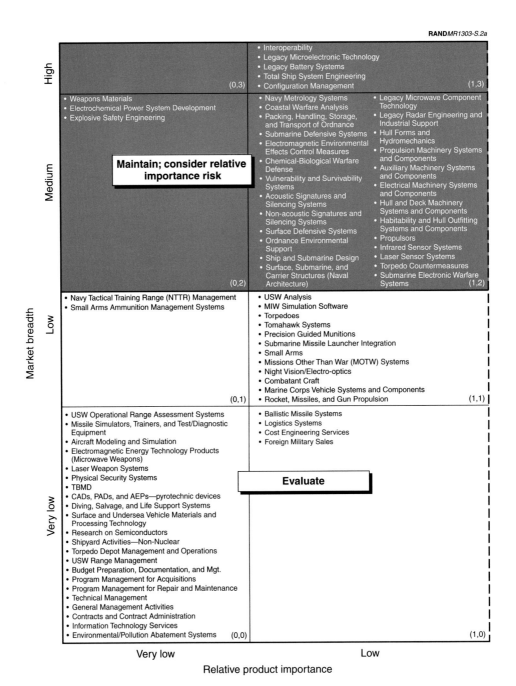

RANDMR1303-S.2a

Figure S.2—All NAVSEA Products Are Plotted for Market Breadth and Relative Product Importance (with product names indicated in each quadrant)

RANDMR1303-S.2b

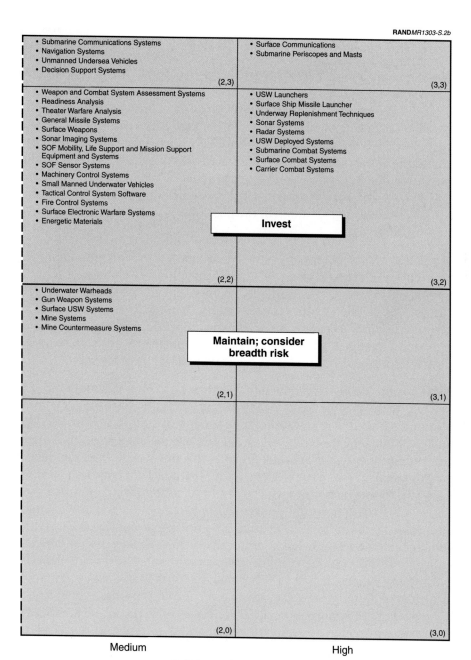

Figure S.2—Cont'd.

for both relative product importance and market breadth. The cell numbering is a convenient code for organizing management decisions.

Among the implications of this plot are that products that are important across a range of markets and are simultaneously of High importance could be considered candidates for new or continued investment; examples of such products are Surface Communications and Submarine Periscopes and Masts. Products that are restricted to few markets and have Low importance are candidates for repositioning in the marketplace: Either find a valuable use for such products in one or two markets or outsource the product. Products that appear to be risks in terms of market breadth only or importance only warrant maintaining, but with continued consideration of the possibility that they might slip into the Evaluate quadrant.

Investment decisions have many dimensions, not just breadth and importance of products, but process change for products, technology change for products, personnel involvement in products, facility use by products, and product/activity associations with business units. The analyses of products and markets involved a succession of two-dimensional grids like Figure S.2, as diagrammed in Figure S.3, which indicates that a manager's decision can be refined by referring back to a grid from the earlier part of the analysis.

Likewise for markets. A market rated High for growing in emphaiss in the drivers part of the market analysis may use products that have only Medium or Low importance. For determining a product's centrality within NAVSEA's portfolio, all markets are not equal. In Figure S.4, we once again plot relative product importance against market breadth, this time weighting each measure by growth factors (rated as 3 for High, 2 for Medium, 1 for Low, and 0 for Very Low growth) for the markets to which the products contribute, summed across all markets. We assign portfolio-level centrality to products that we judge to have at least Medium breadth in markets growing in emphasis or Medium importance in markets growing in emphasis, as long as they are not Very Low on either dimension. The remaining products were submitted to an analysis of their centrality to specific niches. This analysis resulted in a spectrum ranging from products defining at least one market through products that are not defining but are still important in at least one market, to those that are clearly in a supporting role, contributing to the market, but not in a major way (somewhat like indirect labor as opposed to direct labor) (see Figure S.5).

To make the assessments for the associations of products/markets/processes/technology/personnel/facilities, we created spreadsheets listing one set of components along the left side and another set across the top, together with a corresponding score/factor or product/sum. All told, spreadsheets linked

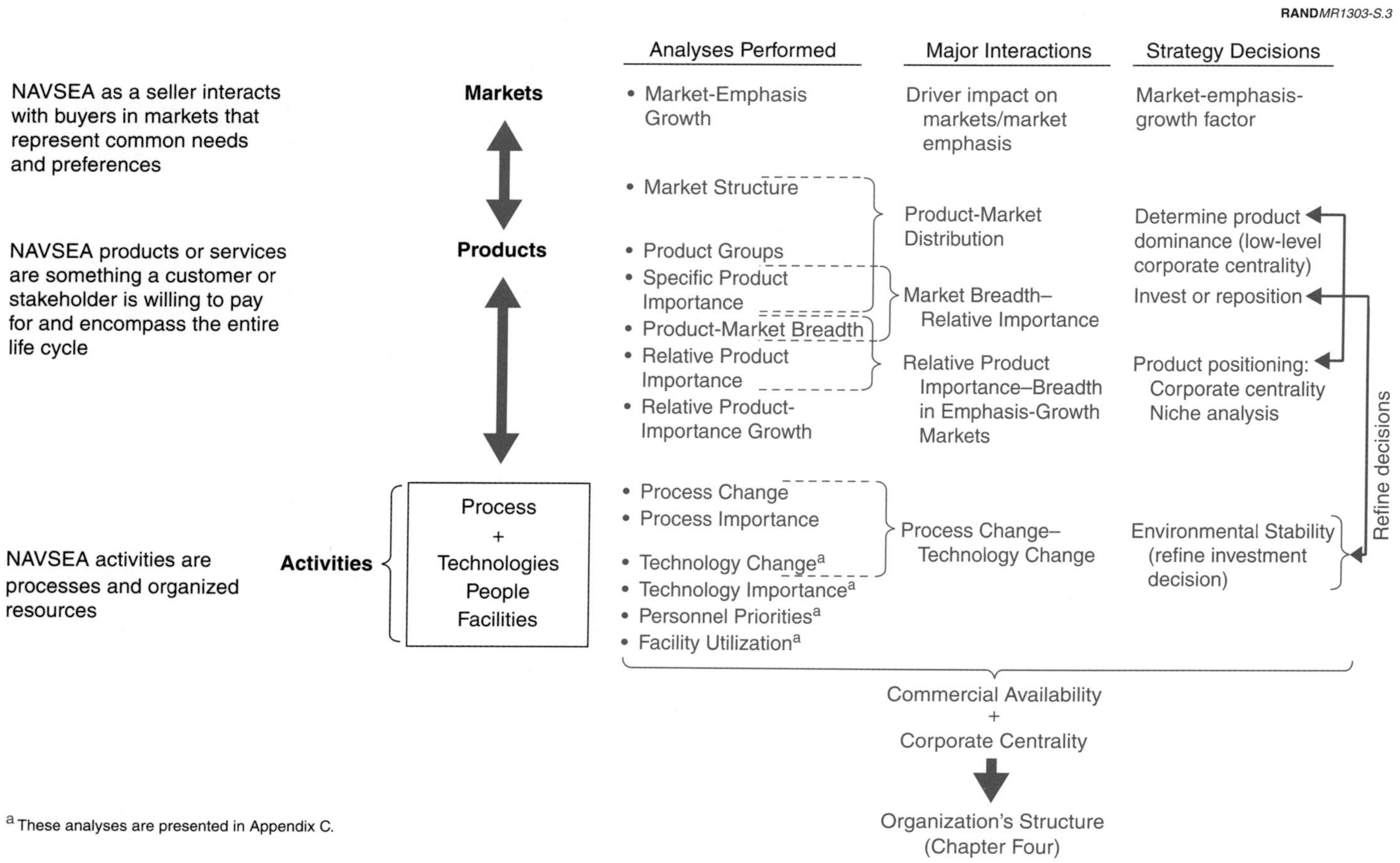

RAND*MR1303-S.3*

Markets

NAVSEA as a seller interacts with buyers in markets that represent common needs and preferences

Products

NAVSEA products or services are something a customer or stakeholder is willing to pay for and encompass the entire life cycle

Activities

NAVSEA activities are processes and organized resources

Process
+
Technologies
People
Facilities

Analyses Performed

- Market-Emphasis Growth
- Market Structure
- Product Groups
- Specific Product Importance
- Product-Market Breadth
- Relative Product Importance
- Relative Product-Importance Growth
- Process Change
- Process Importance
- Technology Change[a]
- Technology Importance[a]
- Personnel Priorities[a]
- Facility Utilization[a]

Major Interactions

Driver impact on markets/market emphasis

Product-Market Distribution

Market Breadth– Relative Importance

Relative Product Importance–Breadth in Emphasis-Growth Markets

Process Change– Technology Change

Commercial Availability
+
Corporate Centrality

Organization's Structure (Chapter Four)

Strategy Decisions

Market-emphasis-growth factor

Determine product dominance (low-level corporate centrality)

Invest or reposition

Product positioning: Corporate centrality Niche analysis

Environmental Stability (refine investment decision)

Refine decisions

[a] These analyses are presented in Appendix C.

Figure S.3—RAND Market-Product-Activity Model, Showing Analyses Conducted in Each Stage

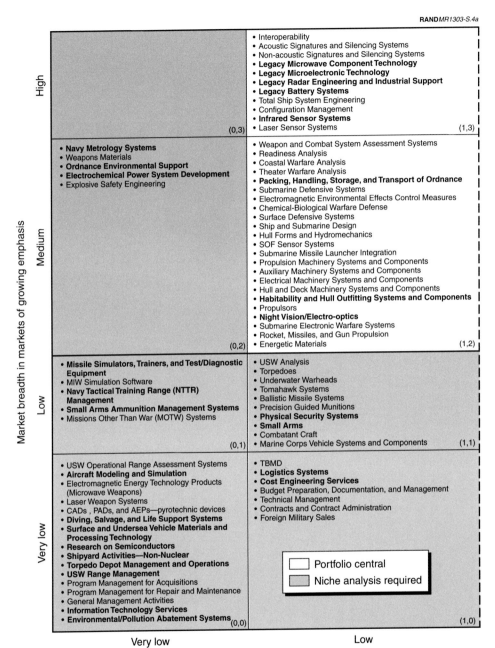

RAND*MR1303-S.4a*

Interoperability etc. (top-right High/Low cell):
- Interoperability
- Acoustic Signatures and Silencing Systems
- Non-acoustic Signatures and Silencing Systems
- **Legacy Microwave Component Technology**
- **Legacy Microelectronic Technology**
- **Legacy Radar Engineering and Industrial Support**
- **Legacy Battery Systems**
- Total Ship System Engineering
- Configuration Management
- **Infrared Sensor Systems**
- Laser Sensor Systems   (1,3)

(0,3)

Medium / Very low cell:
- **Navy Metrology Systems**
- Weapons Materials
- **Ordnance Environmental Support**
- **Electrochemical Power System Development**
- Explosive Safety Engineering

(0,2)

Medium / Low cell:
- Weapon and Combat System Assessment Systems
- Readiness Analysis
- Coastal Warfare Analysis
- Theater Warfare Analysis
- **Packing, Handling, Storage, and Transport of Ordnance**
- Submarine Defensive Systems
- Electromagnetic Environmental Effects Control Measures
- Chemical-Biological Warfare Defense
- Surface Defensive Systems
- Ship and Submarine Design
- Hull Forms and Hydromechanics
- SOF Sensor Systems
- Submarine Missile Launcher Integration
- Propulsion Machinery Systems and Components
- Auxiliary Machinery Systems and Components
- Electrical Machinery Systems and Components
- Hull and Deck Machinery Systems and Components
- **Habitability and Hull Outfitting Systems and Components**
- Propulsors
- **Night Vision/Electro-optics**
- Submarine Electronic Warfare Systems
- Rocket, Missiles, and Gun Propulsion
- Energetic Materials   (1,2)

Low / Very low cell:
- **Missile Simulators, Trainers, and Test/Diagnostic Equipment**
- MIW Simulation Software
- **Navy Tactical Training Range (NTTR) Management**
- **Small Arms Ammunition Management Systems**
- Missions Other Than War (MOTW) Systems

(0,1)

Low / Low cell:
- USW Analysis
- Torpedoes
- Underwater Warheads
- Tomahawk Systems
- Ballistic Missile Systems
- Precision Guided Munitions
- **Physical Security Systems**
- **Small Arms**
- Combatant Craft
- Marine Corps Vehicle Systems and Components   (1,1)

Very low / Very low cell:
- USW Operational Range Assessment Systems
- **Aircraft Modeling and Simulation**
- Electromagnetic Energy Technology Products (Microwave Weapons)
- Laser Weapon Systems
- CADs , PADs, and AEPs—pyrotechnic devices
- **Diving, Salvage, and Life Support Systems**
- **Surface and Undersea Vehicle Materials and Processing Technology**
- **Research on Semiconductors**
- **Shipyard Activities—Non-Nuclear**
- **Torpedo Depot Management and Operations**
- **USW Range Management**
- Program Management for Acquisitions
- Program Management for Repair and Maintenance
- General Management Activities
- **Information Technology Services**
- **Environmental/Pollution Abatement Systems** (0,0)

Very low / Low cell:
- TBMD
- **Logistics Systems**
- **Cost Engineering Services**
- Budget Preparation, Documentation, and Management
- Technical Management
- Contracts and Contract Administration
- Foreign Military Sales

☐ Portfolio central
▨ Niche analysis required

(1,0)

Very low   Low

Relative product importance in markets of growing emphasis

Market breadth in markets of growing emphasis — High / Medium / Low / Very low

NOTE: Bold text indicates that existing credible commercial sources are available.

Figure S.4—Products in Figure S.2 by Market-Breadth Growth and Relative Product-Importance Growth

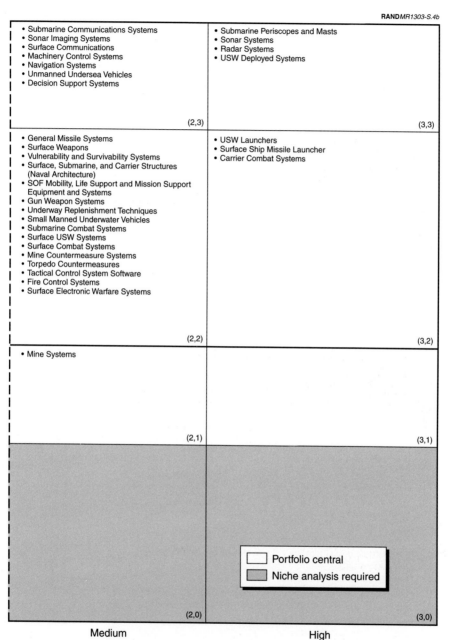

RAND_MR1303-S.4b_

• Submarine Communications Systems • Sonar Imaging Systems • Surface Communications • Machinery Control Systems • Navigation Systems • Unmanned Undersea Vehicles • Decision Support Systems (2,3)	• Submarine Periscopes and Masts • Sonar Systems • Radar Systems • USW Deployed Systems (3,3)

• General Missile Systems
• Surface Weapons
• Vulnerability and Survivability Systems
• Surface, Submarine, and Carrier Structures
  (Naval Architecture)
• SOF Mobility, Life Support and Mission Support
  Equipment and Systems
• Gun Weapon Systems
• Underway Replenishment Techniques
• Small Manned Underwater Vehicles
• Submarine Combat Systems
• Surface USW Systems
• Surface Combat Systems
• Mine Countermeasure Systems
• Torpedo Countermeasures
• Tactical Control System Software
• Fire Control Systems
• Surface Electronic Warfare Systems
 	
(2,2)
	• USW Launchers
	• Surface Ship Missile Launcher
	• Carrier Combat Systems
	
	(3,2)

• Mine Systems (2,1)	(3,1)
(2,0)	☐ Portfolio central ▨ Niche analysis required (3,0)

Medium   High

Relative product importance in markets of growing emphasis

Figure S.4—Cont'd.

RAND*MR1303-S.5*

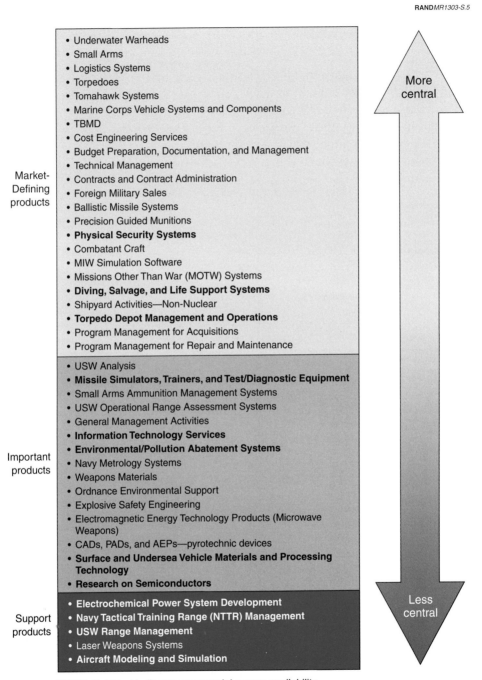

NOTE: Bold text indicates commercial-source availability.

Figure S.5—Spectrum of Niche Centrality for "Niche analysis required" Products in Figure S.4

together 15 markets, 108 products, 49 processes, 1,200 activities, 70 technologies, 319 occupations for 45,000 people, 195 facilities, and 7 major business units.

It is important to realize that the measures are most meaningful when incorporated in the broader context of *strategic intent*—the shifting of *enterprises,* or primary purposeful activities of the organization, what Porter (1990, p. 37) calls positioning for competitive advantage. Such shifts create a need for change in NAVSEA's organizational structure. Consequently, although the research team developed the measures in this phase of the study, we employed them more fully when we analyzed potential organizational structures.

ORGANIZATIONAL STRUCTURE

Our initial plan for this phase had four parts: *industry context,* to describe the scope and structure of industries in which NAVSEA operates; *focus,* to segment NAVSEA's activities into conceptual business units; *shape,* to identify the horizontal and vertical integration of business units; and *size,* to develop a methodology for assessing NAVSEA's size in relation to the focus and shape of the future organization. The plan was revised to exclude the size analysis.

Industry Context

Industry comprises all organizations, public or private, that are in the business of providing, supporting, or disposing of naval ships. More broadly, 95 percent of NAVSEA contract dollars go to 10 industries, Ship-Building and Ship-Repairing being the largest, with Engineering Services next. Over 60 percent of the dollar value of the Ship-Building industry in the United States flows through NAVSEA.

Focus

In this part of the analysis, we segmented NAVSEA into conceptual *business units,* entities that focus on a well-defined set of products, markets, functions, etc., and whose structure is also determined by its customers, which for a NAVSEA unit could be the PEOs, the Type Commanders, or the Fleet; and certain stakeholders in NAVSEA—those accruing the benefits or sustaining the costs of NAVSEA's operations—such as the Chief of Naval Operations and the Assistant Secretary of the Navy for Research, Development and Acquisition. We purposely avoided identifying and characterizing the existing NAVSEA business units. It is not our intent to have readers infer comparisons between the business units we identify and the existing organizational structure of NAVSEA.

Therefore, we have elected to segment NAVSEA into "conceptual" business units that do not reflect the current business-unit structure of NAVSEA.

For its customers, NAVSEA's principal advantage over possible competitors is its knowledge of the Fleet, which has implications for innovation in naval capabilities and efficiency in Fleet support. NAVSEA's stakeholders are primarily interested in fleet readiness and capability improvement—interests that, in turn, have implications for NAVSEA's organization.

To arrive at a basic portfolio of business units, we developed and applied a work activity hierarchy to NAVSEA's future activities, as identified in the preceding phase, taking account of customer and stakeholder interests. Activities fell into groups suggesting seven units: Managing Ships; Providing Program- and Project-Management Services; Resourcing Science, Engineering, and Acquisition Professionals; Managing Infrastructure; Organizing and Managing Existing Knowledge; Creating and Managing New Knowledge; and Providing Systems-Engineering Services. For each business unit, we defined product, market, and competitors; described the benefits it offers to customers relative to those offered by competitors; proposed a strategy; and suggested a structure. Business units and their component structures are shown in Figure S.6.

Shape

The strategic intent of a corporation determines corporate organizational structure. During the course of our study, NAVSEA articulated a comprehensive corporate strategy. This strategy built on the extensive work of the past several years (NAVSEA, 1999a) and was formulated with the participation of the entire NAVSEA organization, parts of which have produced forward-looking business-unit strategies and detailed business plans (NAVSEA, 1999b, n.d.). While not trying to propose a specific strategic intent for NAVSEA in 2007, we used the current corporate strategic plan, other public pronouncements of senior leadership, and our discussions with senior leaders to identify potential statements of strategic intent as it might exist in 2007.

We began with the structure shown in Figure S.6, in which all business units are viewed as organizationally equivalent and report directly to Headquarters. Then, working from our alternative potential statements of intent, we posited four different ways to aggregate those units into business lines reflecting those statements: industry positioning, market/customer, competency, and product life cycle. (We show organization charts for two of these statements.)

Industry Positioning. Product differentiation and low cost are the strategic intent for competing within the industry. For the low-cost part, we made the

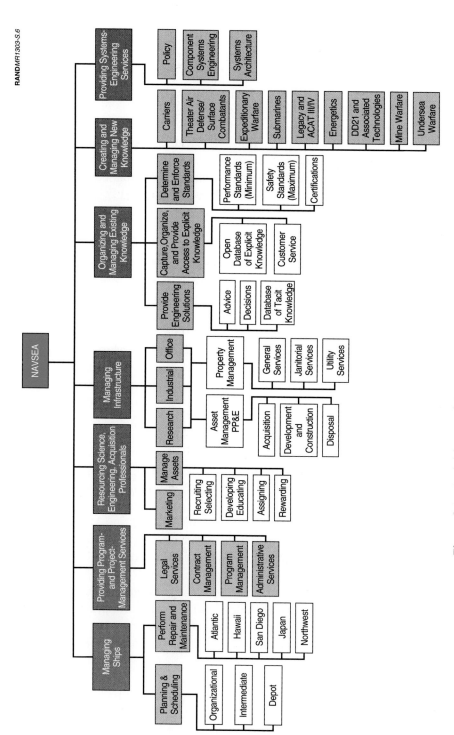

Figure S.6—Activities Portfolio of NAVSEA Corporate Structure

Managing Ships unit a low-cost business line whose products are not well differentiated from those of potential competitors. This business line, which could also be referred to as Readiness Enhancement, provides stakeholder value to the Chief of Naval Operations (CNO) by serving Type Commanders as customers. The other general activities all produce high-cost, highly differentiated products that fall into two major business lines. The first, which provides stakeholder value to the Assistant Secretary of the Navy (Research, Development and Acquisition) (ASN [RDA]), is Managing Knowledge. It comprises not only the business units for managing existing and new knowledge, but also the Providing Systems-Engineering business unit. It serves the PEOs, the Type Commanders, and the operating Fleet as customers. The second, of value to the other two business lines and to the PEOs, is Managing [Critical] Resources, i.e., management of programs and projects, of infrastructure, and of professional staff.

Market/Customer. NAVSEA can be described as in the business of meeting current and future naval needs. If that were the organizing principle, NAVSEA would have two lines of business—Enhancing Readiness and Developing Future Capabilities (see Figure S.7). Viewed from the customer's point of view (instead of as an industry-positioning strategy), Enhancing Readiness must include not only Managing Ships but also Organizing and Managing Existing Knowledge. Developing future capabilities means, in effect, providing support to the PEOs, and includes all the other generalized activities except for Managing [Corporate] Infrastructure, which is here subordinated directly to NAVSEA Headquarters (as it is under the next two alternatives also).

Competency. The third organizational alternative is based on the hypothesis that NAVSEA's basic strategic intent is to identify, develop, and sustain core organizational competencies. If there is a common competency that influences NAVSEA's value to all its stakeholders, it is, as the preceding phase of the analysis revealed, engineering. In this paradigm, then, Creating and Managing New Knowledge, Providing Systems-Engineering Services, and Resourcing Science, Engineering, and Acquisition Professionals are combined with the solutions- and standards-oriented activities of Organizing and Managing Existing Knowledge. Managing Ships, which incorporates the remaining aspects of organizing and managing existing knowledge, and program and project management services are then business lines of secondary importance. These would compete on the basis of cost and, if they turn out to be uncompetitive, could be outsourced.

Product Life Cycle. NAVSEA's strategic view might be that its business is providing full-spectrum life-cycle product support. Indeed, the products in the second phase of the study were viewed as an aggregation of activities

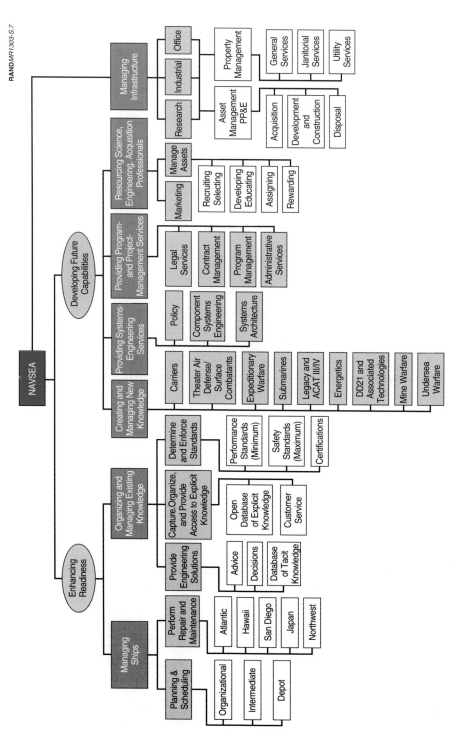

RANDMR1303-S.7

Figure S.7—Organizational Structure of the Market/Customer-Oriented Strategic Intent

throughout a life cycle. If so, three business lines are needed: (1) Creating and Managing New Knowledge, i.e., innovation; (2) Supporting Acquisition, which comprises Providing Systems-Engineering Services, Providing Program- and Project Management Services, Resourcing Science, Engineering, and Acquisition Professionals, and the standards-related aspects of Organizing and Managing Existing Knowledge; and (3) Providing In-Service Support, which would include other aspects of Organizing and Managing Existing Knowledge, together with Managing Ships activities—planning, scheduling, repair, and maintenance (see Figure S.8).

Size

The objectives of the final stage of the organizational analysis were to link activities to specific organizational structure, to further refine the corporate structure based on the importance of the activities, and to delineate what might be inside and what might be outside of NAVSEA's formal boundaries. NAVSEA management decided to perform this analysis. However, we delineate a framework that NAVSEA can use to carry out this analysis. It asks for judgments about which business units contribute more or less to strategic intent, which business units deliver more or less value to NAVSEA customers and stakeholders, and which business units yield products that are more or less central.

The results of the three phases of our completed study provide the basis for NAVSEA to proceed with the organizational sizing analysis. Products, activities, personnel, facilities, and technologies can be linked to NAVSEA organizational elements, and the business units described above can be evaluated individually and within the context of a corporate portfolio. The two-dimensional grids developed in the second phase can be used for answering the questions in the sizing framework. Of particular importance for the sizing stage is the portfolio-centrality analysis, which can be used as the entry point for consideration of organizational design. Understanding NAVSEA markets, products, and activities will be crucial to understanding the core businesses, the vertical and horizontal linkages, and the proper size of NAVSEA in 2007.

RAND would be pleased to work with NAVSEA to implement this framework or a modified version of it.

RAND*MR1303-S.8*

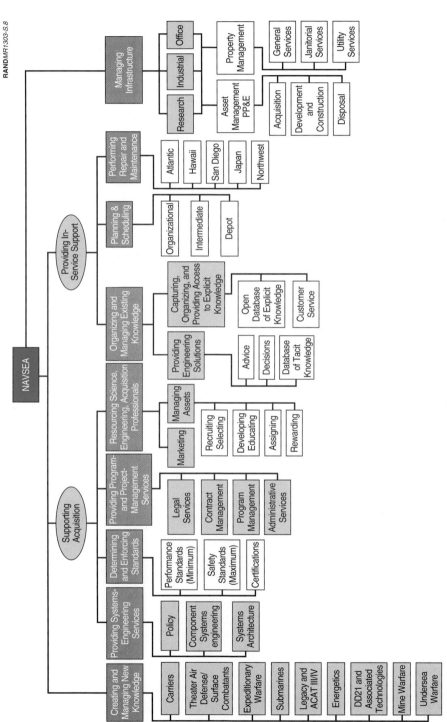

Figure S.8—Organizational Structure for the Product-Life-Cycle Strategic Intent

The work presented here would not have been possible without the efforts of the NAVSEA staff. Through the many availabilities provided by VADM G. P. Nanos, Commander, NAVSEA; RADM Balisle, Vice Commander, NAVSEA; Pete Brown, Executive Director, NAVSEA; and senior leaders throughout NAVSEA, we were able to obtain input of great value. Craig McKay and Jeanie Woods, NAVSEA Corporate Office, assisted us greatly and provided valuable input, for which we are deeply grateful. The research team wishes to thank particularly the many organizations that put enormous effort into preparing and hosting the 38 site visits that were an essential part of the research. We learned a great deal from NAVSEA Headquarters staff, the Program Executive Officers, the field activities, the warfare centers, Naval War College faculty, the Commander of Naval Operations' Strategic Studies Group, Naval Shipyard Commanders, Supervisor of Shipbuilding's (SUPSHIP's) leadership, and representatives from the Fleet. Many individuals from the Los Alamos National Laboratory and MIT were very generous with their time in giving expert opinion on specific technology and process issues. The team extends its sincere thanks for their efforts. The careful reviews of the initial draft of this report by Elliot Axelband and Al Robbert are gratefully acknowledged. The research team extends their thanks to Jim Chiesa, Research Communicator, for structuring many of the briefings involved in this project and for preparing the read-ahead for Commander's Forum IX. Finally, the authors and the management of the National Defense Research Institute at RAND gratefully acknowledge the contribution made by Marian Branch to the final report through her insightful editing.

2-D	Two-dimensional
4π	Full-dimensional
AAW	Anti-Air Warfare [market]
ABM	Anti–Ballistic Missile Treaty
ABP	Assumption-Based Planning
ACAT	Acquisition Category
ACQ	Acquisition Support [market]
AEP	A pyrotechnic device
AMW	Amphibious Warfare [market]
ARG	Amphibious Ready Group
ASN (RDA)	Assistant Secretary of the Navy for Research, Development and Acquisition
ASU	Anti–Surface Ship Warfare [market]
ASW	Anti-Submarine Warfare [market]
ATF	Acoustic Test Facility
C2	Command and control
C3I	Command, control, communications, and intelligence
C4ISR	Command, control, communications, and computers, intelligence, surveillance, and reconnaissance
CAD	Cartridge-Activated Devices [pyrotechnic devices]

CAE	Component Acquisition Executive
CCC	Command, Control, and Communications [market]
CEP	Circular error probable
CF	Commander's Forum
CINC	Commander in chief
CNA	Center for Naval Analyses
CNO	Chief of Naval Operations
COTS	Commercial off-the-shelf
CV	Carrier
CVBG	Carrier battle group
CVNX	Nuclear-powered carrier
DAWIA	Defense Acquisition Workforce Improvement Act
DD	Destroyer
DDG	Guided-missile destroyer
DEF	Defensive Systems [market]
DMR	Defense Management Review
DoD	Department of Defense
DRPM	Direct Reporting Program Manager
EEO	Equal Employment Opportunities
EHF	Extremely high frequency
EM	Electromagnetic
EMP	Electromagnetic pulse
EU	European Union
FAA	Federal Aviation Administration
FFG	Guided-missile frigate
FFTS	*Forward . . . from the Sea*

FMS	Foreign Military Sales
FSO	Fleet support operations
FWG	Federal Wage Grade
FY	Fiscal year
FYDP	Future Years Defense Plan
GDP	Gross Domestic Product
GPCS	Government Process Classification Scheme
GPS	Global Positioning System
GS	General Schedule
H	High
HR	Human resources
ICBM	Intercontinental ballistic missile
ILS	Integrated logistics support
INT	Intelligence [market]
IR	Infrared
IW	Information Warfare [market]
JCS	Joint Chiefs of Staff
JLCC	Joint Logistics Command and Control
JTF	Joint Task Force
JV	Joint Vision
L	Low
LIDAR	Laser infrared radar
LPD	Landing platform–dock
M	Medium
MCM	Mine countermeasure
MGMT	Management

MHD	Magnetic hydrodynamic
MIW	Mine warfare
MOB	Mobility [market]
MOS–NCO	Missions of State–Non-combat Operations [market]
MOTW	Missions other than war
NASA	National Aeronautics and Space Administration
NAVFAC	Naval Facilities Engineering Command
NAVSEA	Naval Sea Systems Command
NCA	National Command Authority
NEO	Noncombatant evacuation operation
NMD	National Missile Defense
NMS	National Military Strategy
NNSY	Norfolk Naval Shipyard
NOC	Navstar Operations Center
NRC	National Research Council
NRFA	Naval Reserve Force–Active
NSB	Naval Studies Board
NSW	Naval Special Warfare [market]
NSWC	Naval Surface Warfare Center
NTTR	Navy Tactical Training Range
NUWC	Naval Undersea Warfare Center
O&M	Operations and Maintenance
OMFTS	Operational Maneuver from the Sea
OMW	Offensive Mine Warfare [market]
ONI	Office of Naval Intelligence
ONR	Office of Naval Research

OOTW	Operations other than war
OPA	Operational Availability [market]
OPM	U.S. Office of Personnel Management
OPNAV	Office of the Chief of Naval Operations
OPNAVINST	OPNAV Instruction
OPTEMPO	Operational tempo
OSD	Office of the Secretary of Defense
OTA	Other Transaction Authority
PAD	Propellant-Activated Devices [pyrotechnic devices]
PEBB	Power electronic building blocks
PEO	Program Executive Officer
PGM	Precision-guided munition
PLAAF	People's Liberation Army Air Force
PP&E	Program Planning and Evaluation
PRC	People's Republic of China
QFD	Quality Function Deployment
R&D	Research and Development
RDA&M	Research, Development, Acquisition and Modernization
RDT&E	Research, Development, Test, and Evaluation
REIT	Real Estate Investment Trust
RF	Radio frequency
RMA	Revolution in Military Affairs
ROC/POE	Required Operational Capability/Projected Operational Environment
RoRo	Roll-on/roll-off [ship]
SAM	Surface-to-air missile

SATCOM	Satellite Communications
SDTS	Self-Defense Test Ship
SECNAV	Secretary of the Navy
SIC	Standard Industrial Classification
SOF	Special Operations Forces
SRBM	Short-range ballistic missile
SSBN	Fleet ballistic-missile submarine
SSGN	Fleet guided-missile submarine
SSN	Attack submarine
STW	Strike Warfare [market]
SUBLANT	U.S. Submarine Force, Atlantic Fleet
SUPSHIP	Supervisor of Shipbuilding
SWEF	Surface Warfare Engineer Facility
TBMD	Theater ballistic-missile defense [system]
TCO	Transnational criminal organization
TOA	Total Obligation Authority
TYCOM	Type Commander
UAV	Unmanned aerial vehicle
UNREP	Underway Replenishment
USW	Undersea warfare
UUV	Unmanned underwater vehicle
UV	Ultraviolet
VADM	Vice Admiral
VIS	Visible
VL	Very low
WDFC	Weapon Development Facility Center
WMD	Weapons of mass destruction

Chapter One

INTRODUCTION

All businesses plan for the future as a way of dealing with uncertainty and change. When a new strategic intent is expressed for a business or organization—when the mission or organizational end changes—and the primary purposeful activities of that organization are perceived to be shifting, the organizational structure is often part of that shift. In January 1999, then–Navy Vice Admiral (VADM) G. F. Nanos, Commander of the Naval Sea Systems Command (NAVSEA), asked RAND to formulate a methodology for making business-planning decisions involving the activities, products, markets, technologies, people, and facilities—the equities—of NAVSEA, initially with a view toward organizational realignment. The time horizon for those plans was 2007, so that the analysis results would be far enough in the future that simply extrapolating from the NAVSEA of today would not be appropriate, yet not so far into the future that forecasts of geopolitical, technological, and business environments would be totally unreliable, and so that a possible implementation of results could influence recommendations for budget cycles before 2007.

BACKGROUND

The Naval Sea Systems Command is the largest of the U.S. Navy's Systems Commands. It employs almost 45,000 people in 310 occupations. NAVSEA's responsibilities span all aspects of the life cycle of ships, submarines, and their components—from acquisition through support to the Navy Program Executive Officers (PEOs), to in-service engineering, maintenance, and retirement.

To provide this full spectrum of services in the twenty-first century in an environment of continuing downsizing, declining Research, Development, Test, and Evaluation (RDT&E) infrastructure and resources, and increasing competition from the private sector for scientific, engineering, and management resources is one of the great challenges confronting NAVSEA leaders. This environment is being constrained further by congressional unwillingness to approve new authority to the Department of Defense (DoD) to close additional bases and facilities. In 1998, the Administration placed this issue back on its agenda for reconsideration, but congressional action was not forthcoming. However, Congress has provided opportunities for structuring a number of new types of relationships between government organizations and the commercial world, such as Other Transaction Authority (OTA), venture capital for leveraging commercial innovation, and private-government partnerships.

Over the past decade, NAVSEA has responded to this environment by significantly reducing its workforce and closing several bases or detachments. Yet, it has also recognized that major changes will continue to affect NAVSEA and its field activities as significant changes continue to occur in the acquisition processes and technologies that have the potential for more efficient operations and improved performance for Navy ships, submarines, and combat systems. For NAVSEA operations to accommodate these changes will be a continuing problem, especially in view of the expectation that DoD will be looking for further reductions in infrastructure and increased organizational efficiencies to help finance future force modernization. Recognizing and accommodating both force modernization and sustainment of vital long-term capabilities as resources continue to decline require examination of those innovative best practices that contemporary organizations, both public and private, experiment with and exercise.

Faced with similar circumstances, other organizations have recognized that they cannot do everything well when there is less to do it with. They have found innovative alternatives to achieving their strategic intents. NAVSEA leaders have recognized that emerging technologies and the exponential acceleration in information processing and computer capabilities are transforming the ways in which both private and public organizations get their business done. They have also recognized that business-process engineering could significantly influence the way NAVSEA operates and is organized. As a consequence, a number of NAVSEA organizational initiatives are under way.

Among these initiatives (e.g., NAVSEA's internal Core Equities Initiative), NAVSEA asked RAND to perform an independent analysis that focuses on the next 10 years (2000–2010) to identify the NAVSEA capabilities needed to support future Navy missions. NAVSEA leaders also asked RAND to analyze alternative NAVSEA organizational alignments for the twenty-first century. A fourth task, examination of options for transitioning the NAVSEA of today to those alignments, was withdrawn.

RESEARCH PLAN

The RAND effort to support NAVSEA organizational decisionmaking involved a three-phase methodology: analysis of the strategic environment in 2007 to identify products, technologies, and activities that are central to the success of current naval strategy and naval strategy for the future; a quantitative analysis of those products, technologies, and activities, as well as the markets that will use them, to further determine which products will have the highest importance and widest breadth for the NAVSEA of 2007; and analysis of potential organizational arrangements to capitalize on commonalities and synergies (combined actions or operation) among products, personnel, and technologies to achieve goals for least cost or high differentiation (i.e., superior value in product quality, special features, or in-service maintenance) for NAVSEA customers.

The three phases of our systems-analysis approach overlapped, and the research team was the same for all phases. Each phase began with a review of documents pertinent to the "system" being analyzed; site visits to Navy, NAVSEA, or defense organizations to gather additional information or to participate in presentations; and discussions among the team members on subject-matter expertise to form a judgment; then selection of a methodology most appropriate for achieving the desired goal; and finally iterations of the methodology to complete a framework for planning. Many times, the methodology for the framework was an adaptation of a RAND-developed tool. The main methodologies underpinning the three analyses are presented in Table 1.1.

The four elements of the national security strategy—deter, shape, prepare, and respond—drive mission capabilities and, hence, frame the analysis. Assumption-Based Planning identifies the assumptions about the future in that strategy and in other national and military planning documents and identifies indicators that could signal the likelihood of the futures assumed in those plans coming to pass. The strategy-to-tasks approach traces the top-level strategy to systems and on to mission capabilities (products and services) that will enable the strategies to be realized. To identify for the Navy the implications of mission capabilities that are likely to be more important than those for the current mission, we began the research by analyzing the external security environment for the next decade and beyond. Projecting the Navy needs onto NAVSEA responsibilities using this framework yields detailed foresight into the future demands for NAVSEA capabilities. This analysis is the subject of Chapter Two.

The mandates examined in Chapter Two provided a bridge to the business analysis of Chapter Three. The missions they specify translate into NAVSEA's markets when NAVSEA is placed in a business context. As a starting point in this phase of the analysis and to relate our assessment of the capabilities needed for the future strategic environment described in Chapter Two to the products (something a customer or stakeholder is willing to pay for), markets (needs and preferences of customers and clients), and activities (processes and

Table 1.1

Methodological Underpinnings of the Study

Strategic Environment and Implications	
Assumption-Based Planning	Identifies the assumptions within planning documents, looks for vulnerabilities in those assumptions, identifies indicators that an assumption is failing, and enables shaping and hedging actions to be taken to add robustness to a plan
Strategy-to-tasks framework	Links national security strategy to NAVSEA mission
Markets and Products and Activities to Fulfill Them	
Market analysis	Identifies forces that will drive growth in emphasis on specific markets
Priority setting/portfolio analysis	Ranks products, markets, activities according to specific measures, then arranges those ranked elements against two of the measures, with different management actions assigned to different ranks
Organization	
Organizational design approach	
Industry structure	Provides context in which the future NAVSEA corporation is intended to operate
Focus	Segments NAVSEA's activities into conceptual business units
Shape	Identifies the horizontal and vertical integration of business units
Size	Develops a methodology to assess NAVSEA's size, given focus and shape, and to determine boundaries for what is inside NAVSEA and what is outside it

RAND*MR1303-T1.1*

organized resources) in NAVSEA, the research team consulted the inventories derived from NAVSEA's internal Core Equities Initiative to identify those areas/activities within each organizational element of NAVSEA that should be retained in-house or that should be outsourced (NAVSEA, 1999a). The Core Equities Initiative is an internal NAVSEA effort to have each of NAVSEA's Centers and elements describe and rank its equities. Intended to bring business planning to NAVSEA's elements, this effort was under way throughout our study. A Core Equity Working Group is still present at NAVSEA, using the RAND results reported here, it is hoped.

Framed by this Market-Product-Activity Model, the analysis begins with an assessment of markets growing in emphasis and continues to describe the databases of products, processes, and organized resources (technologies, facilities, and personnel) and measures that help to quantify the importance, breadth, and growth of each in the markets. Our portfolio-analysis methodology enables a sequence of comparisons of how one element/capability interacts with another. The purpose of this methodology is to narrow options among products and activities so that managers can debate those options without having to deal with too many variables. We concluded this phase of the research with an assessment of the centrality of each product to the corporate mission. The concept of centrality serves as a bridge to the organizational structure analysis. This phase of the analysis is the subject of Chapter Three.

The organizational analysis is likewise concerned with narrowing options. It begins by placing NAVSEA within the context of the industries within which it does business. The narrowing continues through *focus*—segmenting NAVSEA's activities into conceptual *business units,* entities that focus on a well-defined set of activities, products, etc., that meet the needs of specific NAVSEA customers. The focus can be changed by switching, adding, or deleting segments. It concludes the narrowing through *shape*—identifying the horizontal and vertical integration of critical processes or products across business units to achieve major leverage points, economies of scale, or other benefits. For both focus and shape, the team emphasized the importance and implications of NAVSEA strategic intent. This analysis is the subject of Chapter Four.

Originally, *size*—delineating what might be inside and what might be outside of NAVSEA's formal boundaries and its extent—was to be part of Chapter Four. We describe a framework in Chapter Four that NAVSEA can use to analyze sizing issues.

The appendices include background information on this comprehensive analysis. Appendix A provides a list of site visits and presentations, and a survey for gathering data at the sites. Appendix B lists Instructions and Directives from the Secretary of the Navy and Office of the Chief of Naval Operations that clarify NAVSEA's missions and capabilities needed for those missions. Appendix C presents technical aspects of the analysis presented in Chapter Three. It includes the majority of the analysis of activities. The results of that analysis pertain to resource allocations, part of the sizing analysis that was not performed in this study.

Chapter Two

STRATEGIC ENVIRONMENT AND IMPLICATIONS

Strategic analysis illustrates the links between naval strategy and tasks for NAVSEA, as well as between naval strategy and NAVSEA products, services, technologies, and organizations. Its purpose in this study is to establish that the analysis in the two following chapters is based on strategy. In this chapter, we convey our understanding of how changes within U.S. strategic guidance and in dynamics within the Navy and in the international security environment could influence NAVSEA's future missions and mandates. The strategic assessment considers near-term developments (2000–2010) and the potential for pressure on U.S. strategy over the longer term (2011–2020). Our focus is to identify concrete actions that NAVSEA can undertake to improve its position over the remainder of the current decade.

INTRODUCTION

Methodology

The strategic analysis presented here draws on two important RAND methodological tools: Assumption-Based Planning (Dewar et al., 1993) and the strategy-to-tasks framework (Thaler, unpublished). We used Assumption-Based Planning to assess the robustness of U.S. military and naval strategy over the near term and to identify those factors that might put pressure on naval strategy and ultimately require NAVSEA to reorient, reprioritize, or reorganize. The process begins by outlining the principal elements of today's strategy, then identifying the key assumptions upon which those elements depend. Next, the study determines what developments might put pressure on the strategy by undermining important assumptions. Finally, by exploring the international security environment and trends within the Navy and Marine Corps, the study identifies types of events and developments that could serve as indicators or warnings that circumstances are developing that could threaten key, "load-bearing," assumptions.[1]

Next, this chapter makes use of the strategy-to-tasks framework to understand what changes in strategy and the strategic environment mean for NAVSEA. The framework rests on the premise that strategy dictates tasks to the organizations that must help implement the strategy. Thus, NAVSEA finds itself instructed explicitly to perform certain functions and tasks. In addition to the orders, instructions, mandates, and warrants that task NAVSEA, the organization also faces other tasks: those implied and inferred from its explicit orders and instructions. The point of the strategy-to-tasks framework is to follow the threads of guidance from high-level strategy to a level at which giving advice to NAVSEA officials that can be implemented is possible. Those threads run through the doctrine, visions, and implementing instructions from intermediate organizations and officials down to their implications for the activities, outputs, and organizations within NAVSEA to the level of implementation. Figure 2.1 illustrates the threads reaching from the global security environment through U.S. military strategy to NAVSEA's mandates and instructions to its specific contributions of products and technologies to the key elements of the National Military Strategy.

RAND*MR1303-2.1*

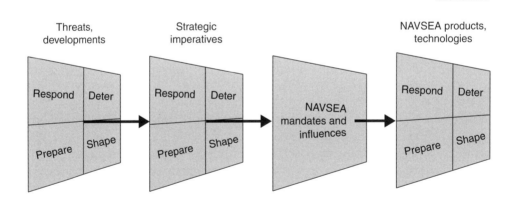

Figure 2.1—From Threats and Strategy to Tasks and Products for NAVSEA

---

[1]Assumptions are said to be "load-bearing" because they function like load-bearing pillars in a building. If the pillars are somehow undermined, the building collapses; if the assumptions are undermined, the plans that rest on them also crumble.

Research Resources

In addition to RAND planning guidelines/tools, the study team made maximum use of official Department of Defense and service documents and experts. The research and analysis presented here are informed by numerous sources inside and outside the Navy and NAVSEA. The research team has undertaken discussions with scholars and analysts at the National Defense University; faculty members at the Naval War College; the deputy director of the Chief of Naval Operation's (CNO's) Strategic Studies Group; and operational officers at Second Fleet Headquarters in Norfolk, Va., Seventh Fleet Headquarters in Yokosuka, Japan, and SUBLANT (U.S. Submarine Force, Atlantic Fleet). We have visited NAVSEA Headquarters and its field activities, which include the Surface and Undersea Warfare Centers, SUPSHIP (Supervisor of Shipbuilding), the public shipyards, and associated Program Executive Officers. We have reviewed a number of documents, ranging from those intended for high-level national security planning, including *Joint Vision 2020*, Joint Publication 3-0, National Security Strategy of the U.S., and various other DoD, Joint Chiefs of Staff (JCS), and Navy publications; to more specific Navy-relevant operational and intelligence assessments, including summer Navy wargames outbriefs, intelligence community assessments, VADM Cebrowski's "Road Ahead" briefing, National Academy of Sciences reports, and numerous Navy Study Board publications; as well as relevant congressional testimony.

Chapter Organization

This chapter is organized into four parts. First, we examine the determinants of U.S. naval strategy gleaned from official planning documents and then from our own assessment of the international security environment. Second, we review the current and planned future capabilities of the U.S. Navy; this review includes a discussion of naval doctrine, force structure, and systems. Third, we analyze the potential vulnerabilities of some of the key assumptions the Navy has made about the future security environment and the behavior of likely adversaries. Fourth, we assess the implications of all these strategic issues for NAVSEA organizations, operations, and technological priorities.

DETERMINANTS OF NAVAL STRATEGY

Official View of the Developing Naval Strategy

Strategic guidance informs NAVSEA's options for designing its transformation. In the current U.S. military strategic planning system, guidance first takes form in the White House's National Security Strategy, which subsequently generates more-detailed strategic guidance in the Department of Defense, first in the National Military Strategy and thereafter in a string of documents and plans that thread their way down the chain of command to major commands and their subordinate commands and activities, ever increasing in the level of detail and specificity, and ultimately providing a complete "strategy-to-tasks" conceptual chain.

The historical record offers widely varied examples of naval strategies, ranging from aggressive global sea-control efforts to simple coastal patrol strategies. Some naval strategies, such as Germany's U-boat campaign in the Atlantic during World War II, have focused on enemy commercial shipping; others, such as American naval strategy for the Pacific in the 1920s and 1930s, have concentrated on destroying the adversary's fleet of capital ships. The record illustrates great latitude and variety in the design of naval strategy, and the fact that countries make significantly different decisions about the size, characteristics, and composition of their naval forces, reflecting their strategic preferences. This is to say that strategy is not over-determined; the Navy and NAVSEA have room in which to be creative in fulfilling their respective roles, especially in a world where the United States enjoys a position as the sole superpower.

In the United States, the President's National Security Strategy sets the tone for security policy and establishes the basis for and the extent of the United States' involvement around the world. The National Military Strategy develops the military aspects of the National Security Strategy, while statements of vision and doctrine such as *Joint Vision 2020*, the *Naval Posture Statement*, *Forward . . . from the Sea*, and *Operational Maneuver from the Sea* determine the specific form of the military instrument and its application to execute the strategy. Finally, a host of strategic guidance papers and plans within each service provide highly specific and more-detailed instructions relevant to their specific subordinate commands.

National Security Strategy. The Clinton Administration released its security strategy, *A National Security Strategy of Engagement and Enlargement,* in 1994 and its principal tenets endure with the Bush Administration today (The White House, 1995). The reigning security strategy engages the United States actively with its global neighbors and embraces a broad vision of national security that includes issues such as population flows, transnational criminal activity, and environmental degradation. In this role, the United States is cast not only as a model of democracy, market economics, and human rights, but also as their champion. This posture creates both the basis for U.S. military involvement in regions and some issues that historically would fall beyond the scope of U.S. interests deemed worthy of military commitments (for example, sub-Saharan Africa).

National Military Strategy. The National Military Strategy translates the principles and objectives embodied in the security strategy into terms of action by the uniformed armed forces. The current edition of the National Military Strategy organizes around the terms "deter, shape, prepare, respond" (Joint Chiefs of Staff, 1997). The strategy prepares the military for energetic employment around the globe as one of the United States' principal instruments of international relations. In this role, the U.S. military is called upon to deter potential adversaries, shape the international environment in ways favorable to the United States and its principles, respond to the demands of current contingencies, and prepare for longer-term security challenges.

Joint Vision 2020 (JV2020) offers an advanced conception of how U.S. joint forces will operate in a decade or so (Joint Chiefs of Staff, 2000). It envisions that those joint forces will work closely with other governmental agencies and foreign allies and/or partners to exploit first-class personnel and cutting-edge technology as a means of coordinating their activities for achieving powerful effects throughout the battlespace of the future. JV2020 conceives of military forces that can see the battlespace in great depth and detail, discriminate between friend and foe, and attack the foe with precision and lethality. The concept embodied in JV2020 relies on network-centric warfare (Cebrowski and Garstka, 1998) and also calls for high-efficiency logistics and support activities, and reliable force-protection capabilities. These attributes culminate in a sophisticated ability to find and dominate a wide variety of adversaries under various conditions and circumstances.

The Naval Posture Statement. The specific U.S. Navy and Marine Corps roles in implementing JV2020 and upholding the tenets of the National Military Strategy take shape in the pages of the *2000 Posture Statement* (Department of the Navy, 2000). This document discusses the Department of the Navy's mission, its direction for the future, and the priorities informing Navy decisionmaking. The current document argues that the United States will retain its position as the world's only superpower for some years to come, but that the processes of globalization and technological diffusion are creating many opportunities for capable adversaries to use asymmetric strategies to challenge American military might. Ballistic missiles and information warfare are but two of the threats mentioned in this area. The statement argues that naval forces offer a number of unique traits to national leaders in the coming era, such as long-term forward presence in unstable regions, scalable combat power against a spectrum of threats and contingencies, and increasingly long-range precision striking power that does not need to be launched from forward bases. In Section IV, "The Force of the Future," the posture statement identifies the key technologies the Navy and Marine Corps are counting on to deliver the capabilities they envision. Elements of this part of the posture statement reflect some of

NAVSEA's products, programs, and initiatives (Department of the Navy, 2000, pp. 5–8).

Other Documents and Influences. Both the Navy and Marine Corps are implementing compelling visions of their own operations, such as today's *Forward . . . from the Sea* and tomorrow's *Operational Maneuver from the Sea* (U.S. Marine Corps, 1997) and *Network Centric Warfare* (Cebrowski and Garstka, 1998). Usually, the implementing and supporting technologies to bring these doctrinal visions to fruition emerge from the Naval Studies Board, the Naval War College, and similar bodies that have chartered or undertaken analyses of future naval system requirements. The nine-volume study *Technology for the United States Navy and Marine Corps, 2000–2035* (Naval Studies Board, 1997a) is one of the best examples of this type of influence upon naval strategy.

Finally, the overall force-structure parameters within which the Navy and Marine Corps must carry out their doctrinal visions are set by the congressionally mandated Quadrennial Defense Reviews (Cohen, 1997).

Intelligence assessments also bear directly on the form and substance of naval strategy, especially studies of foreign technology development, weapon manufacturing, and arms-transfer arrangements. The Defense Intelligence Agency's recent report (1999), *Future Technology Impact on Global Security Trends by 2025*, and similar estimates influence strategic options by illustrating how foreign military technology R&D and procurement could present the Navy with new capabilities that would place additional demands on NAVSEA for the maintenance of technological hegemony. Ultimately, the conceptual drivers of strategy, such as the *National Security Strategy* and the National Military Strategy, combine with the operational visions of military activities, such as JV2020 and *Operational Maneuver from the Sea*, as well as the technology surveys just cited, to give specific form to U.S. naval strategy.

RAND Appraisal of the International Security Environment

To complement the baseline determinants of naval strategy seen in official policy planning documents, the research team conducted an independent assessment of the international security environment to see if the most plausible trajectory into the future meshes well with the doctrinal and operational visions found in official DoD and Navy publications. Our view ultimately reflects discussions with a range of international relations and naval power experts, the findings from a number of articles and books from both the academic political science and contemporary defense policy literature, and quantitative analysis based upon official U.S. government data (for example, Joint Publication 3-0, the Summer Navy War Games outbriefs, National Academy of Science reports, and numerous Naval Studies Board publications). We present the outlooks for the decades 2000–2010 and 2011–2020 in the following subsections.

2000–2010. From our analysis, we conclude that there will not be enough significant change in the international political and/or military environment to increase the challenge to the United States during the next 10 years. The United States will probably remain the sole superpower and will not likely face a peer competitor or any organized coalition of near-peer competitors. This is not to say that the United States will not face any significant security challenges in the near term, only that in the arena of the Great Powers, the United States will continue to enjoy a comfortable edge over potential challengers. The justification: there simply is no country out there that is threatening to develop the same kind of robust state power based on the portfolio of capabilities that this country now possesses. Some nations may challenge the United States in certain spheres, perhaps through state-sponsored terrorism, but a serious threat to U.S. primacy seems very unlikely. The United States will remain a significant global force in all the main categories of power measurement: military, economic, demographic, political, and cultural.

It is clear from our analysis and interviews that the most likely combat scenarios for the U.S. Navy in the 2000–2010 time frame will probably feature littoral operations against medium-sized powers employing asymmetric strategies. At the lower end of the conflict spectrum, a robust forward presence in critical regions such as East Asia and the Persian Gulf will remain necessary to shape the local environment along favorable lines and to provide ready forces that can assist in low-intensity operations such as embargo enforcement and noncombatant evacuation operations (NEOs). Simply put, *Forward . . . from the Sea* seems well-suited to the world as we expect it to be over the next 10 years. The remainder of this subsection is devoted to a brief review of the highlights of our near-term environmental appraisal.

Militarily, the United States is currently well ahead of other large nations in the so-called Revolution in Military Affairs. It has been able to integrate advanced sensors, broadband communications technology, and large-scale data processing more effectively than any other state, and thus is creating a new paradigm of theater warfare. The United States also retains an unparalleled capacity for global force mobility; its ability to project power to distant regions is of a different scale than that possessed by other large states, most of whom can project power only in their own regions.

Economically, the United States has the world's largest Gross Domestic Product (GDP), with about 22 percent of the world's total GDP. Even more telling, though, is the fact that the United States' economic lead over other industrialized nations has been increasing and there are indications that this trend may well continue. For example, since 1990, the U.S. GDP has increased by 27 percent, whereas the European Union (EU) and Japan have seen GDP increases of only 15 and 9 percent, respectively (Office of the Secretary of Defense [OSD], 1999). America's current lead in such cutting-edge technologies as Internet commerce, biotechnology, and software makes it plausible that this pattern will continue, perhaps for decades.

In terms of demographics, the U.S. population is continuing to grow at a steady rate, thanks to a fertility rate close to replacement and to immigration flows. In the changing rankings for the world's 10 most populous states, shown in Table 2.1, the United States maintains its rank as third-most-populous state.

As the table indicates, China and India, two potential military competitors of the United States, will retain their top positions in the population rankings. However, two other important world actors, Russia and Japan, will drop in the world population rankings, Russia falling from 6th to 10th place, and Japan dropping off the list altogether. Both nations face declining populations. None of the countries of the European Union is on the top-10 list. The United States' slowly rising population will shield it from some of the extreme worker-shortage and aging-population problems that face its most-advanced economic competitors. Fundamentally, however, population size per se will not be as central to any future strategic competition as will the quality of a country's human and intellectual capital.

Table 2.1

World Population Rankings

1997	Population (millions)	2025	Population (millions)
1. China	1,200	1. China	1,430
2. India	960	2. India	1,330
3. United States	272	3. United States	332
4. Indonesia	203	4. Indonesia	275
5. Brazil	163	5. Pakistan	268
6. Russia	147	6. Nigeria	238
7. Pakistan	144	7. Brazil	217
8. Japan	126	8. Bangladesh	180
9. Bangladesh	122	9. Ethiopia	136
10. Nigeria	118	10. Russia	131

Finally, the analysis considered the elements of political and cultural power, or "soft power" as Harvard's Joseph Nye dubbed them several years ago in *Bound to Lead* (1990). In both areas, American ideas and innovations have more global appeal than do those developed by potential near-peer competitors. Indeed, the whole process of globalization in many ways is the diffusion of American ideals of free trade, open markets, and representative government. Its high levels of soft power in the Information Age make the United States a desirable honest broker in many of the more-difficult international disputes occurring today, such as the religious strife in Northern Ireland, the Israeli-Palestinian conflict, and the reintegration of Bosnia. At this writing, the only real model of political philosophy that challenges American-style liberal democracy on a wide geographic scale is Islamic fundamentalism. However, fundamentalist Islam is not the guiding philosophy of any of America's potential major competitors. Its appeal is found mainly in small and medium-sized states in North Africa, the Levant, and the Persian Gulf.

Some limited strategic competition from Russia and China is also likely, fueled by their fears and suspicions of Washington's plans and motives. Russia will probably compete with the United States through limited modernization of its strategic nuclear force; Moscow's focus here will be on deploying a new generation of road-mobile intercontinental ballistic missiles (ICBMs) and a handful of quiet, next-generation ballistic missile submarines (SSBNs). Specifically, the Russian Strategic Rocket Forces can be expected to continue to acquire 35–40 of the new SS-27 Topol single-warhead road-mobile ICBMs each year until a force-size target of 450 SS-27s is met sometime around 2010 (U.S. Naval Institute Periscope Database, 1999). The SS-27 is both accurate and very difficult to target. Additionally, there is substantial evidence that the Russian military is investing significant funds in new underground strategic command and control facilities at Yamantau Mountain and Kosvinsky Mountain (U.S. Naval Institute, 1999). While these programs do not threaten the viability of the U.S. strategic nuclear deterrent, the fact that Moscow is investing heavily in strategic nuclear modernization while Russia is in dire economic straits indicates that Russian leaders place the highest priority on maintaining a modern, robust (if somewhat smaller) strategic nuclear threat to the United States through the next decade and beyond.

To maintain its weapon industries, Russia will continue as a major exporter of sophisticated armaments to emerging Third World countries, including China. The recent Russian sale of a Sovremenny-class guided missile destroyer to the People's Republic of China (PRC), along with advanced SSN-22 anti-ship missiles, is an excellent example of this practice (U.S. Naval Institute, 1999). Despite this combination of selective strategic modernization and increased arms exports, Russia's overall military capability will continue to decline, because

Russia's conventional forces will not have the funding to meet their recapitalization needs during the current decade. Procurement shortfalls are especially evident in the Russian Air Force.

As it modernizes both its strategic forces and its conventional power-projection capabilities, the People's Republic of China could pose a more multifaceted challenge. The PRC is moving aggressively to expand its air and naval power-projection capabilities in the Western Pacific. Chinese capabilities to detect and counter U.S. Navy battle groups in the region and bombard Taiwan with short-range ballistic missiles have already increased since the spring 1996 tensions in the Taiwan Strait.

China's procurement patterns reveal a fairly ambitious effort at power-projection modernization. In the tactical air area, the People's Liberation Army Air Force (PLAAF) is planning to deploy 250 Russian-designed Su-27s by 2012—aircraft that will be armed with advanced AA-11 radar-guided beyond-visual-range missiles (U.S. Naval Institute, 1999). These aircraft would give the PLA's Air Force a margin of superiority over Taiwan's air force, if Taipei is unable to purchase additional American fighters. The Chinese are pursuing an aerial-refueling capability for their Su-27 force by converting up to five older B-6 bombers into refuelers. If China successfully builds an aerial-refueling force, it could extend the range of its Su-27 fleet so that targets in the Philippines and Singapore could be in reach. The final element of the aerial power-projection picture for the PLAAF is the formerly proposed acquisition of an Israeli-manufactured Phalcon airborne command and control aircraft. Although this transaction was canceled by the Israelis under pressure from Washington, it indicates a Chinese desire to increase its situational awareness greatly over the South China Sea.

Chinese naval forces are also being bolstered by Russian imports. Beijing has purchased four Kilo-class diesel submarines and two Sovremenny-class guided missile destroyers from the Russians; these capabilities will give the Chinese the ability to put U.S. naval forces at greater risk in the littoral areas of the Western Pacific (U.S. Naval Institute, 1999).

Tensions may continue to rise as the PRC deploys increasing numbers of ballistic missiles aimed at Taiwan. The PRC's short-range ballistic missile force is expanding to the point where it can execute a devastating first strike against the major Taiwanese ports, air bases, and command and control facilities. China could deploy up to 600 M-9 short-range ballistic missiles (SRBMs) opposite Taiwan in the current decade (U.S. Naval Institute, 1999). These air, naval, and missile capabilities will not give the Chinese the ability to invade and occupy Taiwan, but they may give the Chinese the ability to coerce a Taiwanese leadership feeling isolated and vulnerable into acceding to Beijing's demands for major political concessions on reunification.

Both Russia and China face significant security challenges that could weaken them during the present decade. Russia is facing the prospect of a long, draining guerrilla war in Chechnya, as well as the drift of both Ukraine and the Baltics toward NATO and the West. China, meanwhile, is confronting secessionist movements in Tibet and Xinjiang province, as well as an India that is developing a strategic nuclear deterrent force against Beijing.

At the regional level, a few rogue states, such as North Korea and Iraq, will continue to be a threat to U.S. interests in key regions. Rather than challenge the United States or its interests directly with conventional forces, these states might reorient their strategies toward obtaining advanced military weapons of mass destruction and the long-range ballistic and cruise missiles to deliver them. This approach might appeal especially to adversaries who appreciate the weapons' potential to intimidate U.S. regional allies into denying American military forces overflight and basing rights.

A wild card at the regional level is that all of the rogue-state regimes face domestic pressures, instability, and/or leadership transitions. North Korea, while still suffering the lingering effects of famine, is also now facing the prospect of increasing Western investment affecting its domestic political environment. Iran faces a burgeoning reformist movement, which has taken control of the national parliament and much of the press and is challenging the remaining power of the conservative clerics. Iraq's domestic environment is more stable, but dissent does exist among some of the nation's tribal leaders, as well as the Kurds. Syria is now facing the post–Hafez Assad era with uncertainty and the possibility of increasing openness to the outside world. These pressures and instabilities could result in changes in the policies and behavior of current regimes toward their neighbors and the United States; or they could lead to the replacement of current regimes, with unpredictable political ramifications.

Outside of those regions where threats to U.S. interests might draw the United States into large-scale conventional wars, such as southwest and northeast Asia, we expect to see continued instability in local hot spots that have simmered over the past few years and where second-order U.S. or NATO interests—those of moderate importance—may be at stake. For example, the ongoing narco-insurgency in Colombia could threaten regional stability and democracy in northern Latin America. Continued ethnic strife in the Balkans, in both Kosovo and Bosnia, is likely to continue through the present decade, requiring a long-term peacekeeping presence by the United States and NATO. Indonesia, with its simmering secessionist conflicts in Aceh and Papua and proximity to the critical Strait of Malacca, is a third potential flashpoint to watch over the next 10 years.

Transnational threats increase. Terrorist groups, such as the Bin Laden organization, become more preeminent and more dangerous in this decade. Some of the world's smaller nuclear powers, such as Pakistan, implode under the twin stresses of ethnic strife and overpopulation, creating the risk of "loose nukes" (nuclear weapons in unauthorized hands) in very unstable regions.

No matter how the geopolitical environment develops, one can say with some certainty that the task of protecting and securing its information networks will be vital for the Navy. The Navy is becoming more operationally dependent on information networks spanning the organization. Much has been written recently about information warfare (IW) threats (Denning, 1999; Schwartau, 1996; Rattray, 2001; Schleher, 1999; Adamy, 2001; Forno and Baklarz, 1999; Duncan et al., 2000; Alexander and Swetnam, 1999; Campen and Dearth, 2000; Waltz, 1998; Sharp, 1999; Khalilzad et al., 1999); these threats will only become more sophisticated with the passage of time. Offensive IW against the Navy could easily be conducted by non-state actors or even individual malcontents.

Finally, certain political and economic factors can hamper the Navy's operational and development programs, as well as its abilities to perform its missions. Specifically, any new U.S./Russian arms-control measures reducing strategic nuclear weapons and modifying the Anti–Ballistic Missile Treaty (ABM) could alter the Navy's strategic posture, reducing, on the one hand, the size of the SSBN fleet, and influencing, on the other hand, decisions on the development of a sea-based National Missile Defense (NMD) capability. Political considerations may also inhibit or prevent the export of advanced U.S. military weapons and platforms to allies who help maintain a regional balance of power that favors U.S. interests. Although major budget surpluses are predicted for the next several years, deciding whether to maintain military spending at its current levels in a time of relative peace, let alone increase it, is fraught with uncertainty and may be politically difficult to do, especially if domestic claimants on the budget become more aggressive (for example, increased Medicare and Medicaid benefits, and the need to rescue Social Security).

2011–2020. Our assessment of the state of the international security environment during the 2011–2020 time frame produced more uncertainty about the appropriateness of evolving naval strategy. It is not clear that the future doctrine of *Operational Maneuver from the Sea* and *Network-Centric Warfare* will be well-suited to the types of security threats that will emerge in the next decade. For example, in this time frame one might see open-ocean threats to the U.S. Navy from a robust near-peer competitor or the international acceptance of space as a combat medium. In either case, today's visions of U.S. naval strategy would need to be altered. Littoral warfare could well be of decreasing importance to the United States in this period.

Estimates looking further into the future become less reliable. There is the possibility of unanticipated challenges to the United States' strategic primacy from regional competitors. The most dangerous and discussed example is that of a possible PRC quest to militarily dominate the Western Pacific, challenging U.S. influence there. However, other events in which hostile geopolitical alignments might emerge—such as a possible link between Russia and China, or one between Russia and Iran to challenge American interests in the Persian Gulf and Caspian regions—also seem plausible. Although Russia and China are now well behind the United States in taking advantage of the Revolution in Military Affairs, this gap may decrease with the passage of a number of years, particularly if Russia continues to sell its advanced military technology and hardware to the PRC and other nations who challenge U.S. interests.[2]

At the regional level, the possibility is high that governments of rogue states will survive the decade now beginning and increase their military prowess in the following one. States such as Iran might be better able to challenge U.S. dominance in the littoral if they acquire better military technology, weapons, and platforms from Russia, China, and other industrial nations. They could have longer-range missile systems, both cruise and ballistic, enabling them to attack U.S. allies and ships at much greater distances—and with greater accuracy—if they successfully exploit the increasing opportunities they will have to access commercial satellite imagery. If some of them manage to integrate their surveillance and reconnaissance capabilities into fairly sophisticated information-gathering and -processing complexes, the resulting systems might allow them to locate and attack enemy ships with their longer-range weapon systems. If such circumstances came to pass, the Navy's ability to maintain local sea control could be sorely tested.

In addition to conventional nation-state–type threats, the Navy would also be prudent to ponder the implications of a possible surge in major non-state security threats during the 2011–2020 time frame. The realm of information warfare is tailor-made for non-state, transnational actors such as transnational criminal organizations (TCOs), ethnic diasporas, and peace/social justice organizations. It is plausible that the 2011–2020 time frame might see the emergence of powerful transnational groups with massive offensive IW capabilities that could seriously threaten the infrastructure of the United States. Another possibility could be that the current wave of subnational warlordism that is inundating parts of

---

[2]Of particular interest here are Russia's efforts to transfer nuclear reactor technology to Iran—technology that has conceivable military applications.

west and central Africa might also appear in other parts of the developing world, such as south Asia and the Andes region of Latin America. Such warlordism could result in an onset of social anarchy in those regions and could spur large-scale refugee flows and destroy regional infrastructures. A systemic crisis of this sort might trigger U.S. intervention, much of which would likely be led by amphibious forces.

Summary. In summary, the political/military environment is not expected to change to any significant degree in the decade ending in 2010. In this decade, only small and a few moderate-sized military threats to the United States and its interests are expected, mostly from smaller rogue states, but possibly moderate-sized threats from North Korea, and perhaps China later in the decade. Iraq, for the time being, remains hobbled by its defeat in Desert Storm and by the major economic sanctions imposed on it in its aftermath, although Baghdad has become increasingly creative in its attempts to free itself from Western penalties. Political trends in Iran have been toward greater moderation in international matters and toward the pursuit of economic development. The environment of the following decade raises many uncertainties. What will transpire in the decade beyond 2010 is most difficult to discern.

PLANNED NAVY STRATEGY AND CAPABILITIES BEYOND 2000

The Navy is responding to the future challenges just outlined with doctrinal, force-structure, and technology initiatives.

Current and Future Doctrine

Current Doctrine. Current naval doctrine is a major departure from that promulgated during the later stages of the Cold War. Instead of seeking to keep Soviet submarines away from the North Atlantic sea lanes, by bottling up and destroying the Soviet Navy on the Kola Peninsula, today's doctrine of *Forward . . . from the Sea* (Department of the Navy, 1994) emphasizes the importance of littoral operations across the spectra of both conflict intensity and geographic location. The current doctrine must grapple with a broader repertoire of tasks, both new and traditional. This subsection highlights the key features of the prevailing naval doctrine and then outlines likely future naval doctrine. It discusses the current strategy with reference to the four pillars of the present National Military Strategy (NMS): deter, shape, prepare, respond.

Forward . . . from the Sea (FFTS) is the title that has been given to the current Navy doctrine. First published in 1994, it remains the official doctrinal statement of the U.S. Navy (Department of the Navy, 1994). The cornerstone of FFTS is a regular forward-presence posture in key regions. From this stems two critical attributes of American naval forces in the present day. First, naval forces, by virtue of their regular day-to-day operations in key theaters, are constantly helping to favorably influence the local security environment in ways that periodic deployments of ground-based forces cannot. Second, because of their presence posture, carrier battle groups and amphibious ready groups can be the first responders to a serious crisis or conflict and serve as the foundational building blocks upon which a larger joint force can be constituted over time if the conflict escalates.

FFTS, because it is about USMC tactics, appears to slightly de-emphasize the strategic-deterrence mission, but still gives this mission a prominent mention. Open-ocean combat operations and multitheater global warfare are glaringly absent from the current doctrinal vision. FFTS places a priority on the shape and respond elements of the National Military Strategy and appears to put the deter and prepare functions into a category of lower priority. We now take a brief look at the implications of FFTS for the four pillars of the NMS.

Shape. Although *shaping* has always been a component of naval strategy, it has become a particularly vigorous element in FFTS. The reigning National Security Strategy relies heavily on U.S. military forces to represent the nation abroad and to help foster appreciation of the United States' values and institutions. Today, in addition to the traditional forms of shaping, such as maritime patrol, port calls, and freedom-of-navigation activities, shaping includes increasing numbers of exercises with foreign navies, expanded staff contacts and workshops, wargame simulations, senior official visits, and nation-building activities in which sailors and Marines play a major role. A clear example of the importance of the shaping function for the Navy is provided by the recent activities of the Seventh Fleet in the Western Pacific. The Seventh Fleet participates in an average of 100 multinational exercises per year. In 1998, it conducted exercises with Russia, South Korea, Japan, Australia, Brunei, the Philippines, Hong Kong, Singapore, Malaysia, Indonesia, Thailand, Bangladesh, India, and the Maldives. In addition, this fleet made port visits to 21 different regional states during the same period. Figure 2.2 illustrates that the overall Fleet spends about 62 percent of its time away from home, much of it devoted to shaping and forward-presence operations.

Respond. The *respond* function has to do with handling actual contingencies, ranging from blockade enforcement and counter-drug surveillance at the low end of the spectrum to major theater wars at the high end. Clearly, the conclusion of the Cold War has not reduced the frequency of this function for the Navy and Marine Corps; to the contrary, the contingency operations have increased for these services since 1990. Whereas U.S. military forces conducted

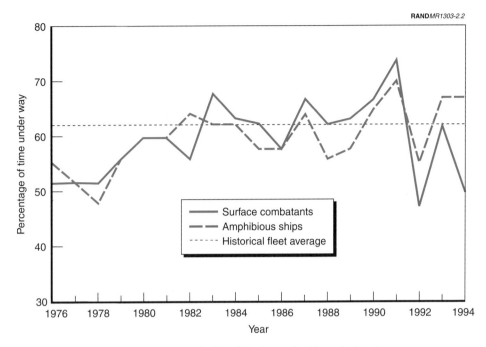

SOURCE: Adapted from Center for Naval Analyses, *Avoiding a Hollow Force: An Examination of Naval Readiness*, Alexandria, Va.: CRM-95-238, April 1996, p. 47.

Figure 2.2—Percentage of Time Select Ship Classes Spend Under Way

59 operations during the 44-year Cold War, they had carried out 133 operations in the decade since the end of that era.[3]

As FFTS notes, the higher the level of intensity of a contingency, the more likely it is that, to finish the job, naval forces will need to be supplemented by Air Force and Army units. Because of their scalability and flexibility, naval forces are usually the leading wedge of a combat effort, especially one that begins on short notice. For example, 1998's coercive air strikes against Iraq (Operation Desert Fox) were launched on short notice, and sea-launched cruise missiles and carrier-borne aircraft played a major role in that effort. The advance of technology is also allowing naval forces to strike deep into the adversary's hinterlands with high accuracy at the outset of a conflict; this capability makes naval forces ideal tools for sudden punitive attacks upon the strategic command and control of a hostile state.

---

[3]The 133 operations cited include some still ongoing in the Balkans and Southwest Asia. See the Federation of American Scientists' web site at http://www.fas.org/man/dod-101/ops/index/html#post.

Often, *responding* in today's strategy involves long residual commitments that make additional demands on Navy and Marine Corps forces. Many of the post–Cold War uses of force have left the adversary in power, with the means to resist more or less intact. Therefore, U.S. military forces have been directed to patrol no-fly zones, to monitor zones of separation, and to implement similar post-conflict mechanisms. As a result, Navy and Marine Corps air sometimes participate in no-fly-zone enforcement and naval ships assist in monitoring cease-fires. Doing so means that these forces are not immediately available for other tasks.

Deter. Deterrence has long been a part of the Navy and Marine Corps' role in national defense. The Navy contributes to strategic nuclear deterrence through its fleet of 14 ballistic missile submarines. Their high level of quietness means that these Ohio-class boats remain virtually undetectable in the open ocean, providing the National Command Authority (NCA) with an assured second-strike capability. Indeed, many experts believe that, as America's ICBM force ages and its bomber force becomes more oriented to conventional missions, the Navy's SSBNs will become the sturdiest and most important leg of the nation's nuclear triad.

The Navy and the Marine Corps together contribute to conventional deterrence. Through their presence in theaters of operation where major regional adversaries are located, they demonstrate both strong U.S. intentions and capabilities, dissuading most would-be adversaries from actions that could jeopardize U.S. interests and allies. A classic example of naval conventional deterrence at work is the March 1996 deployment of two U.S. carrier battle groups off the Taiwanese coast during extensive Chinese missile-firing exercises. The presence of those carriers deterred Beijing from making stronger attempts to intimidate Taiwan on the eve of its presidential elections.

Prepare. In today's naval strategy, *preparing* means developing long-range capabilities that will be robust against a wide array of potential contingencies and enemies. The *prepare* function of today involves readying the forces for non-traditional missions and tasks, such as noncombatant evacuation operations, shallow-water mine countermeasures, and counter-drug support, in addition to having weapons, platforms, and tactics that can deal with more-standard threats, such as anti-ship cruise missiles and advanced surface combatants.

Recapitalization is at the core of the *prepare* function for the Navy and Marine Corps. New procurement programs such as the DD21 land attack destroyers and nuclear-powered carrier (CVNX) are aimed at giving the Navy a new generation of tools with which to meet the wide range of threats that will be possible in the 2011–2020 time frame. Recently, however, recapitalization funding has been below desired levels, because the Navy has concentrated on maintaining short-term readiness and operational tempo (OPTEMPO). This deficit will likely result in a procurement "bow wave" of backlogged requirements in the 2005–2010 time frame that would severely tax the Navy's budget, absent any major defense-spending increases or reductions in threat.

Future Doctrine. Naval doctrine appears to be developing in step with technology as the service looks to the future. Both the Navy and the Marine Corps are trying to exploit fully those advances in computing and communications technologies that will allow them to extract more fighting power from smaller forces, expose fewer personnel to danger, and shock and disorganize adversaries through the use of speed and superior situational awareness. In short, both services appear to see great potential in information dominance.

With respect to warfare missions, the Navy is moving from its *Forward . . . from the Sea* doctrine, which emphasizes forward-presence, environment-shaping, and early response to regional conflict, to a doctrine of network-centric warfare. With respect to Fleet support missions, the Navy is moving steadily toward implementing on-time maintenance and logistics.

Network-centric warfare has as its objective the connection of ships in a battle group with other friendly naval and military groups in the region and beyond in such a way that situational awareness and action are greater than what could be attained by the individual battle group elements acting alone. These networked battle groups will be able to acquire real-time data on enemy movements and locations from worldwide sources for ship-based sensor and data processing. As a consequence, the battle group can more efficiently allocate its different defensive countermeasures and weapons against incoming enemy air and missile threats and simultaneously engage and defeat enemy ships and submarines that endanger the battle group.

In addition to the operational advantage of seamlessly integrating weapons and sensors within a battle group, network-centric warfare offers advantages for the force planner as well. First, network-centric warfare may, over time, allow the U.S. Navy to do more forward presence without today's reliance on carrier battle groups (CVBGs) and Amphibious Ready Groups (ARGs). Second, network efficiencies may allow the Navy to focus on developing fewer new weapon systems for each mission, since different platforms will be able to share targeting data more easily. For example, new anti-submarine warfare (ASW) research could focus on helicopter-mounted torpedoes at the expense of surface-ship ASW systems, because the helicopter's weapons would be linked directly to sensors on surface ships in the battle group and thus could be used to defend the surface ship as rapidly as the ship could deploy its own weapons.

Operational Maneuver from the Sea (OMFTS) is the Marine Corps' doctrinal vision for the future. Essentially a prescription for next-generation littoral warfare using light amphibious forces, OMFTS is based on the premise that the traditional force-on-force model of amphibious assault, as typified by the Iwo Jima landing in World War II, needs to be replaced and can be replaced. OMFTS entails the movement by helicopter and tilt-wing rotorcraft of small groups of Marines over the shore, behind enemy coastal positions; the Marines are then to be supported mainly by sea-based firepower and supply ships. These Marine attack teams would carry little organic firepower ashore (no tanks or heavy artillery) and would seek to overcome enemy positions primarily by calling on long-range sea-based firepower, and by conducting erosive infiltration attacks against an enemy's infrastructure: communications, transportation, and similar targets. In essence, fortified enemy shore positions would be steadily eaten away from the rear by small, autonomous cells of Marines backed by precision gunnery from surface ships. OMFTS holds the promise of low-casualty amphibious operations and offers the prospect that future national leaders will be able to use light naval infantry that are routinely present in distant theaters to destroy concentrations of entrenched enemy heavy forces—a capability that the United States does not currently possess.

As a complement to network-centric warfare, the Navy intends to pursue a logistics paradigm optimized to deliver the requisite support "just in time," thereby reducing the size of the burdens of accompanying spares and stores on the combatant forces. Designs for focused logistics have long sought to ensure that resulting logistics systems are robust enough for the circumstances under which they must operate. One of the challenges for logistics in the future strategy could arise from an enemy ability to delay, damage, or destroy logistics and supply ships. These circumstances would place greater premiums on at least three areas: (1) improved defenses for logistics elements, (2) longer-endurance products and expendables, and (3) greater ability to project these types of support further ashore. Therefore, in addition to improving defenses for logistics ships and facilities, prudence suggests taking steps to reduce the demand on logistics to begin with by pursuing more fuel-efficient, lightweight vehicles, longer-life batteries, and more-effective ammunition, thus reducing the frequency when focused logistics must replenish combat forces. Prudence further dictates developing the capability to project support further ashore, over extended distances, as a hedge against the advent of enemy weapons that force Navy ships to remain farther out at sea.

Finally, no future naval doctrine of the United States would be complete without attention being paid to the threat and opportunities posed to the Fleet by information warfare. U.S. national doctrine as embodied in JV2020 is already taking IW into account, and future naval doctrine will inevitably follow. U.S. information systems have already suffered enough attacks to prompt establishment of the Joint Task Force (JTF)–Info Protect, the first joint task force devoted to information operations, within U.S. Joint Forces Command. The legal constraints on offensive information operations are under review. Reliance on radio transmissions—the medium that electronic warfare and signals intelligence can most easily target—has been gradually reduced among the United States' potential adversaries, in favor of other media such as fiber optics. As a result, naval and Marine forces will often confront opponents who are fully cognizant of the risks posed by U.S. communications-intercept capabilities and thus follow advanced communications security procedures. These opponents will also be eager to embrace offensive information-warfare techniques as a powerful weapon against the U.S. Navy. Note that, in this arena, non-state opponents may be more dangerous than state actors. Malignant non-state actors, such as organized-crime syndicates and religious fundamentalist terrorist fronts, generally do not have large bureaucracies that inhibit rapid innovation with new technologies and thus will be among the first organizations in the world to embrace new IW concepts and methods.

Current and Future Force Structure

Force Structure and Modernization. The Navy is replacing and upgrading elements of the Fleet to ensure that it can meet its mission requirements for the remainder of this decade. At the same time, overall fleet size and age pose potential challenges during the latter part of this decade. We discuss these trends below and summarize their implications.

Additions to the Fleet. Navy procurement funding has varied more sharply with changes in the defense budget than have other aspects of the Navy's total obligation authority (TOA). Figure 2.3, derived from official DoD budget data, shows past trends and future estimates for the various elements of Navy TOA (in FY00 dollars) from FY76 through FY05, the end of the prevailing future-year defense plan. The procurement spike during the Reagan Administration buildup is apparent, as is procurement's reaction to the decrease in the defense budget after the fall of the Berlin Wall. The graph also shows the current and planned trends in procurement as the Navy tries to take advantage of potential defense budget increases to recapitalize in response to future challenges.

According to the Navy's planned shipbuilding program, the median production rate over the next two decades will be five ships per year.[4] Over the next 10

---

[4]As another benchmark, the Honorable H. Lee Buchanan, Assistant Secretary of the Navy for Research, Development and Acquisition, presented a statement before the House Authorization Subcommittee on March 14, 2000, describing the Department of the Navy's Fiscal Year 2001 Procurement and RDT&E budget request. This request calls for construction of 39 ships across the Future Years Defense Plan (FYDP), which is an average of 7.8 ships per year—somewhat higher than we have shown in Figure 2.4 for those years.

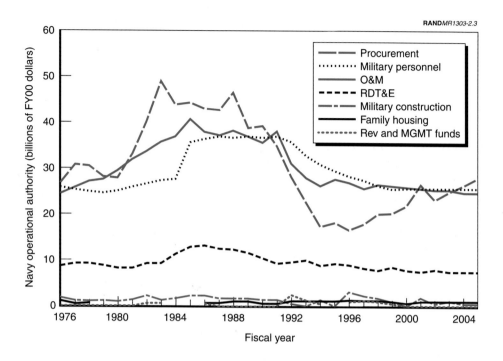

Figure 2.3—Trends in the Navy Budget

years, most of the shipbuilding will be for the conclusion of the construction program for the DDG51 Arleigh Burke–class destroyers, and most of the remainder will be for the LPD17 San Antonio–class amphibious ships (Figure 2.4, dark hatched and light hatched bars, respectively). Between 2010 and 2020, most of the new ships commissioned will be DD21s or Virginia-class attack submarines (light gray and dark blue bars).

Fleet Size and Age. Today, the Navy maintains a fleet of battle ship forces of slightly more than 300 ships—down sharply from the beginning of the past decade. Projections are that the Fleet will stay within 5 percent of that number for a while (see Figure 2.5). After 2006, the size of the force is projected to decrease until it stabilizes again after 2010 at around 250 ships. This projection assumes that the Los Angeles–class SSNs will remain in the Fleet for 30 years, the FFG-7s will retire at 25 years, and the Spruance-class destroyers will retire at 30 years. This projection is, of course, subject to the uncertainty of these assumptions and future decisions that may be made within DoD or by Congress. That uncertainty is greater for specific classes, e.g., SSNs, than for the Fleet as a whole. Assuming that the general downward trend in total fleet size is approximately correct, it can be seen from Figure 2.5 that the number of ships decommissioned between 2005 and 2020 would exceed the new acquisitions by

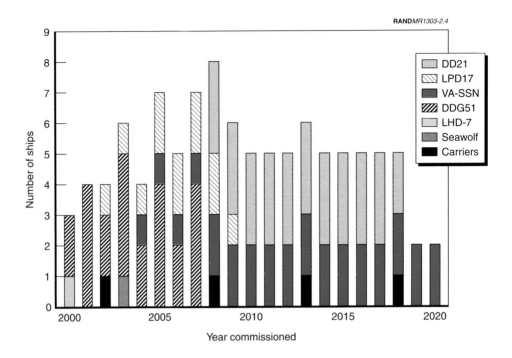

Figure 2.4—The Navy Plans to Average Five New Ships per Year over the Next 20 Years

20 to 30 ships in that time period. The procurement budget beyond the FYDP is very uncertain because it depends on how threatening the international environment will be and the impact of that environment on the overall future U.S. defense budget.

The decreasing force structure projected here may challenge the Navy's ability to continue the scope of its current forward-presence operations. If demand increases, the Navy may have to consider alternative solutions: perhaps re-designing task groups and task units around fewer ships or employing some ships in roles originally not envisioned for them.

Despite the challenges that may confront the Fleet's ability to support widespread presence, two of the core instruments of U.S. Navy power, carrier battle groups and Amphibious Ready Groups, are still present in sufficient quantity to accomplish most of the forward-presence mission assigned to the Navy and Marine Corps today. Figures 2.6 and 2.7, which are based on Center for Naval Analyses (CNA) analysis, illustrate this fact and show global coverage probabilities for different numbers of ARGs and CVBGs, respectively. Both amphibious ships and aircraft carriers are assumed to be available one-third of the time, because the average ship spends one-third of its time in pre-deployment preparations and training, one-third at sea, and the final third in maintenance

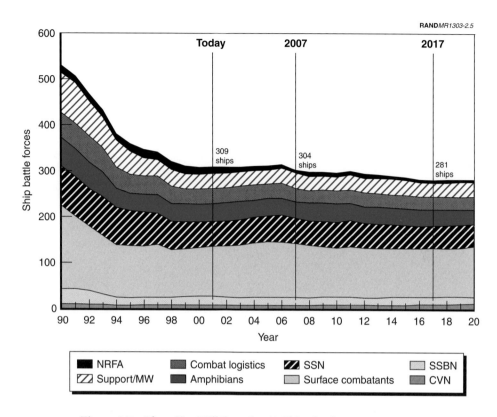

Figure 2.5—Fleet Size Will Drop by 28 Ships in the Next 20 Years

and recovery after its cruise. Based on this logic, Figure 2.6 shows the number of amphibious ships needed to provide for the presence of a standard three-ship ARG at five percentages of time for two, three, four, and five regions of the world.

As the figure suggests, the current and forecast inventory of amphibious ships can maintain a three-ship ARG in all five key regions of the world while leaving some ships available for extended maintenance and other downtime.

Aircraft carrier coverage can be calculated the same way. It is less robust and, because it depends on a smaller number of ships than amphibious coverage does, is more sensitive to small changes in carrier availability. This sensitivity is somewhat offset by the fact that carrier coverage is required in fewer regions than ARG coverage, since some areas (such as sub-Saharan Africa) do not have conventional forces strong enough to warrant a significant carrier presence. However, as Figure 2.7 illustrates, in the current force structure, if even one carrier becomes non-deployable (as is usually the case, since one carrier is almost always in reactor overhaul), the consequences are significant. With 11

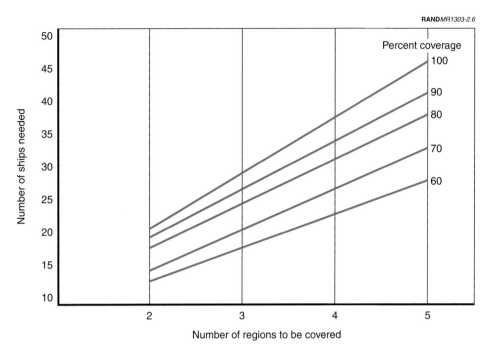

Figure 2.6—Number of Amphibious Ships Needed for Regional Coverage

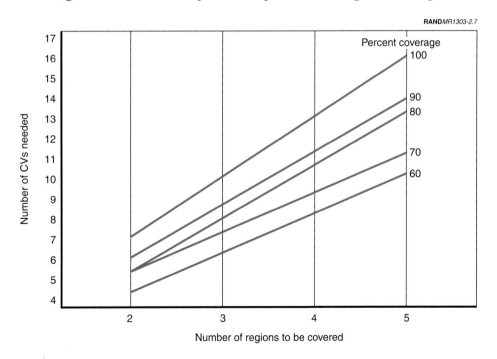

Figure 2.7—Number of CVs Needed to Sustain Regional Coverage

carriers available, the Fleet can cover three regions fully (i.e., 100 percent of the time) and provide limited presence in a fourth area. If carrier availability drops to 10, however, the Fleet can maintain full-time coverage for only three regions, or must reduce coverage to approximately 90 percent to maintain significant presence in all four regions.

Ship age could be an important consideration, since the average age of ships in the Fleet is rising, from about 17 years in 1990 to about 22 years in 2020, assuming that planned retirement and commissioning dates hold (see Figure 2.8, which is based on the *Naval Vessel Registry*). But close examination indicates that some parts of the Fleet are aging more gracefully than others. At the aggregate level, the Fleet ages five years over the course of 30 years if the programmed acquisitions of new ships take place. However, SSBNs, support, and mine warfare ships age chronologically—one year for every year, or linearly. On the other hand, the SSN force will age more slowly because of the introduction of the Virginia-class attack submarines. The changing age

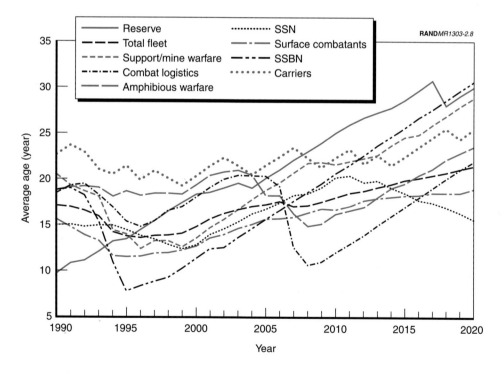

Figure 2.8—Fleet Age Is Increasing, but at Very Different Rates for Different Ship Types, Current and Future Systems

structure could have implications for maintenance practices and, possibly, ramifications for NAVSEA's responsibilities for Fleet in-service support.

Technological advances, especially if combined with decreases in force structure, will act along with resource constraints to create both opportunities and the need for innovative types of support options. Such options as mobile offshore bases, globally prepositioned supply and logistics, and advanced underway replenishment systems could allow the Navy to keep ships, if not the crews, on-station for far longer periods of time. The Navy may also find itself required to construct a new class of Marine fast-logistics ships beyond the current medium-speed roll-on/roll-off ships to support Operational Maneuver from the Sea. This class would be designed for very large payloads and the capability to precisely deliver supplies over the horizon to small networked units ashore. Finally, we anticipate the need to meet the configuration-control challenges posed by rapid data processing and computer system hardware and software turnover.

A potential impediment to the Navy's ability to do littoral power projection at an acceptable level of risk is the ongoing proliferation of cruise missiles. In response, the Navy is incorporating Single Integrated Air Picture capability, which will coordinate detection, tracking, and intercept capabilities between the airborne and sea-based elements of the battle group into its doctrine. This defense capability will require continued upgrading as enemy cruise missiles become faster, more maneuverable, and more stealthy. Improvements will also be needed to overcome enemy countermeasures to distort or yield spurious signals that could thwart detection and tracking.

The Navy is pursuing new methods for detecting the need for shipboard maintenance. Significantly reducing the time ships need in port, these methods will rely, in part, on electronic data chips that detect the status of shipboard operational equipment and signal that status to remote Navy locations, which can coordinate the replacement or repair of that equipment at the nearest port or while the ship is still under way at sea. Similarly, ship supplies may also be delivered in a timely manner at the nearest port, by commercial airfreight, or while the ship is still at sea, by helicopter or another ship, reducing the Navy's need for maintaining large land-based storage facilities at locations around the world.

The new Navy ships are expected to be much more capable than their predecessors. Therefore, even though they are being procured in smaller numbers, they should add considerably to the Navy's littoral warfare capability while featuring newly designed elements that are expected to reduce personnel and Operations and Maintenance (O&M) costs. The LPD17 will have an advanced, fully integrated self-defense system, and new composite materials and shape to reduce its hull signature. The Virginia-class attack submarine will possess an open command, control, communications, and intelligence (C3I) architecture that will enable refreshing with advanced commercial off-the-shelf (COTS) hardware and software as it is developed. The DD21 will be able to actively manage its signature characteristics. It will have an integrated power system, and automation to reduce manning. The CVNX, the advanced carrier class to follow the Nimitz, is going to have electromagnetic catapults and a new and improved nuclear-propulsion plant. It will feature a zonal electric distribution system, and its hull will be of modular construction.

Possible nonplatform acquisitions should also enhance Navy mission capability. Among those that have been either proposed or funded are the following:

- Conversion of SSBNs to Tomahawk-missile-firing SSGNs

- Upgrade of the SPY radar systems on Aegis-class destroyers

- New sonar systems for attack submarines

- Development and incorporation of extended range guided precision munitions into the Navy's gunfire systems

- Shipboard defenses against chemical and biological warfare

- Ship-based theater ballistic-missile defense (TBMD) systems

- Improved broadband information and communications networks

- Development of a cooperative engagement capability for defense of the Fleet against missile and aircraft attacks.

OPERATIONAL UNCERTAINTIES AND VULNERABLE ASSUMPTIONS

As with all complex plans, the current and anticipated naval strategies rest on a number of critical foundation assumptions—what we call "load-bearing" assumptions—some of which are explicit and some implicit. If the future security environment were to prove one or more of these assumptions to be faulty, then the effectiveness of the associated naval doctrine would be placed in jeopardy. This section first identifies the key, load-bearing assumptions underpinning naval strategy, then assesses the current evidence—signposts—that these assumptions are becoming vulnerable.

Key, Load-Bearing Assumptions

Identifying assumptions requires content analysis of key strategy and planning documents. The technique, developed by RAND colleague James A. Dewar and his colleagues, involves searching the key documents for certain words and phrases that—experience indicates—point toward assumptions. Sample words include *will, must,* and *is expected.* Thought in today's U.S. Navy on future strategic, doctrinal, and force planning rests on at least seven such assumptions:

- Navy and Marine Corps force packages are of a size adequate for the tasks they face. Naval and amphibious battle groups have the skilled personnel, major platforms, equipment, weapons, and munitions in the numbers they need to prevail, or to continue operations until reinforced or relieved. All are based on the premise that the wars the Navy and Marine Corps will fight in the future will be against regional adversaries with limited strategic depth and limited numbers of technologically advanced weapons.

- Naval and Marine forces can be projected successfully to the scene of trouble. The forces have the speed necessary to arrive on-scene in time to be effective, and they have the means to overcome efforts to interfere with their arrival.

- The forces have the means to operate on-scene effectively and at an acceptable level of risk. Some combination of active and passive force-protection measures is adequate against enemy capabilities.

- Forces can be sustained and supported on-scene. The logistics, maintenance, and replenishment systems can overcome enemy attempts at interdiction and similar disruptions to support the deployed force. Expendables, especially ammunition, can be replaced at rates that will support the pace of combat.

- Forces will participate in joint warfare. Not only will the Navy and Marine Corps continue to operate in their long-standing partnership, but U.S. Army and Air Force elements will be able to reinforce the initial naval and Marine forces for those contingencies that develop into sustained combat operations.

- Core allies will remain resolute in the face of pressure from rogue states and will provide forces and bases to support U.S. naval combat operations.

- The aircraft carrier will remain the dominant tool in naval combat operations. While submarines and advanced cruisers will have very powerful effects on war in the littoral, the aircraft carrier will hold on to its status as the premier capital-ship type in the world.

Signposts of Vulnerability

Threats to these assumptions are of three types: domestic politics, external security environment, and military/operational. These assumptions might become vulnerable as a result of changes in the global security environment or enemy force postures; it is also possible that changes and dynamics within the Navy and Marine Corps themselves will call some of the assumptions into question. The Navy must be prepared to hedge against the demise of one or more of these assumptions.

Domestic Politics. A number of changes in the domestic political climate could force the Navy and Marine Corps to adopt a new outlook. If a future administration were to cut the Navy's procurement budget below requested levels, the service might see its force structure shrink further, which could force the Navy either to reduce the size of individual battle groups to the point where they are capable of providing basic forward presence but are unable to conduct sustained combat operations, or to simply maintain fewer battle groups and reduce global forward presence. Alternatively, should the Navy lose internal Pentagon political battles to the Army and Air Force, the other services could acquire missions and capabilities that would free them from the need to work jointly with the Navy. Finally, should the country come to a decision to pursue sea-based national missile defense, the Navy could find some of its forces becoming more of a strategic tool for the NCA and less of a theater instrument for the combatant commanders. It might be required to stay on-station or maintain a patrol route designed to optimize its missile defense capabilities and would not, therefore, be available to the regional commander in chief (CINC) to respond to local contingencies.

Signposts suggesting the current vulnerability of the key, load-bearing assumptions arising from domestic factors are not evident. The current administration has endorsed national missile defense, but the technical architecture of the system is yet to be determined, leaving the future of sea-based systems shrouded in ambiguity. The FY01 defense budget estimate, at least at the macro level, offers no clues suggesting that the Navy's fortunes are waning relative to those of the other services.

That said, there are indications that U.S. military investments in engagement—crucial to the shaping function of U.S. strategy—are down. Figure 2.9 offers four metrics of declining investment in engagement: The number of exercises essential to engagement have declined about 34 percent; manpower for joint exercises has been reduced almost 32 percent; Operations and Maintenance funds within each of the services' budgets for support to engagement also reflect significant decrements for FY00; and transportation funds earmarked to move forces to the site of exercises have likewise been reduced.

External Security Environment. The emergence of a near-peer competitor would challenge the Navy's assumptions about future combat. All of the candidates for near-peer status (Russia, PRC, India) have vastly greater strategic

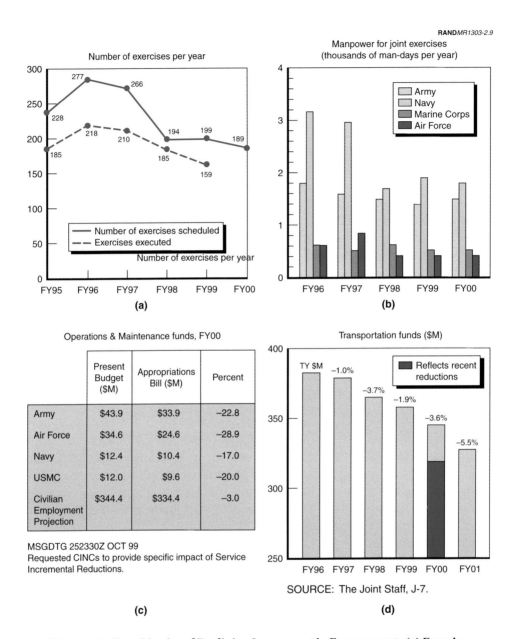

Figure 2.9—Four Metrics of Declining Investment in Engagement: (a) Exercise
numbers down 34 percent; (b) man-days reduced 31.7 percent;
(c) congressional reductions for FY00; and (d) 92-percent
reduction in transportation funds in FY00
compared with FY96.

depth—territory in which to operate—and many more weapon systems than the rogue states the Navy has been planning to fight. A Kosovo-level naval air and missile campaign would have little effect on a nation the size of China. More-intense operations with more-powerful weapons would be warranted.

Another challenge would be increasing sophistication on the part of medium-sized adversaries. Some of these adversaries might wish to pursue formal alliances with larger states (e.g., a Russia-Iran Entente) in order to deter decisive U.S. attacks against the regime in power. In general, more-capable adversaries might render today's force packages—carrier battle groups and Amphibious Ready Groups—less adequate for their tasks and might also be able to raise force-protection risks to unacceptable levels, especially for operations for which relatively minor U.S. interests hang in the balance. More-capable adversaries might be able to interdict critical support and replenishment tasks, undercutting naval and Marine force effectiveness. As an alternative, more-capable foes, perhaps those armed with chemical, biological, or nuclear weapons and short-range ballistic missiles, might be able to intimidate local U.S. allies sufficiently that they withdraw the right for U.S. forces to use their ports, airfields, and other facilities and to fly through their airspace. Such a development could severely complicate some operations, especially reinforcements by Air Force and Army elements.

As Figure 2.10 suggests, since the demise of the Soviet Union (the highest columns for the years through 1991), defense spending has been fairly modest and consistent in much of the world. Only East Asia has experienced much real growth—mostly for new equipment focused on ground forces.

Focusing more specifically on some of the countries the United States most often views with concern, in Figure 2.11 we see that their individual defense-spending habits have been modest and fairly constant. Expenditures by Iran, Iraq, Pakistan, and Syria have been even smaller than North Korea's, and none has risen more than 20 percent over the period shown.

Turning to arms transfers, Figure 2.12 shows that, with few exceptions, the arms transferred have been in fairly small quantities. Supersonic combat aircraft were transferred in the greatest numbers, but most often the aircraft types involved were older: MiG-21s and similar-vintage obsolescent aircraft.

Given the wide distribution of fairly small numbers of major weapons transferred over the 12 years 1986–1997 and the modest defense budgets over a similar period of time, it seems doubtful that the countries considered will be able to mount a Revolution in Military Affairs within the near-term horizon of this study. The level of investment that we can see and the arms transfers that

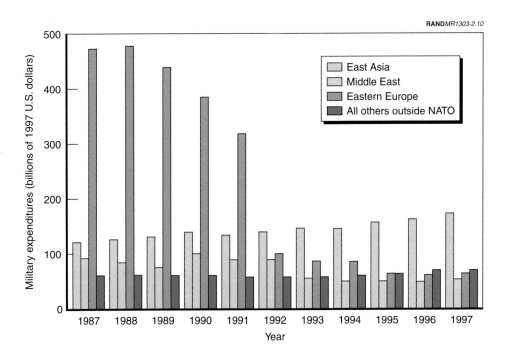

Figure 2.10—World Military Spending Has Been Modest and Consistent Since 1992

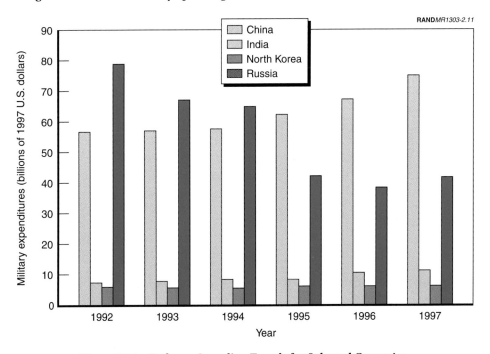

Figure 2.11—Defense-Spending Trends for Selected Countries

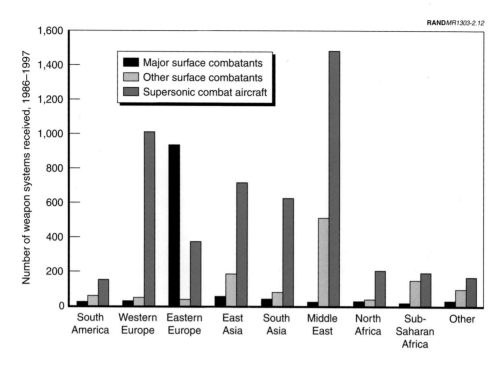

Figure 2.12—Major Weapon Systems Have Been Transferred in Fairly Small Quantities

we can track do not suggest the emergence of a peer competitor within the near term, either.

Military/Operational. Finally, we cannot dismiss the prospect that developments in military technology and operations will make it easier for medium-weight adversaries such as Iraq to resist the types of precision attacks the Navy conducts and to threaten Navy ships and friendly ports. Advances in camouflage and signature-reduction technologies would permit adversary forces to be more easily hidden in urban areas, among masses of civilians. Major developments in quiet diesel submarine technology, such as air-independent propulsion, could allow regional powers to begin to threaten U.S. battle groups in the open ocean as they transit to or from a combat theater. Further advances in communications encryption and fiber optics might cut U.S. naval information-gathering capabilities to low levels, thus complicating surveillance and targeting. In extreme cases, such developments could allow a perpetrator who has attacked U.S. personnel or facilities to "cover his tracks" so well that the United States could not muster the political consensus to retaliate. Last but not least, new strides in offensive IW technologies, such as electromagnetic pulse (EMP) weaponry, could place individual battle groups at risk for a surprise attack.

The same indicators—trends in global defense spending, military investments of selected potential adversaries, and records of arms transfers—suggest that the security environment is not likely to produce a peer competitor within the planning time frame considered in this study and that the military/operational factors are also unlikely to affect the Navy significantly in the near term. Indeed, the Navy is becoming more capable in such key categories as strategic lift. For example, the large, medium-speed roll-on/roll-off (RoRo) ship acquisition program will deliver 10 million square feet of capacity needed for strategic lift (Joint Staff, n.d., Chapter 5).

IMPLICATIONS FOR NAVSEA

Equipped now with a sense of the main elements of current and future naval strategy and the environment in which they are intended to operate, we must now follow the threads down to specific implications for NAVSEA. In doing so, this section employs the strategy-to-tasks framework to identify the strategic priorities driving the current and anticipated naval strategy and then to suggest technical, organizational, and operational contributions that NAVSEA can make, based upon the command's mandate and warrants, summarized in Table 2.2.[5] Simply put, this last section suggests areas for NAVSEA emphasis that will support the needs and preferences of warfighters with respect to current and future naval strategy over the next decade.

The strategy-to-tasks framework for NAVSEA is represented in Figures 2.13 through 2.16. The first three sections of this chapter produced a conception of naval strategy and of the threats and developments that might influence it. The remainder of this section elaborates on the *strategic imperatives*—those capabilities and mission areas the Navy and NAVSEA should strive to maintain and grow because of their centrality to the success of overall naval strategy—that result from the strategic plans and the environment in which the strategy must be executed. Next, the section considers how NAVSEA's mandates and other influences suggest ways for the command to contribute toward preserving and improving the viability and vitality of naval strategy. The section concludes by identifying those areas within NAVSEA that are likely to make the greatest contributions.

Strategic Imperatives

Recall the "deter, shape, prepare, respond" template developed in the first section of this chapter as shorthand for the major elements of the National Military

---

[5]Appendix B includes an exhaustive list.

Table 2.2

NAVSEA Influences, Warrants, and Mandates

Influences on Mandates:	Secretary of the Navy (SECNAV) and Office of the Chief of Naval Operations (OPNAV) Mandates
National Security Strategy	Ship and ship system acquisition
National Military Strategy	Ships, submarines, submersibles
Joint Vision 2020	Aviation interface
Navy Posture Statement	Expendable ordnance
Forward . . . from the Sea	Small arms, infantry equipment, body protective armor, and in-shore undersea warfare equipment
Operational Maneuver from the Sea	Special explosive ordnance disposal tools and equipment
	Chemical, biological, radiological warfare defense materials and equipment
	Respiratory protective devices, diving methods and equipment
	Equipment for towing and salvage
	Coordination of shipbuilding, conversion, and repairs

RAND*MR1303-T2.2*

Strategy and, ultimately, naval strategy. This shorthand also supports the discussion of the strategic imperatives that underlie the template. This subsection follows the threads of strategy deductively from the various strategic imperatives underpinning "deter, shape, prepare, respond" down through NAVSEA mandates and influences to specific systems, products, and services: the strategy-to-tasks pathway.

Deter. As Figure 2.13 below suggests, deterrence rests upon two strategic imperatives: information dominance, which ensures that the United States can always identify attackers, and potent forces, which gives the country the ability to promise that the United States will retaliate if attacked, to produce unacceptably costly losses for the enemy, and to deny an adversary the ability to achieve a quick, decisive victory over a U.S. ally.

As the arrows in the figure indicate, these strategic imperatives, interpreted through NAVSEA's mandates and influences, imply specific contributions from NAVSEA. First, the command should contribute toward accurate and timely identification, location, and tracking of adversaries. Doing so requires integrated and networked combat systems from NAVSEA. The subsystems appear the next tier down, as radars, infrared sensors, undersea warfare systems, sound interoperability among systems, and communications, both on the surface and beneath it.

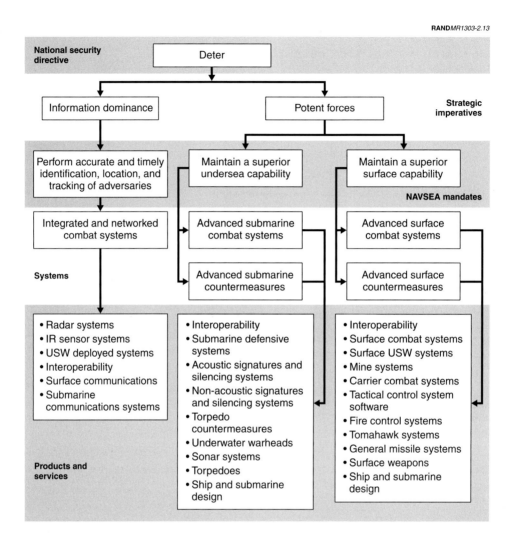

RAND*MR1303-2.13*

| National security directive | Deter |
| Strategic imperatives |
| NAVSEA mandates |
| Systems |
| Products and services |

Figure 2.13—Strategy-to-Tasks Framework for Deterrence

The second strategic imperative is maintenance of potent forces: a strong, sur-
vivable, and reliable deterrent force that will have high credibility with potential
enemies. Contributing to potent forces are specific NAVSEA systems in the next
tier down, including advanced submarine combat systems and advanced surface countermeasures. The specific products and services central to this improvement, at the bottom of the figure, include surface combat systems, carrier
combat systems, and Tomahawk systems.

Shape. The shaping function is about exerting positive regional influence. It
rests on two strategic imperatives: (1) forward presence and (2) force protection

for U.S. allies in the region. The basis for forward presence is obvious: U.S. forces must be present in the region to be influential there. Allied force protection is less obvious, but critical. Extending protection to allies will help prevent their intimidation by others and prevent them from being blackmailed into withholding access to their ports, airfields, and facilities in times of crisis. As Figure 2.14 illustrates, each of these strategic imperatives produces specific influences on NAVSEA.

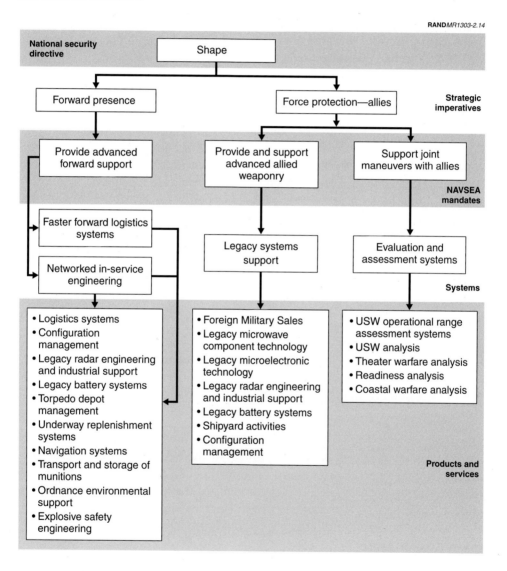

Figure 2.14—Strategy-to-Tasks Framework for Shaping

Consistent with its mandates, NAVSEA should provide advanced forward support by developing faster forward logistics systems and networked in-service engineering, thus helping to maintain the U.S. military presence in regions of importance to the United States. NAVSEA should also support force protection for allies by providing and supporting advanced allied weaponry and supporting maneuvers with allies.

At the level of NAVSEA systems, contributions to forward presence take the form of faster forward logistics systems and network engineering. The command's contributions to allied force protection at this level include support for legacy systems and evaluation and assessment systems.

At the products and services level, NAVSEA's contributions appear as specific systems and capabilities, including logistics systems for forward presence and Foreign Military Sales and assistance for allied force protection.

Prepare. Preparing for the future means, in part, developing the most powerful approach to warfare possible. Navy preparations depend upon three strategic imperatives: (1) effective engagement, (2) complex terrain operations, and (3) standoff operations support. Each of these imperatives contributes toward the most capable and fully prepared forces possible, as Figure 2.15 illustrates.

NAVSEA's contribution toward effective engagement is in capabilities for the littoral—more specifically, cooperative engagement systems. The products and services box at the bottom left in Figure 2.15 lists specific NAVSEA products that contribute directly toward cooperative engagement capabilities, enabling multiple means of attack and synchronization of the actions of many combatants in a single engagement.

Complex terrain capabilities depend upon full-spectrum situational awareness, which, in turn, depends upon advanced networked sensors. These sensor capabilities reside in sonar systems, infrared sensors, undersea warfare systems, radars, and even in submarine periscopes and masts.

Standoff operations support involves development of a new generation of brilliant munitions and new delivery options. At the NAVSEA-systems level, this means precision strike systems and systems that can hover/orbit/loiter for extended periods, awaiting appropriate targets. At the level of NAVSEA products and services, energetic materials, propulsion, weapons, and the systems as shown in the bottom tier of Figure 2.15 constitute the NAVSEA contribution to standoff operations.

Respond. Future naval responses will be shaped by three strategic imperatives: (1) network-centric warfare, (2) littoral warfare, and (3) improved force protection for U.S. forces. Figure 2.16 summarizes the framework.

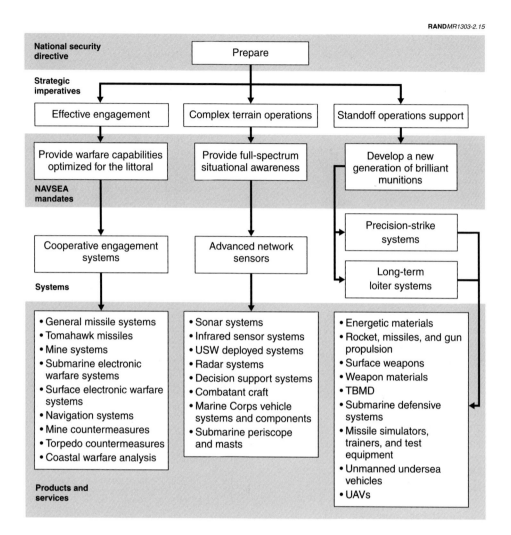

RAND*MR1303-2.15*

Figure 2.15—Strategy-to-Tasks Framework for Prepare

Given the strategic imperative for network-centric warfare, NAVSEA should respond by providing appropriate advanced warfare systems. At the systems level, the NAVSEA contribution is in high-bandwidth networks and advanced command, control, communications, and computers, intelligence, surveillance, and reconnaissance (C4ISR) systems that make network-centric warfare possible. These, in turn, rest on NAVSEA products and services, including submarine and surface communications systems, sonar imaging, and a host of sensors.

NAVSEA's mandates in support of littoral warfare should lead the command to help with new concepts for maneuver and amphibious forces. That help should

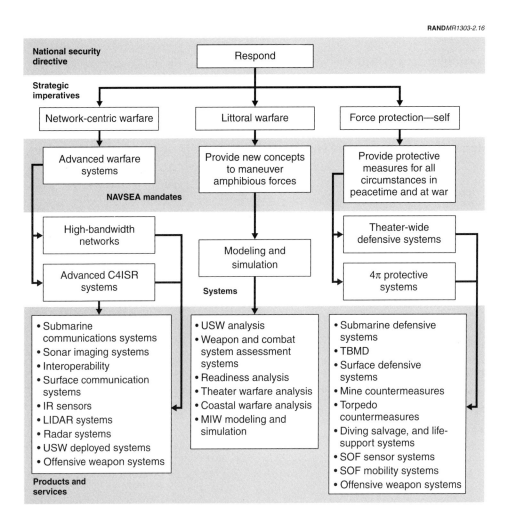

RAND*MR1303-2.16*

Figure 2.16—Strategy-to-Tasks Framework for Respond

come in the form of modeling and simulation that will support the representation and testing of new concepts. The specific analytical tools appear on the bottom tier of the figure.

NAVSEA could contribute a great deal to force protection, the third strategic imperative, by providing appropriate protective measures. As Figure 2.16 indicates, these include theater-wide defensive systems, full-dimensional (4π) protective measures in foreign ports' coastal waters, and further ashore. The specific NAVSEA products and services involved include submarine and theater missile defense systems, mine countermeasures, and offensive weapon systems.

NAVSEA'S ROLE IN COPING WITH THE UNEXPECTED

In addition to doing its part to satisfy warfighter requirements and preferences as described above, NAVSEA also has a responsibility to ensure that the current naval strategy remains robust in the face of developments in domestic politics, the international security environment, and military operations and technology. Fulfilling this responsibility requires the management of uncertainty. Managing uncertainty in large, complex organizations generally involves coping actions. Coping is meant to prepare for uncontrollable developments— for example, the sudden emergence of an alliance between a rogue state and a large nuclear power. For example, if a long-term technological threat is detected in a hostile power, the appropriate coping action would be to develop countermeasures before the original threat is even operationally deployed. Shaping actions, on the other hand, are more proactive. They attempt to influence controllable developments. Ideally, coping actions are grounded in the key assumptions that undergird current and anticipated U.S. naval strategy. As we have seen, some of these assumptions could be vulnerable. NAVSEA should always be in a position to support rapid Navy adjustments in case one or more of the foundation assumptions become invalid. Therefore, NAVSEA should consider developing some products, programs, and technologies because of their value to coping actions rather than for their direct contributions to existing Navy doctrine. Given the assumptions discussed earlier in this chapter, NAVSEA might take the following actions:

- Deal with the prospect that foreign military developments may render current naval force packages inadequate by building more capabilities into existing platforms and more operational capability into smaller units and battle groups.

- Anticipate the prospect of the sudden loss of port access in an allied state by deploying advanced underway replenishment systems and fast logistics ships that can compensate temporarily.

- Plan against the increasing threat of enemy interdiction's delaying the arrival of U.S. forces into a theater by improving capabilities that can counter interdiction efforts, including advanced ASW techniques (possibly including non-acoustic sensors), additional minesweepers, and reliable ship-based TBMD.

- Anticipate the eventuality of Army and Air Force units, not being able to reach the scene of a crisis in a timely manner, leaving Navy and Marine

Corps forces to face the prospect of sustained combat. Make targeted investments in weapons that are suited for extended combat (e.g., more capable artillery support for the Marines, long-endurance reconnaissance and surveillance platforms).

- Address the possibility that future adversaries may have significantly more strategic depth and size by developing longer-range precision-strike systems with multiple warheads—e.g., theater ballistic and intermediate-range ballistic missiles using Global Positioning System (GPS) guidance targeted in near-real-time from space.

- Build and improve incentives for regional partners to cooperate within the current strategy by supporting training-and-equipping initiatives for improving allied force protection and interoperability with U.S. forces.

- Influence would-be weapons of mass destruction (WMD) proliferators by developing means to preempt the deployment and use of WMD-delivery vehicles.

SUMMARY

This chapter has identified the key NAVSEA products, technologies, and activities that are central to the success of current and future naval strategy. However, simply knowing which of various products and activities enjoy high strategic priority is insufficient. For NAVSEA to optimize them, it must first understand the needs and preferences of the Navy markets that will consume the command's products, since these factors will influence the specific characteristics of individual products, the way they operate, and the way they are maintained. The next chapter, therefore, examines Navy markets and the positions that NAVSEA products and activities hold within them.

Chapter Three

NAVSEA MARKETS AND THE PRODUCTS AND ACTIVITIES TO FULFILL THEM

We have examined the military template for NAVSEA, which framed what that command does in terms of needs of the strategic imperative for the Navy as a whole and of the National Military Strategy. We now look at a different template, a business template, which views NAVSEA's core competencies as a business not unlike other, large private-sector, for-profit organizations as NAVSEA participates in the general government move to become more business-like.

INTRODUCTION: FROM MILITARY STRATEGY TO BUSINESS STRATEGY

Answering the Call to Accept Business Practices

The United States government is in the throes of a movement to behave more like "business." The current effort at governmental reform—making government more "business-like"—has its roots in the Progressive era of public administration, from 1890 to 1910. In that era, the public rejected the budgetary abuses of machine politics at all levels of government. The outstanding successes of the new techniques of "scientific management" associated with Frederick Winslow Taylor, Thorstein Veblen, and Henry Ford in the business community created for the first time the movement for making government more like a business. Under scientific management, all work was dissected into an irreducible set of activities combining the most efficient process and the minimum set of resources to accomplish a well-defined set of goals, or to provide a component or service needed in the next stage of the manufacture of a specific product. This set of activities was viewed as the "best" way or the most efficient way to provide the component or product or to meet the goals (Moe, 1993, p. 46).

The great success of scientific management in the United States at the end of the nineteenth century and the beginning of the twentieth century transformed the Industrial Revolution of Europe into a uniquely American economic force and established the United States as an economic rival of Europe. The Progressive Movement in public administration transformed the way government conducted its business so that the work of government, likewise, was dissected into an irreducible set of activities representing the "best" way in which the products and services of government can be provided. The Progressive era in government created the phrase "doing it by the book," because it was in this era that the book was written (Moe, 1994, p. 111).

Just as there was a call at the beginning of the past century for government to adopt the successful practices of the business community of that era, so too is there a call for government at the beginning of this century to adopt the practices of the business community of today. But they are business practices that are radically different from those of the earlier century. The rulebook is being tossed out the airlock to adapt to the rapidly changing economic conditions, the advent of new knowledge and technologies, and the rise of an ever-more-sophisticated consumer public. The most successful businesses of today are those that have the agility and adaptability to learn and to innovate in an environment of constant change. The "best way to do something" is a concept that is constantly changing, making rigid rule sets both inefficient and ineffective, and restricted discretionary power of responsible managers, inappropriate. Discretionary decision power wielded by responsible and committed officials is needed now more than ever before.

However, the organizing principle—combining activities involving processes and organized resources to produce a product or service needed by a customer or client, either internal or external to the organization—is still valid. But none of its components is cast in concrete. There could be more than one best way to be both efficient and effective. The past 20 years of management practice and research has shown a shift away from managing assets by assuming implicitly that the processes were a given to managing processes under the assumption that the required assets are determined by the set of best possible efficient and effective processes. A report of the National Research Council (NRC, 1996, p. 9) provides an example of such a shift:

> . . . many builders of small vessels are currently competitive and even leading in the international market for their products. These builders of smaller vessels have been examined by the committee for beneficial practices. Factors for successful competition cited by small shipyards include improved efficiency from less complex management organizations, the ability to change products quickly to enter new markets, and a willingness to price products at a loss in order to enter new markets.

Understanding the Clients' Needs

Another essential ingredient for commercial success in the current business environment is a thorough understanding of the evolving needs and preferences of increasingly more-sophisticated customers and clients. Not only is a business required to know what the customer needs of today are, it must also anticipate what those needs will be in the future—the risk NAVSEA now faces.

"The needs and preferences of customers and clients" is one way to define a *market* in conventional business parlance. Other parts of a definition of *market* include reasonably well-defined sets of product characteristics and competitors. The components of *market structure*, then, are needs and preferences, product characteristics, and competitors.

How the customers perceive the value of a company's products determines how the product will be positioned in the marketplace and reveals a specific choice in how the company achieves a sustainable competitive advantage: "A firm creates value for its buyer . . . if it lowers its buyer's cost or raises the buyer's performance in ways the buyer cannot match by purchasing from competitors" (Porter, 1990, p. 43). *Lower cost* is "the ability of a firm to design, produce, and market a comparable product more efficiently than its competitors" (Porter, 1990, p. 37); a buyer's performance is enhanced by *differentiation*, "the ability to provide unique and superior value to the buyer in terms of product quality, special features, or after-sale service" (Porter, 1990, p. 37) over the other organizations competing for market share. If a customer's demand for a particular product is high, the customer values the product highly and the product occupies a high ranking in the marketplace and within the producer's portfolio, or full array of products. Some products are present in multiple markets, requiring that product characteristics be optimized carefully to achieve a sustainable competitive advantage in those markets.

U.S. shipbuilders offer a good example of a positioning dilemma (NRC, 1996, p. 34):

> U.S. shipbuilders must target niche markets because the yards will find it difficult to compete in high-volume production markets where foreign competitors are well entrenched. . . . They must select shipbuilding market niches in which they can be competitive, adapt the technologies required to develop competitive products, apply the product technologies required to differentiate their products (ship designs) from competitors' products, develop the process technologies required to design and build these products competitively, and last but not least, develop strategies for the procurement of everything the yard cannot make efficiently.

Just as drastic declines in U.S. defense spending have forced many large U.S. shipbuilders to translate their skills from military to commercial markets if they are to thrive or simply survive, those declines have forced military organizations such as NAVSEA to look closely at its mission and its structure.

Viewing Military Capabilities Through Business-Planning Analyses

In assisting NAVSEA to look closely at its mission and its structure, we reconsider the military capabilities identified as important to future military strategy from the perspective of market analysis—e.g., industry facts,[1] advances in technology, growth in emphasis on the intended market (as opposed to size of market, which is usually studied in private-sector market analysis), identified market niches, growth-emphasis history and trends in the target market, identified customers and competitors, and trends in product or service development; investment planning—e.g., a portfolio analysis of products as "stocks," in which characteristics of those products are traded off against those of other products and the markets to answer specific questions on future risk, competition, priorities, etc., to which managers need answers; market structure; and other concerns such as *value chains*—an interdependent network of activities in a particular industry—and the *linkages* that connect that network—that will affect how NAVSEA is structured as an organization (see Chapter Four).

One such "business-like" concern is risk. In his *The Applications of Best Practices to Unmanned Spacecraft Development: An Exploration of Success and Failure in Recent Missions*, Sarsfield (2000, p. 147) points out that,

> Risk and the value of a space project are closely connected and must be evaluated together (NRC, 1997). To enjoy long-term political support, all Federal agencies, even one like NASA with an exploratory mission, must in practice evaluate risk in terms of responsiveness to a national mandate. This must be accomplished in a constrained budget environment, which usually precludes following the risk-abatement practices of the past. . . . a Federal agency cannot afford to purposely eliminate risk or blindly court it. Some means of dealing with risk is needed while reaching an assurance that Federal funds are being invested most effectively.

In his analysis of risk management in the space program, Sarsfield draws an analogy to stock-portfolio optimization, which teaches that a "most effective portfolio" can be defined as representing maximum return for a given level of risk; a superior portfolio must contain high-risk elements, even at the lowest desired levels of risk; and the least desirable option contains only low-risk elements.

_____

[1] In this chapter, we present quotations from sources about industries that NAVSEA is in and whose challenges are similar to those NAVSEA faces. Explicit information on the industrial context within which NAVSEA operates is presented in Appendix C (the companion to this chapter) and Chapter Four.

For NAVSEA, the risk of knowing the customer needs of today and anticipating the needs of tomorrow can be viewed as a two-edged dilemma in which failure is measured both in investing in unneeded technology, capacity, and/or personnel and, as a consequence, being unable to maintain the Fleet, and in being unable to bring new technology/capability online in a time frame that allows the Fleet to make full use of the capability in a current engagement. *Shipbuilding Technology and Education* (NRC, 1996, p. 25) proposes a taxonomy for the technologies that will need to be invested in for the shipbuilding industry of the future—"business-process technologies, system technologies, shipyard production-process technologies, and technologies for new materials and products"—and goes on to clarify that

> These categories are useful for considering investments in technology, but in operation they interact and overlap. "Technology" is discussed in its full sense, that is, as a practical application of knowledge (or capability thus provided) or a manner of accomplishing a task, especially using technical processes, methods, or knowledge. The concept of technology is interpreted in the larger sense because, . . . , the biggest challenges to a genuinely competitive U.S. industry are often matters of "soft technology," such as better marketing and cost-estimating techniques, as well as "hard technology," such as new hull designs.

In this chapter and in Appendix C, we endeavor to provide a similarly comprehensive taxonomy of the capabilities needed by the Navy in the future and the technologies to achieve them.

Dealing with Declining Budgets Through Portfolio Analysis

Another business-like concern, this time for the Navy's Science and Technology efforts, is dealing with declining budgets when there is not a corresponding reduction in mission requirements. Instead of giving every program's advocates an equivalently smaller portion of the available resources or looking for immediately visible payoffs, Gaffney and Saalfeld propose an investment strategy whose first aim is stabilizing funding, then looking at the technology base on which national naval responsibilities rest (1999, p. 15):

> National naval responsibilities are research areas like ocean acoustics that are essential to the Department of the Navy, but areas that no other mission agency or private enterprise can reasonably be expected to support.

Continuing the investment metaphor, the authors point out that "an effective science and technology investment strategy must also provide prioritized naval and Marine capabilities."

NAVSEA, a federal agency, is facing the constraints of the Navy as a whole and of the space program, and is under increasing pressure to demonstrate the value of its products based less on peer evaluations and more on returns, using measures employed by the private sector. The principles of stock optimization reinforce the notion that returns from NAVSEA products can be more thoroughly evaluated, and that a balanced portfolio of both *central products*—products important to all markets—and *niche products*—products that are essential to one or two markets—is the best way to achieve national mandates in a cost-constrained environment. However, as Gaffney and Saalfeld (1999, p. 17) note for Naval Science and Technology at the Office of Naval Research, "the return on investment we look for . . . is not *profits,* but *capabilities.*" The analysis in this chapter looks for a similar return on investment.

RAND MARKET-PRODUCT-ACTIVITY MODEL

The analysis in this chapter is directed at evaluating different aspects of product value relative to other products, processes, and markets for which NAVSEA should be configured for the year 2007 planning time horizon. (Potential configurations are presented in Chapter Four.)

The time horizon was set at 2007 so that the analysis results would be far enough in the future that simple extrapolations of the status quo would not be appropriate, yet not so far in the future that forecasts of future geopolitical, technological, and business environments would be totally unreliable. Moreover, this planning time horizon was chosen so that a possible implementation of analysis results could influence recommendations for earlier budget cycles. All of our analysis results are for the NAVSEA of 2007: The changes in market demand will be those that the NAVSEA of 2007 experiences, and the products will be those that the NAVSEA of 2007 will create with the processes of 2007, in response to those market needs.

In this chapter, we provide two types of analysis. The first is a market analysis to determine market-emphasis growth and market structure. The second is a portfolio analysis, which treats the products much like stocks in an investment portfolio viewed on different measures—or dimensions—of the product against questions that a decisionmaker—manager—would ask. The purpose of the latter analysis is to determine which products and markets are most central and/or essential to the business of NAVSEA so that a manager can make informed investment decisions. Each step of the analysis provides graphic tools to enhance the discretionary decision power of NAVSEA decisionmakers. Once centrality is established, we go on to determine the structure of the NAVSEA organization, or corporation, in 2007, in Chapter Four.

Both analyses are combined into what we call the RAND Market-Product-Activity Model, represented in Figure 3.1. Following partly the analytic

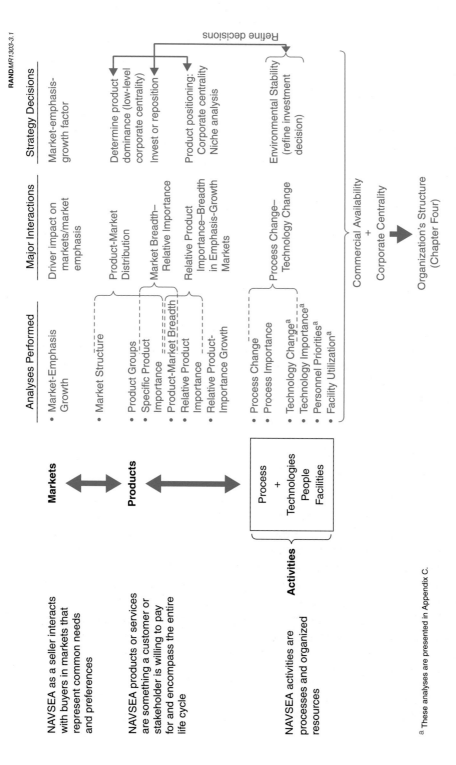

Figure 3.1—RAND Market-Product-Activity Model, Showing Analyses Conducted in Each Stage

framework in an earlier RAND report by Saunders et al. (1995), *Priority-Setting and Strategic Sourcing in the Naval Research, Development, and Technology Infrastructure,* the model is built on databases, or lists, of all the aspects of NAVSEA included in the figure.

Although the analysis in this chapter begins with markets, the research team began their study with activities, using the *Core Equities—Red Team Review* (Naval Sea Systems Command [hereafter, NAVSEA], 1999a) as a starting point. Intended as a means for identifying which functions within a NAVSEA Center[2] must be retained (core functions, or "floor functions") or can be performed by another source ("flex functions"), the Core Equities study provides an inventory of facilities within NAVSEA, including capabilities provided,[3] knowledge (e.g., for Submarine Imaging and Electronic Warfare Systems, knowledge is of design of surveillance antenna systems, early-warning receivers, RF systems, and infra-red imaging systems, among others, and testing and calibration of similar systems), functions and services, business base (experience, in work years), associates (employee affiliations), and specific facilities and amount budgeted. The research team aggregated the information for NAVSEA as a whole, creating separate lists of all activities, all processes, all technologies, and all personnel to be analyzed for crosscutting importance to and redundancies in the command as a whole. This focus is in keeping with the Navy's acquisition concerns for efficiencies that might be realized from vertical integration if budget activities became mutually supporting (Gaffney and Saalfeld, 1999, p. 13). It is also in keeping with the imperative stated in the Naval Studies Board–National Research Council overview of the twenty-first-century force, for the Department of the Navy and the naval forces to change their way of thinking about building and financing the forces (NSB–NRC, 1997a, p. 8):

> They must think in terms of life-cycle costs; people, platforms, weapons, and mission subsystems designed together as single systems; and investment in total and enduring capabilities, rather than system acquisition, support, and manning separately. "Affordability" must be thought about in terms of value received for money that is spent within allocated budgets to achieve a desired or necessary capability, rather than as simply spending the least amount of money in any area, as the term has often come to be used.

---

[2]We have used *Center* to represent an element of the NAVSEA organization—e.g., Naval Undersea Warfare Center (NUWC) or Naval Surface Warfare Center (NSWC). In reality, our study included other NAVSEA organizational elements, such as Headquarter Elements, Divisions of Centers, Field Activities, and Cost Centers.

[3]The scope of this study did not include an assessment of the shipyards managed by NAVSEA. Also, the Nuclear Propulsion Organization (SEA 08) was excluded from the scope of this study at the request of the NAVSEA Commander.

Additions were made to these lists of functions, products, markets, etc., after detailed discussions during site visits (see Appendix A for a list of these visits), and from documents by the Office of Naval Intelligence (ONI, 1998), Naval Studies Board–National Research Council (NSB–NRC, 1997a), and NRC (1996) documents, and from input from individuals in naval shore and Fleet operations. To ensure an accurate assessment of market-product-activity elements' characteristics and their interactions, the research team made significant use of a survey instrument constructed for the 38 site visits conducted as part of the research, which is also included in Appendix A. It enabled us to gather firsthand opinions on a wide variety of issues, including organizational mission, goals, and staffing location and size; programs, products, and services; internal equities; operating budget and investment in capital equipment; research and technology programs and activities outsourced during downsizing actions; and technical journal articles and reports published.

An *activity* in our model can be characterized in terms of a process and the organized resources that are set in motion by the process. Therefore, the team developed a process model tailored to the needs of the NAVSEA organization and categorized each activity according to its embedded process, organizational unit in NAVSEA, and, ultimately, to the technologies, personnel, and facilities that are needed for its execution.

The research team next analyzed the products, building them from the fundamental activities that supported their creation. For each product, the research team considered the list of activities that would encompass all aspects of the life cycle. Thus, the description of the product itself is embodied in the activities through which it is supported. After several iterations of input from the Strategy phase of the research program on the future geopolitical situation (Chapter Two), the initial product list and descriptions were projected into the planning time horizon, 2007, with support from ONI (1998), NSB–NRC (1997a), and NRC (1996) documents, and from the expertise of the RAND team. As a result, some new products were defined and existing ones redefined to include new performance requirements, advancing technologies, and changes in business processes. The product descriptions that flowed from the activities fundamental to a product were used for matching the needs and preferences of customers in the NAVSEA markets. In total, 108 NAVSEA products emerged, which the team aggregated into several product groups to facilitate further analysis at a higher level of summary, much as, say, Johnson and Johnson in the commercial world might think of baby lotions, cotton balls and swabs, and medical supplies as its product groups. Such groups share common technologies, skill sets, facilities, customer groups, and other features that make strategic planning in their regard a coherent effort.

The research team based the building of the NAVSEA markets in large measure on the Instruction by the Office of the Chief of Naval Operations (OPNAVINST) that defines the traditional Navy warfighting missions—OPNAVINST C3501.2J, *Naval Warfare Mission Areas and Required Operational Capability/Projected Operational Environment (ROC/POE) Statements*—and on additional directives from the Chief of Naval Operations and Secretary of the Navy (SECNAV) (see Appendix B). What emerged were 15 NAVSEA markets with well-identified "customers" with clear needs and preferences. To project these markets into the planning time horizon of 2007, the research team considered the input from the Strategy phase of the research on the future geopolitical situation (Chapter Two) and on forecasts of business and technology drivers of change available from ONI (1998), NSB–NRC (1997a), and NRC (1996) studies.

This structure was used to analyze the interactions listed in the middle of Figure 3.1. Although the individual components of our analysis model have distinct characteristics, they interact with each other. For example, corporate-level decisions on products depend on the characteristics of various dimensions of the market—such as structure and demand for a product—evaluated at the planning time horizon. In the commercial world, these interactions involve positioning. *Positioning* in the broadest sense is a firm's overall approach to competing. It involves making choices about the characteristics of a product and the product's relationship to current or emerging customer needs and preferences and to competing products. To facilitate management decisions on what actions should be taken toward structuring the organization, we then developed measures of interactions of products with markets. Similarly, corporate-level decisions on products depend on the characteristics of product-activity interactions evaluated at the planning time horizon. In the commercial world, these interactions involve all aspects of the activity, including associated processes and organized resources, or internal equities—technologies, facilities, people—and the extent to which these components must change to at least maintain the current product position in the marketplace.

At the outset of this study, we anticipated carrying our analysis through to include sizing (details of numbers of and resources to be allocated to personnel, activities, and facilities) of the NAVSEA organization in view of the potential organizational structures we arrive at and the activities taking place within those structures. However, NAVSEA elected to carry out an analysis of sizing in-house as a way of dealing with sensitive areas. Our analysis stops at potential structures. For this reason, this chapter focuses primarily on markets, products, and processes (as a proxy for activities). Our overall analysis of activities is confined to Appendix C, together with technical details of the product and market analyses. See Figure 3.2.

RAND*MR1303-3.2*

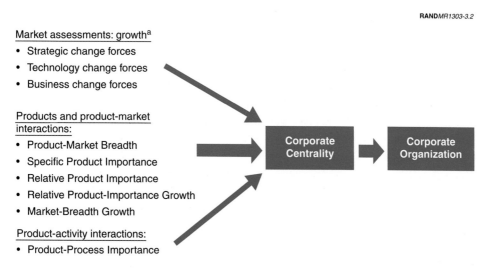

Market assessments: growth[a]
- Strategic change forces
- Technology change forces
- Business change forces

Products and product-market interactions:
- Product-Market Breadth
- Specific Product Importance
- Relative Product Importance
- Relative Product-Importance Growth
- Market-Breadth Growth

Product-activity interactions:
- Product-Process Importance

[a]Here, growth is indicated not so much by the increase in the size of a market but by the increase in the emphasis placed on that market.

Figure 3.2—Road Map for Chapter Three

Products are at the center of all the evaluations. The value of the products in the external markets can be projected back onto the activities internal to NAVSEA that created those products. From this interaction perspective, our analysis model provides the inputs for management decisions ranging from investment and divestment strategies; to market-positioning alternatives; to facility, personnel, and technology priorities; to organizational alignments.

The research team also assessed which NAVSEA products can be obtained from commercial sources—*commercial availability*—as a guide for how NAVSEA should align itself with the commercial markets. The product interactions with the market are also used in our analysis to develop the concept of *corporate centrality*, which addresses a crucial issue: How central, or key, to the core mission of the NAVSEA corporation are the products and services they provide?

ORGANIZATION OF THIS CHAPTER

This chapter begins with a description of the framework for the methodology used in this chapter. It then proceeds through the framework, first with an analysis of NAVSEA markets and market-emphasis-growth factors. It then describes products and the interactions between products, markets, and processes, measured by such factors as product relative importance and breadth, and process change. It then translates these interactions into two-dimensional grids (the measures forming the dimensions) from which management decisions on market structure can be made. Finally, commercial availability and corporate centrality are assessed and provide a segue to organizational structure. Similar analyses are included in Appendix C for activities and their interactions. These interactions are translated into two-dimensional grids that can be further assessed against the grids in this chapter and in Appendix C. From those grids, finer-resolution management decisions can be drawn.

NAVSEA MARKETS

Understanding the needs and preferences of the Navy as a whole and the responsibilities those needs and preferences imply for NAVSEA is central to understanding NAVSEA in the twenty-first century. Those needs and preferences are summarized in the regularly updated OPNAVINST C3501.2J, which details all the naval warfare and support missions exercised by the United States Navy and Coast Guard organizations and further assigns the specific mission areas and operational capabilities required of each naval unit. These ROC/POE Statements provide the needed inputs for resource planning, training requirements, and platform design specifications.

In the commercial world, such statements of market segmentation (mission areas) and customer needs and preferences (mission requirements and operational capabilities) are essential planning and marketing tools and are discovered only after much research and analysis of customer value and market structure. This information leads to an understanding of whether or not a market is profitable and how to achieve a sustainable competitive advantage in that market. In the world of the Navy, this OPNAVINST informs our analysis of how the Navy market as a whole is segmented, who the customers are, what their needs and preferences are, and who pays the bills.

OPNAVINST C3501.2J provided the basis for bridging the gap between the commercial and the military in these important dimensions; moreover, it provides a window into the terminology and parlance of the Navy itself.

From Warfare Areas to NAVSEA Markets

Eight warfare missions and nine support missions are traditional to the Navy (Table 3.1). The Instruction refers to them as Naval Warfare Mission Areas and divides them further into many secondary Naval Warfare Mission Areas[4] that

---

[4]In Table 3.1 we have labeled the secondary Naval Warfare Mission Areas as "Support missions."

Table 3.1

Traditional Navy Warfare Areas

Warfare missions	Support missions
• Anti-air warfare • Amphibious warfare • Anti–surface ship warfare • Anti-submarine warfare • Mine warfare • Command and control warfare (IW) • Navy special warfare • Strike warfare	• Command, control, and communications • Intelligence • Logistics • Fleet support operations • Mobility • Construction • Missions of state • Non-combat operations • Strategic sealift

RAND*MR1303-T3.1*

fully describe the duties required. In some cases, such as the Construction mission area, NAVSEA products do not contribute to a warfare area. Few of the NAVSEA activities have very much to do with construction of Navy buildings and facilities, a market area to which the Naval Facilities Engineering Command (NAVFAC) contributes. Likewise, some of the secondary mission areas in the Fleet support operations mission area, such as supporting the base hospital or the chaplaincy, are not provided by NAVSEA products. These market areas represent the needs and preferences of the Fleet as a customer group.

Not directly represented by these market areas are the needs and preferences of another group of customers: the Program Executive Officers (PEOs).[5] A large number of additional OPNAVINSTs detail the services that NAVSEA must provide to the PEOs and other groups of customers. The research team studied all the instructions relevant to NAVSEA products and services (see Appendix B). Broadly speaking, these are the mandates for the organization.

---

[5]PEOs act for and exercise the authority of the Assistant Secretary of the Navy (Research, Development and Acquisition) to supervise directly the management of seven assigned programs, or major product lines: Theater Surface Combatants, DD21, Expeditionary Warfare, Carriers, Submarines, Undersea Warfare, and Mine Warfare (see Figure 4.2 in Chapter Four). NAVSEA fulfills much of its purpose by supporting PEOs. NAVSEA ensures that the Department of the Navy has superior and operational ships and ship systems by ensuring that the PEOs and Fleet have access to the institutional knowledge of naval engineering needed to design, construct, modernize, and repair ships and ship systems. See Chapter Four for a more complete description of the NAVSEA–PEO relationship.

NAVSEA Mandates

The Naval Sea Systems Command exists to perform certain functions and activities for the U.S. Navy. To comprehend the NAVSEA of today and to envision NAVSEA 2007, we needed to fully understand NAVSEA's responsibilities and contributions to the Navy and to other naval organizations. As a result, we analyzed instructions issued by the Secretary of the Navy (SECNAV Instructions) and the Chief of Naval Operations (OPNAV Instructions) that specifically assign NAVSEA responsibilities. This mandate analysis, in turn, informed our activity and organizational analyses.

The research team compiled an initial list of NAVSEA's mandates through a search on the Navy Electronic Directives System (http://neds.nebt.daps.mil), which yielded a long list of unclassified OPNAV and SECNAV Instructions that assign NAVSEA responsibilities. A list of these instructions can be found in Appendix B.

These instructions mandate NAVSEA to do a number of activities, ranging from very detailed items, such as maintaining certain databases, to larger and broader responsibilities that are very closely aligned to NAVSEA's mission, such as developing naval architectural limits. For analysis purposes, we needed to understand how the detailed mandates became embedded in the existing NAVSEA products and services and whether these products served a set of customers that we did not have already represented as a market.

Our review of these instructions yielded the following broad potential market areas:

- Acquisition support and execution

- Systems engineering

- Naval architecture

- Maintenance and repair

- Ship modernization and upgrade planning

- Technical expert for diving and salvage

- Submarine safety

- Technical expert on naval explosives

- Logistics management

- Explosives ordnance disposal.

Many of these areas are already represented in the products and services listed in Figures 2.13 through 2.16. However, the "Acquisition support and execution" area is not. We have created a separate market for it in our analysis. Its customers are the PEOs.

We used these encompassing mandate categories to guide the refinement of market definitions extracted from the traditional Naval Warfare Mission Areas, as follows:

- Created a new market area termed "Acquisition Support": We combined NAVSEA's contribution to the Logistics and Strategic sealift warfare areas and (for manuals) part of the Fleet support operations warfare area with other mandated acquisition support activities to create this new market.

- Created a new market area termed "Defensive Systems": Many NAVSEA activities and related products support defensive measures, whereas the warfare areas are largely offensive in character. To make this Defensive Systems market complete by reflecting the needs and preferences of customers, we moved the use of mine countermeasures from the Mine Warfare market to the Defensive Systems market and moved the defensive use of Information Warfare from the Command and Control Warfare market to the Defensive Systems market.

- Renamed Mine warfare mission area the Offensive Mine Warfare market: The defensive use of mine countermeasures is now in the Defensive Systems market.

- Redefined Fleet support operations (FSO) the "Operational Availability" market: We restricted the FSO market definition to encompass only maintenance and repair activities. This market includes all in-service and shipyard activities, integrated logistics support (ILS) for new spare parts, updating of manuals, and all in-service engineering.

- Combined Missions of State with Non-combat Operations: The needs and preferences of the customer groups for these two warfare areas are very similar; we therefore combined these warfare areas into one market.

- Used Information Warfare to describe Command and Control Warfare: As stated in OPNAVINST C3501.2J, Information Warfare is a more inclusive term and anticipates command and control (C2) warfare as it may be conducted in 2007.

- Eliminated Construction as a market area for NAVSEA: No NAVSEA activities directly contributed to this area.

This refinement resulted in the following NAVSEA markets and definitions, many of which are taken directly from OPNAVINST C3501.2J (see Table 3.2 for a side-by-side view of these markets with the mission areas):

- Anti-Air Warfare (AAW): The detection, tracking, destruction, or neutralization of adversary air platforms and airborne weapons, whether launched by the adversary from the air, surface, subsurface, or land platforms.

- Amphibious Warfare (AMW): Attacks launched from the sea by naval forces and by landing forces embarked in ships or craft designed to achieve a shore presence in a littoral zone. Such attacks include fire support for troops in contact with adversary forces through the use of close air support or shore bombardment.

Table 3.2

Side-by-Side View of Warfare/Support Missions and NAVSEA Markets, for Comparison

Warfare missions	NAVSEA markets
• Anti-air warfare • Amphibious warfare • Anti–surface ship warfare • Anti-submarine warfare • Mine warfare • Command and control warfare (IW) • Navy special warfare • Strike warfare	Anti-air warfare Amphibious warfare Anti–surface ship warfare Anti-submarine warfare Command, control, and communications Information warfare Intelligence Operational availability Offensive mine warfare Mobility Missions of state–non-combat operations Acquisition support Naval special warfare Strike warfare Defensive systems

Support missions

- Command, control, and communications
- Intelligence
- Logistics
- Fleet support operations
- Mobility
- Construction
- Missions of state
- Non-combat operations
- Strategic sealift

- <u>Anti–Surface Ship Warfare (ASU)</u>: The detection, tracking, and destruction or neutralization of adversary surface combatants and merchant ships.

- <u>Anti-Submarine Warfare (ASW)</u>: The detection, tracking, and destruction or neutralization of adversary submarines.

- <u>Command, Control, and Communications (CCC)</u>: Providing communications and related facilities for coordination and control of external organizations or forces, and control of one's own unit's capabilities.

- <u>Information Warfare (IW)</u>: Actions taken to achieve information superiority by affecting adversary information, information-based processes, information systems, and computer-based networks. The defense of one's own information, information-based processes, information systems, and computer-based networks is now in the Defensive Systems market and includes the integrated use of psychological operations, military deception, operations security, electronic warfare, and physical destruction to achieve such superiority.

- <u>Intelligence (INT)</u>: The collection, processing, and evaluation of information to determine location, identity, and capability of hostile forces through the employment of reconnaissance, surveillance, and other means.

- <u>Operational Availability (OPA)</u>: The repair and maintenance activities and processes associated with maximizing operational availability. These activities include all in-service and shipyard activities and ILS of new spare parts, updating of manuals, and all in-service engineering.

- <u>Offensive Mine Warfare (OMW)</u>: The use of mines for control or denial of sea or harbor areas. The defensive use of mine countermeasures to destroy or neutralize an adversary's mines is now in the Defensive Systems market.

- <u>Mobility (MOB)</u>: The ability of naval forces to maneuver and maintain themselves in all situations over, under, or upon the surface. This market includes the use of sealift and logistics ships.

- <u>Missions of State–Non-combat Operations (MOS–NCO)</u>: Operations supporting the historical role of naval forces to conduct preventive or punitive diplomacy and/or to achieve strategic national objectives. This market includes naval diplomatic presence, peacekeeping, interdiction, counterterrorism, and counterdrug operations, as well as humanitarian and other forms of assistance. Non-combat Operations include all the necessary support activities or special missions that are required of a unit but that are not directly related to the other mission areas. The services NAVSEA provides to other parts of the government are included here as well.

- Acquisition Support (ACQ): A new market that combines NAVSEA's mandated acquisition support activities with the following: (1) NAVSEA's contribution to the Logistics warfare area (design of ILS and first provisioning); (2) purchase of all Navy ships and submarines, including Strategic Sealift ships; and (3) the part of Fleet Support Operations that prepares manuals for the warfare areas. Acquisition support for other parts of the government is also included here.

- Naval Special Warfare (NSW): Naval operations that are generally accepted as being nonconventional and, in many cases, clandestine. This market includes special mobile operations, unconventional warfare, coastal and river interdiction, beach and coastal reconnaissance, very-shallow-water mine countermeasures (MCMs), and certain tactical intelligence operations.

- Strike Warfare (STW): The destruction or neutralization of adversary targets ashore through the use of conventional or nuclear weapons. Such targets include, but are not limited to, strategic targets, building yards, and operating bases from which the adversary is capable of conducting air, surface, or subsurface operations against U.S. or allied forces.

- Defensive Systems (DEF): The self-defense of ships and submarines from hostile attack, whether from above the surface or below the surface, through the use of stealth, countermeasures, or active point defense. Such self-defense, including all mine countermeasures and defensive information warfare.

These markets and their abbreviations are listed in Table 3.3.

Customers

The individuals and groups who create these markets, such as the PEOs for Acquisition, are *NAVSEA customers.* NAVSEA enjoys a far richer relationship with these individuals and groups than customers and firms in the commercial world typically have enjoyed (Mintzberg, 1996, pp. 75–83). Far more than customers, these market participants are clients, colleagues, and coworkers as well. The traditional customer-supplier relationship has been a distant, almost anonymous one that many corporations are rejecting. As a corporation, NAVSEA is closer to the needs and preferences of its clients—sometimes being collocated with them—and understands the short- and longer-term changes in these preferences. As a colleague, NAVSEA is a collaborator on projects that are of mutual value to the U.S. Navy. And as a coworker, NAVSEA promotes warfighters by supporting the individuals and organizations seeking service.

Table 3.3

NAVSEA Markets and Their Acronyms

AAW	Anti-air warfare
AMW	Amphibious warfare
ASU	Anti–surface ship warfare
ASW	Anti-submarine warfare
CCC	Command, control, and communications
IW	Information warfare
INT	Intelligence
OPA	Operational availability
OMW	Offensive mine warfare
MOB	Mobility
MOS–NCO	Missions of state–non-combat operations
ACQ	Acquisition support
NSW	Naval special warfare
STW	Strike warfare
DEF	Defensive systems

RAND*MR1303-T3.3*

Realizing that the relationship between NAVSEA and the Navy is a far richer one than "customer," we use *customer* as shorthand to capture all of the above characteristics. The revised list of markets above corresponds to the major NAVSEA customers, clients, and colleagues and their needs and preferences, in Table 3.4.

Market-Emphasis-Growth Factors

The above list and definitions of markets will not remain static between now and 2007. As part of our market analysis, we need to forecast where new and emerging opportunities will be. Growth in market emphasis is that forecaster. *Market-emphasis growth* is measured primarily by how the needs and preferences of the customers in a given market are changing and what those needs will be in the future. To understand and forecast such growth, it is necessary to understand the major change forces, or *drivers,* that are changing the structure of the markets themselves and to understand how these forces will change the needs and preferences of the customers in these markets (see Figure 3.3).

Table 3.4

NAVSEA Primary Customers

1. Program Executive Officers
   • Acquisition of new ships and submarines (subs)
   • Modernization and upgrade of existing ships and subs
2. The Chief of Naval Operations and the Operational Fleet itself
   • Technological hegemony in warfighting systems
   • Sustainment of high operations tempo
   • Fulfillment of naval missions
3. Type Commanders
   • Repair and maintenance of ships and subs
4. Other U.S. government organizations
   • Acquisition support for watercraft
   • Diving and salvage expertise
5. Foreign Nations
   • Foreign Military Sales (FMS)

RAND*MR1303-T3.4*

RAND*MR1303-3.3*

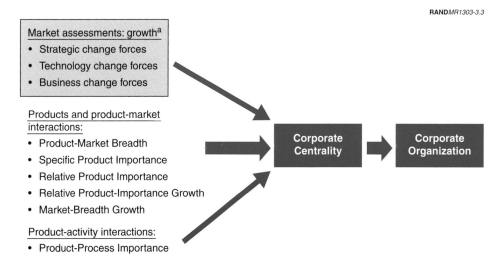

Market assessments: growth[a]
• Strategic change forces
• Technology change forces
• Business change forces

Products and product-market interactions:
• Product-Market Breadth
• Specific Product Importance
• Relative Product Importance
• Relative Product-Importance Growth
• Market-Breadth Growth

Product-activity interactions:
• Product-Process Importance

Corporate Centrality → **Corporate Organization**

[a]Here, growth is indicated not so much by the increase in the size of a market but by the increase in the emphasis placed on that market.

Figure 3.3—Road Map for Chapter Three, Showing That We Are at the Market Assessments: Growth Stage of the Analysis

For the NAVSEA markets, the customers' needs and preferences of the future are shaped by three major drivers: strategic drivers, technology drivers, and business drivers. Our analysis of all three drivers and their effects was an outgrowth of the assessments performed for the Strategy portion of this project. We had volumes of reference material on the Navy and Marine Corps technology assessment for 2000–2005 to draw on, plus intelligence material. On the business side, we also had a large volume of reference material to draw from. We determined the drivers from criteria derived from the Naval Studies Board work on the future of the Navy (NSB–NRC, 1997a), on NRC (1996) and ONI (1998) documents, and on the results evolving from the Strategy phase of the research (Chapter Two):

- Strategic drivers: Forces that arise from the evolution of the geopolitical situation for the year 2007. In this analysis, we use the results from the Strategy phase of the research. (See Table C.1.)

- Technology drivers: Forces that arise from the anticipated trends and directions for technologies and capabilities of direct relevance to NAVSEA markets. Information is one such trend (NSB–NRC, 1997a, p. 54):

  > Observation and processing capacities and the ability to communicate the results to multiple users are growing explosively with modern sensing, computing, and communications technologies. Today's military forces exist in a mass of information—an "infosphere"—that is essential to their existence and their effective functioning. All naval force elements must be designed to operate in this information environment.

  (See Table C.2.)

- Business drivers: Forces that are created by macroeconomic trends, by the adoption of industrial best practices, and by the use of recommendations from acquisition-reform efforts. An example is modeling and simulation, "because it affects every aspect of military force design, equipment, and operation" (NSB–NRC, 1997a, p. 18). (See Table C.3.)

See Appendix C, the Analyses Related to Growth in Market-Emphasis Factors section, for a further discussion of these drivers.

These groups of drivers will influence the growth in market *emphasis*. Within each of these groups are from four to 10 detailed contributing drivers. Each market was assessed with respect to these contributing drivers and assigned an aggregate score for the driver group in answer to the basic question:

> In 2007, will this technology, or strategy, or business driver be forcing the emphasis on a certain NAVSEA market to grow or increase as a response?

Each driver was given a score of 0 for No and 1 for Yes. For example, we would expect zero growth in emphasis in the NAVSEA CCC market in response to the "Increasing use of commercial firms for maintenance and support functions" contributing driver (although it is a business driver for NAVSEA markets), given the statement in *Technology for the United States Navy and Marine Corps, 2000–2035* (NSB–NRC, 1997a, p. 18) that "logistics and support, in addition to communications, are areas in which commercial services will be used extensively for the foreseeable future." Details of the analysis are presented and discussed in Appendix C.

Considering all NAVSEA markets in the aggregate, strategic developments in network-centric warfare, information dominance, and effective engagement should be given a high level of attention by NAVSEA because these areas have more potential for increasing the emphasis of NAVSEA markets than do other strategic drivers.

Two technology drivers are receiving emphasis in the majority of NAVSEA markets: the advent and continued development of very-high-speed computational tools, and very-high-bandwidth networks. The other drivers have nonzero scores, but the computational-tools driver score is by far the strongest, indicating that NAVSEA should stay very aware of developments in and foster the progress of very-high-speed computational tools and very-high-bandwidth networks—not to the exclusion of other drivers, but placing the most emphasis here. In considering the total technology impact within a given market, we see that the DEF market shows the strongest sensitivity to technology drivers. This means that when technology drivers are considered in the aggregate, NAVSEA should watch the Defensive Systems market more closely than other markets.

The most important business driver for NAVSEA market emphasis is the increasing use of commercial firms for maintenance and support functions. The market most sensitive to changes in the business environment is the Operational Availability (OPA) market.

Overall Market Emphasis

To arrive at an overall assessment of market emphasis, we combined the results from the three major driver categories, summing the total driver impact for each market for each of the driver categories. We first normalized the driver categories so that they contribute equally, then varied driver weighting to show changes in emphasis, as described in Appendix C. We then looked at the final percentages, derived from the score for each market divided by the total score for all markets, for discontinuities to separate High emphasis from Medium, Medium from Low, and Low from Very Low. Sometimes the discontinuity is half a percentage point, and sometimes it is two or more percentage points.

The final determination relied on the judgment of the research team, as do those for the other figures in this chapter. These determinations should not be viewed as correct or incorrect but as part of a consistency check of a complex process whose value resides in the entirety and iterativeness of a process in which judgments cannot be made all at once. The final results were put into the corresponding four bins in Figure 3.4 (and Figure C.4); the thresholds for the bins are provided in the figure note.

Weighting the market-emphasis drivers uniformly, we see that the Operational Availability (OPA), Acquisition Support (ACQ), and Defensive Systems (DEF) markets are increasing in emphasis more rapidly; Naval Special Warfare (NSW), Anti-Air Warfare (AAW), Missions of State–Non-combat Operations (MOS–

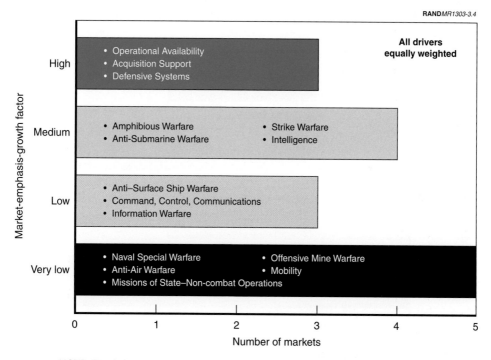

NOTE: The following binning decisions represent thresholds for the total normalized value of all market scoring, based on the apparent separation of percentage bands that came out of the analysis:

    High ~ 13.8–10.6 percent
    Medium ~ 10–8.5 percent
    Low ~ 5.8–4.3 percent
    Very low ~ 2.7–0 percent

Figure 3.4—NAVSEA Market-Emphasis-Growth Factors, with Uniform Weights for Drivers

NCO), Offensive Mine Warfare (OMW), and Mobility (MOB) are increasing in emphasis the least.

The sensitivity analysis of technology emphasis in Appendix C reveals that the DEF market has a technology emphasis, whereas the emphasis of the ACQ and OPA markets is only weakly coupled to technology.

Given a strategic emphasis, the intelligence (INT) market has moved into the High category with DEF and ACQ. The OPA market has moved to the Medium level, whereas NSW, MOS–NCO, OMW, MOB, and AAW have remained Very Low. The Anti-Submarine Warfare (ASW), Strike Warfare (STW), and Amphibious (AMW) markets remain at a Medium emphasis-growth rate (see Figures 3.5 and C.6).

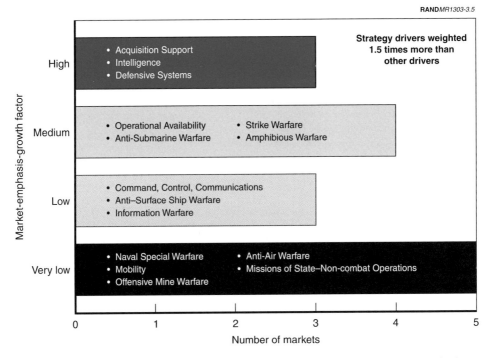

Figure 3.5—NAVSEA Market-Emphasis-Growth Factors, with Strategy Drivers
Weighted 1.5 Times More Than Other Drivers

Because the Navy is a strategy-driven organization and looks to technology and business to implement that strategy, we adopt the strategy-weighted growth factors in the market-structure analysis later in this chapter and in Appendix C.

A few market-emphasis-growth forecasts remain constant regardless of the weighting scenario:

1. NSW, OMW, MOB, AAW, and MOS–NCO markets are always rated at the Very Low emphasis-growth level. The capabilities needed for the NSW market in 2007 will differ substantially in character or number from those of today. Recall that all defensive use of mine countermeasures or Naval Special Warfare for mine clearance is in the DEF market. The needed sealift capability and logistics support will be completed by 2005 and will not be driving the MOB market in 2007: Enough capability will exist.[6] There will be no peer air force in 2007; thus, emphasis on the AAW market will not be growing. The offensive use of mine warfare, OMW, has enough capability now and will not be different in 2007. The MOS–NCO market has enough capability today and will also not be different in 2007.

2. That the Defensive Systems market is always at the High emphasis-growth level follows from the emphasis on the littoral, the availability of advanced sophisticated submarine designs to adversaries, and the extended use of subs in the littoral. Also, electronic intelligence for mines and torpedoes, anti-ship cruise missiles with challenging flight characteristics, and other systems will be inexpensive and readily available to adversaries in 2007.

3. That Intelligence is High for strategic weighting and Medium otherwise follows from there being dominant strategic drivers and smaller technology drivers for this market

4. That the AMW, ASW, and STW markets are always rated at Medium emphasis growth fits in with all the available literature and with the opinion of the research staff.

The following interesting observations can be made with regard to the weighting:

---

[6]One of the reviewers, Elliot Axelband, observed that the U.S. Navy might not be completely done with increasing of the sealift capability, although the growth rate of sealift will have reached its peak and is expected to be decreasing. However, given the current emphasis on the war on terrorism since September 11, 2001 (one year after the cutoff date for information currency in this report), the United States may need even more capacity.

1. The Information Warfare (IW), Anti–Surface Ship Warfare (ASU), and Command, Control, and Communications (CCC) markets are rated Low for all weights.

2. The OPA market is rated Medium for both technology and strategy weights but High for equal weights, which follows from business being the driver for this market. The market is not sensitive to changes in technology or strategic weights.

Generally, the market-emphasis-growth scores are fairly insensitive to differences in the weighting scheme we employed. These examples illustrate that our results are robust in the face of reasonable changes in emphasis.

Signposts for Changes in Market-Emphasis Growth

The emphasis-growth forecasts we have developed are subject to assumptions (in the Assumption-Based Planning sense) about the external environment of which they are a part. The basic assumption from the Strategy phase of the research is that there is not an international Revolution in Military Affairs (RMA), in the true Marshall Ogarkov[7] sense (Simon, 1988, p. 547), going on now nor will there be one in 2007. Such an RMA would involve the development and evolution of a reconnaissance-strike complex—a system that can find targets, pass data to weapons, and engage.

What signposts would indicate changes in market-emphasis growth? In the Anti-Air Warfare (AAW) market, for example, the emergence of foreign and indigenous low-observable technology for aircraft and missiles would be a certain sign that new emphasis in research in these areas in a foreign country is changing the performance characteristics of foreign airborne platforms. Such a change could trigger an increase in the United States' own efforts in AAW, simply because the signatures of hostile forces will have changed. Similarly, if the flying hours of foreign pilots increase drastically, new long-range surface-to-air missiles (SAMs) come to the fore, or a major buildup of strike, attack, or bomber forces is noted, then an increase in emphasis on the U.S. domestic AAW market could follow.

Similarly, the Offensive Mine Warfare (OMW) market will be influenced by changes in the international environment. For example, a hostile nation could acquire significant mine countermeasures (MCMs) capability or a new MCM technology may emerge, compelling the United States to develop more and

---

[7]Marshall Ogarkov, formerly Soviet Chief of Staff, was telling Soviet leadership in the 1980s that to stay in the game of strategic competition, the Soviet Union had to modernize the economy, especially its technology base.

better mine systems of its own. Likewise, an adversary could emerge with large naval forces distributed over many harbors, diluting the United States' current OMW capabilities and requiring new acquisition in this area. A significant foreign naval shipbuilding program could also trigger more emphasis being placed on the OMW market.

For the Missions of State–Non-combat Operations (MOS–NCO) market, the emergence of new and rabid anti-U.S. or anti-Western ideologies, such as the radical Islamic terrorist position against the United States and other Western cultures, could increase the emphasis on products in this market. Similarly, if a major catastrophe occurs in the Second or Third World and the United States is perceived as being at fault, an increase in operations in this market and the need for more and new products may result. Likewise, an acrimonious end to a U.S. alliance or the spread of international organized crime could trigger similar increases in emphasis on this market.

For the Mobility (MOB) market, if the new-build program planned by the Navy is not realized, then the Fleet will age less gracefully than discussed in Chapter Two, the Strategy phase. The ensuing increased downtime for extant resources could trigger new emphasis on this market. Additionally, the appearance of major interdiction air, sea, or submarine forces in a hostile country or the withering of U.S. regional relations in an important strategic area may put pressure on existing resources and attendant loss of basing and overflight privileges.

For the Naval Special Warfare (NSW) market, an increase in the very sophisticated targets that these forces interdict would contribute to greater emphasis being placed on this market area. The emergence of new and sophisticated coastal and riverine facilities in hostile areas or the emergence of new beach and coastal reconnaissance targets may cause an increase in emphasis on this market.

NAVSEA PRODUCTS

The preceding subsection describes how new products may result in the future from geopolitical changes that require markets to react. We now look at the products that resulted from our analysis in Chapter Two of the geopolitical situation.

NAVSEA products are a collection of activities that support the life cycle of an end product such as Special Operations Forces (SOF) systems. In the following discussion, we use "Submarine Combat Systems" as a sample product. It is a collection of activities involving advanced and applied research; the setting of standards and specifications; technology assessments; technical oversight for acquisition; in-service engineering; and other activities. The totality of activities that make up the complete Submarine Combat System product is far more extensive, involving organizations in the Navy other than NAVSEA, DoD, and outside contractors. We consider here only those activities from across NAVSEA that contribute to the product and use the product name to describe that activity collection. In making the assessments, we used the detailed collection of NAVSEA activities (by names and by process code, as described in Appendix C) as a descriptor for the product characteristics.

Just as the description of markets provides a business context in which to view Navy and national strategy, the following description of products indicates a balancing act between markets/missions and the processes and organized resources/internal equities—technologies, facilities, and personnel—that create the products.

As with the three drivers in the NAVSEA Markets section, the process for identifying the NAVSEA products for 2007 was iterative, evolving over the course of the study. The 94 separate products and services listed in Figures 2.13 through 2.16 provide a starting point for a list of NAVSEA products. Many of those were derived from the *Core Equities—Red Team Review* (NAVSEA, 1999a). However, some activities were not included in that initial study. Therefore, after substantial input from the Strategy phase of the research program on the future geopolitical situation and from ONI (1998), NSB–NRC (1997a), and NRC (1996) documents, we added to the original list of products and redefined existing products to include new performance requirements, advancing technologies, and changes in business processes.[8]

NAVSEA offers a wide variety of products, from a concrete set of objects, e.g., "Submarine Combat Systems," to a set of behaviors comprised by "Program Management for Acquisition." For each of these products, we assume that the product title encompasses all parts of the life cycle of the product, from initial requirements definition through research and industrial development to deployment, in-service engineering, and de-commissioning. Thus, we have the product "Torpedoes," rather than "Torpedo Research," and "Machinery Control Systems," rather than "In-Service Engineering for Machinery Control Systems."

In the commercial world, large product groups are used as organizing tools specifically because they interact with very different markets and because their

---

[8]The scope of this study did not include the Navy nuclear program, which is a separate organization that reports to the Chief of Naval Operations and Commander of NAVSEA. Consequently, products having to do with Navy nuclear reactors have been omitted. This omission will bias the analysis to de-emphasize job titles such as "Nuclear Engineer" or "Health Physics Series." Although the technology and facilities needed for Navy reactors are rich and varied, none of them is included in this analysis.

production requires very different skills, knowledge, abilities, facilities, and technologies (i.e., the product groups have different business models). So too for NAVSEA: Product groupings can be useful in analyzing interactions with markets and internal activities. Therefore, we organized the products into groups, corresponding to the major heading (boldfaced) for the final list of NAVSEA products for 2007, shown in Table 3.5:

- **Test, evaluate, assess**
- **Bullets**
- **Communications systems and capabilities**
- **Launching systems**
- **Defensive systems**
- **Engineering services**
- **SOF systems and capabilities**
- **Management services**
- **Platform systems**
- **Sensor systems**
- **Vehicles**
- **Warfare systems**
- **Explosives RDA&M.**

The products subsumed under each heading indicate the range of each part of this taxonomy. The overall type of product will have similar interactions with the markets in our analysis later in this chapter (and will interact similarly with activities, which we analyze in Appendix C). For example, products that are part of the **Management services** group will have interactions with markets and internal processes and organized resources that are markedly different from those of the **Warfare systems** group.

The names of many of the products in 2007 are familiar, but many of the products themselves are going to be very different from those of today, reflecting the needs and preferences of the customers, which will be changing in response to changes in the three major drivers of the markets for NAVSEA: strategy, technology, and business. Substantial changes in the needs and preferences of customers owing to significant changes in strategy, technology, and business are indicated in blue in Table 3.5.

Table 3.5

NAVSEA Products for 2007, Ordered by Product Group

Test, evaluate, assess	Defensive systems
• USW Operational Range Assessment Systems	• Submarine Defensive Systems
• USW Analysis	• Electromagnetic Environmental Effects Control Measures
• Missile Simulators, Trainers, and Test/Diagnostic Equipment	• Chemical-Biological Warfare Defense
• Weapon and Combat System Assessment Systems	• Vulnerability and Survivability Systems
• Readiness Analysis	• Acoustic Signatures and Silencing Systems
• Navy Metrology Systems	• Non-acoustic Signatures and Silencing Systems
• MIW Simulation Software	• Physical Security Systems
• Coastal Warfare Analysis	• TBMD
• Aircraft Modeling and Simulation	• Surface Defensive Systems
• Theater Warfare Analysis	• Mine Countermeasure Systems
	• Torpedo Countermeasures
Bullets	**Engineering services**
• Torpedoes	• CADs, PADs, and AEPs—pyrotechnic devices
• Underwater Warheads	• Ordnance Environmental Support
• Packing, Handling, Storage, and Transport of Ordnance	• Diving, Salvage, and Life Support Systems
• Tomahawk Systems	• Ship and Submarine Design
• General Missile Systems	• Surface and Undersea Vehicle Materials and Processing Technology
• Ballistic Missile Systems	• Surface, Submarine, and Carrier Structures (Naval Architecture)
• Electromagnetic Energy Technology Products (Microwave Weapons)	• Legacy Microwave Component Technology
• Surface Weapons	• Legacy Microelectronic Technology
• Weapon Materials	• Legacy Radar Engineering and Industrial Support
• Precision Guided Munitions	• Research on Semiconductors
• Laser Weapon Systems	• Legacy Battery Systems
Communications systems and capabilities	• Total Ship System Engineering
• Submarine Communication Systems	• Hull Forms and Hydromechanics
• Sonar Imaging Systems	• Logistics Systems
• Interoperability	• Shipyard Activities—Non-Nuclear
• Surface Communications	• Electrochemical Power System Development
Launching systems	• Cost Engineering Services
• USW Launchers	• Configuration Management
• Submarine Missile Launcher Integration	**SOF systems and capabilities**
• Gun Weapon Systems	• SOF Mobility, Life Support, and Mission Support Equipment and Systems
• Surface Ship Missile Launcher	• SOF Sensor Systems
• Small Arms	

Table 3.5—Cont'd.

Management services	Sensor systems
• Torpedo Depot Management and Operations	• Sonar Systems
• USW Range Management	• Night Vision/Electro-optics
• Navy Tactical Training Range (NTTR) Management	• Infrared Sensor Systems
• Small Arms Ammunition Management Systems	• Radar Systems
• Budget Preparation, Documentation, and Management	• USW Deployed Systems
	• Laser Sensor Systems

Management services
- Torpedo Depot Management and Operations
- USW Range Management
- Navy Tactical Training Range (NTTR) Management
- Small Arms Ammunition Management Systems
- Budget Preparation, Documentation, and Management
- Program Management for Acquisitions
- Program Management for Repair and Maintenance
- Technical Management
- General Management Activities
- Contracts and Contract Administration
- Information Technology Services
- Foreign Military Sales

Platform systems
- Missions Other Than War (MOTW) Systems
- Environmental/Pollution Abatement Systems
- Propulsion Machinery Systems and Components
- Machinery Control Systems
- Auxiliary Machinery Systems and Components
- Electrical Machinery Systems and Components
- Hull and Deck Machinery Systems and Components
- Habitability and Hull Outfitting Systems and Components
- Propulsors
- Navigation Systems
- Underway Replenishment Techniques
- Submarine Periscopes and Masts

Sensor systems
- Sonar Systems
- Night Vision/Electro-optics
- Infrared Sensor Systems
- Radar Systems
- USW Deployed Systems
- Laser Sensor Systems

Vehicles
- Unmanned Undersea Vehicles
- Combatant Craft
- Marine Corps Vehicle Systems and Components
- Small Manned Underwater Vehicles

Warfare systems
- Submarine Combat Systems
- Surface USW Systems
- Surface Combat Systems
- Mine Systems
- Tactical Control System Software
- Decision Support Systems
- Carrier Combat Systems
- Fire Control Systems
- Submarine Electronic Warfare Systems
- Surface Electronic Warfare Systems

Explosives RDA&M
- Rocket, Missiles, and Gun Propulsion
- Energetic Materials
- Explosive Safety Engineering

Products that have undergone substantial changes

New NAVSEA products

RAND*MR1303-T3.5b*

Examples of such changes in the coming decade are a rise in the sophistication of adversaries' technology as advanced sensor and guidance systems become less expensive and more available worldwide. In particular, a rapid rise in the sophistication of the detection, tracking, homing, and attack electronics on-board adversaries' torpedoes and mines is forecasted (ONI, 1998; NSB–NRC, 1997a)—a development that is significant enough to call for the realignments in the major warfare mission areas to emphasize the very real threat these systems will pose in 2007. (These expected changes in the adversaries' technology advances by 2007 are reflected in the changes to the list of markets discussed in the preceding section.)

The rise of sophisticated threats with cheap and available technology will place great emphasis on customer needs and preferences associated with stealth and platform protection in all directions: both active and passive cancellation and reduction of acoustic and non-acoustic signatures. The sophistication of de-perming and degaussing of ships and subs will become crucial as cheap mine and torpedo sensors become readily available (ONI, 1998; NSB–NRC, 1997a). In addition, the rise of laser infrared radar (LIDAR)-based standoff wake-detection systems for hydrodynamic and wake effluent signatures will make signature re-duction in these nontraditional areas a high priority.

Moreover, effluent signatures have an environmental impact beyond stealth. In the coming decade, Navy ships will become subject to similar environmental restrictions on effluents that private ships are now subject to. The strategic need for a reduced signature adds more significance to products in this area.

The rise of new wake-detection techniques also means both understanding the signature of hostile vessels and reducing the signatures of U.S. ships. With the rise of new fuel-cell technologies and advanced propulsion (pump-jet) con-cepts, these signatures could be very different in 2007 from what they are today (ONI, 1998; NSB–NRC, 1997a).

The rise in automation technologies and robotics, combined with the lower manning for future Navy ships, places enormous emphasis on the customer need for unmanned underwater and airborne vehicles, as warfare by proxy be-comes the new way to consider engaging hostile forces.

Likewise, *Operational Maneuver from the Sea* (OMFTS) calls for placing great emphasis on precision-guided munitions (PGMs) and promoting development of new and advanced energetic materials. The ability to custom-design molecules is only now becoming mature enough for application in this area. Precision-guided munitions with precision-designed explosives will be the new products in this area. Although precision-guided munitions are available to U.S. forces today, they will be beyond the reach of hostile forces until the decade of 2010–2020 (ONI, 1998; NSB–NRC, 1997a). The attack of shore facili-ties will be possible by 2007, but the circular error probable (CEP) for missiles without terminal guidance is far too great to make them a threat to U.S. ships. In the decade beyond 2007, such threats will be very real. In 2007, the theater ballistic-missile defense (TBMD) system must be in full R&D and need not be deployed until the threat matures.

Designer molecules and other technological advances will enable a new gener-ation of weapons for operations other than war (OOTW) (ONI, 1998; NSB–NRC,

1997a) and the tactics they would enable, as well as a host of other SOF-related sensors and weapons.

In a different arena, the advance of genetic engineering, microbiology, and basic chemistry will enable hostile nations significantly greater access to chemical and biological weapons than in earlier eras. A defense against such attacks is needed and emphasized in one of the re-emphasized products in the above list: SOF Mobility, Life Support, and Mission Support Equipment and Subsystems.

The new emphasis on reduced manning aboard ships calls for major technological and operational changes in damage control and diagnostic systems; Brilliant machinery, which anticipates problems before they happen; and the automation of many mechanical ship functions. Such reduced manning also presents challenges for logistics. Underway-replenishment techniques that require less manning need to be developed, and the entire logistics system for the Navy needs to be updated to just-in-time logistics, so that a part is available in the most-convenient location before it is needed.

Finally, the revolution in computers and networking will transform the entire Navy and the products of NAVSEA. The new network-centric-warfare concept will change dramatically the NAVSEA products so that they can be incorporated into a networked system (Cebrowski, 1998; "The Cooperative Engagement Capability," 1995; Joint Staff J-6, 1997). In Table 3.5, we have added a new product called "Interoperability" to capture these changes in customer needs and preferences.

Beyond the current emphasis on networks, the research team sees a need for enhanced decisionmaking assistance for field commanders, who are currently bombarded with information. What is needed in 2007 will be a software executive officer who transforms the data into knowledge for commanders about what should be acted on. This new product, "Decision Support Systems," is highlighted in black in Table 3.5.

In the field of naval architecture, the manner in which ships and subs are designed will be transformed. With the advent of ultra-high-speed massively parallel computing and algorithms for solving nonlinear partial differential equations by 2007, the full coupling of finite-element analysis for computational fluid dynamics and rigid-body dynamics will be complete, enabling a totally new methodology for designing and building Navy ships. In particular, the research team forecasts the de-emphasis of tow tanks for testing such new designs and the advent of towing at far lower Reynolds numbers than before.[9]

---

[9]Tow tanks and scale models of ships are currently used to determine the ship hull design for the expected range of operational conditions. With the advances in computational capabilities, it is ex-

Linkages

The source of the novel products just described—and of the products that will not be much different from what they are today—is activities, the final locus of our Market-Product-Activity Model. Certain activities are mentioned in the preceding subsection that will accommodate the changes in 2007: just-in-time logistics to handle the challenge presented by robotics and lower manning on ships, and the activities that make up the Interoperability product to ensure that other NAVSEA products are truly network-centric. These accommodations will be one way that NAVSEA gains competitive advantage in 2007. Such accommodations are also called *linkages* (Porter, 1990, pp. 41–42):

> Linkages occur when the way in which one activity is performed affects the cost or effectiveness of other activities. Linkages often create trade-offs in performing different activities that must be optimized. . . .
>
> Linkages also require activities to be coordinated. . . .
>
> . . . Obtaining the benefits of linkages requires both complex organizational coordination and resolution of difficult trade-offs across organizational lines, which is rare.

The organizational coordination of such linkages is described in Chapter Four. Our analysis of activities themselves comprises many details on components of the organized resources that make up the activities and their importance to resource-allocation decisions, which we do not treat in this report. Our focus in this chapter remains on market structure. For this reason, we have moved the discussion of the Activities portion of the model to Appendix C (although information in that appendix will refer back to two-dimensional charts in this chapter, for refinement of decisions). Our discussion of markets and products next focuses on interactions of products, markets, and (since they govern organized resources and since product-process interactions contribute to our understanding of the market structure in 2007) processes to arrive at market structure.

INTERACTIONS WITH PRODUCTS

To complete our analysis of market structure, we next associate processes, technologies, personnel, and facilities with all the products in turn, thereby balancing knowledge of how the products are valued in the external marketplace and how the internal activities reflect that value. These valuations are calcu-

---

pected that, in the future, computational fluid dynamics will advance to the point where the ship hull design can be determined quantitatively and verified by a scale model of the ship's hull.

lated according to how the elements in one list, or database, interact with those of another—become a function of the other—magnifying or diminishing a given metric. The initial valuations involve a simple scoring system, with numbers corresponding to perceptions of importance.

The interactions we consider in this section are of products with the NAVSEA markets and products with processes (see Figure 3.6). Processes are proxies for activities because they encompass all of the organized resources. The separate resources and their interactions are evaluated in Appendix C, which assesses product-activity interactions, product-process interactions, product-technology interactions, product-facility interactions, and product-personnel interactions. These interactions are by no means divorced from those described in this chapter. Refined decisions will rely on a cross-checking of results in one two-dimensional grid with those in the grids presented in this section.

The total score for a product divided by the total score for all products results in a certain percentage. The range of all the percentages can be divided into four parts corresponding to the four ranks of High, Medium, Low, and Very Low. The interaction result aggregates an element—a product, in this case—into one bin of four bins corresponding to the rank assigned to the one part of the four parts of the range of percentages into which the score falls. The height of

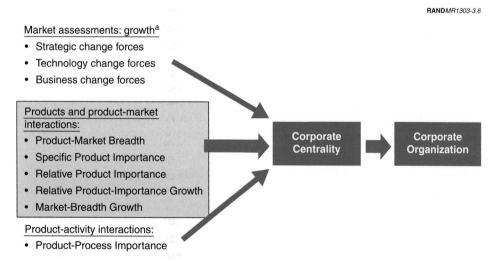

RAND*MR1303-3.6*

Market assessments: growth[a]
- Strategic change forces
- Technology change forces
- Business change forces

Products and product-market interactions:
- Product-Market Breadth
- Specific Product Importance
- Relative Product Importance
- Relative Product-Importance Growth
- Market-Breadth Growth

Product-activity interactions:
- Product-Process Importance

Corporate Centrality

Corporate Organization

[a]Here, growth is indicated not so much by the increase in the size of a market but by the increase in the emphasis placed on that market.

Figure 3.6—Road Map of Chapter Three, Showing That We Are at the Products and Product-Market Interactions Stage of the Analysis

the bins indicates the distribution of elements by measure, or observable. These measures are then evaluated against each other to refine a portfolio analysis for identifying risks in the future, whether the product has many markets and High importance—is *portfolio central* or *central to the corporation*—or has High importance in only one or two markets—is a *niche product*—as well as other questions.

The scoring looks at one measure at a time. After all the measures have been evaluated, the scores for two measures are then placed on a grid to show their relative positions on the grid. Succeeding grids enable a process of elimination—a narrowing of managerial options—that ends with the products most central to the corporation. As questions arise about the placement of one of the products in a less desirable portion of the grid, an iterative process is used to go back through lower-level grids to refine the evaluation.

This section begins with a description of the product-market interactions, the product-rating system for those interactions, and how these interactions will affect market structure in 2007. A similar analysis is presented for product-process interactions.

The concept of growth in market emphasis can be projected onto products, markets, and processes alike and can be used to gain insights into a product's centrality to a market and to the NAVSEA corporation. Such centrality is assessed at the end of this section, as is the commercial availability of NAVSEA products. The main question the following analyses seek to answer is,

> Am I positioned well relative to customer needs?

The scoring and interactions of those scores are part of a technique for analysis. As we have already indicated, assignment of the scores relies on information gained from background documents, site visits, and the expertise of the research team. What is important about a valuation system such as the one we present here is not whether it is "right" or "wrong" but that it presents a consistency determination that reveals internal checks and balances in an organization. The preferred valuation system will be the one that best captures the idea of centrality by realizing the strategic vision of the senior management and by capturing the culture of the organization.

Product-Market Interactions and Observables

NAVSEA has 108 products and 15 markets in which these products may or may not be important. These products are components of a much bigger whole that represents a composite of all the products that contribute to the needs and preferences of customers in the NAVSEA market. No single product answers the needs and preferences of all the customers in a market; each product contributes to those needs, but there is not a one-to-one correspondence between product and need. Interactions of the product with processes, technologies, and other organized resources must be analyzed to determine whether the product indeed meets a need or preference.

We used the needs and preferences extracted from OPNAVINST C3501.2J for the markets we created for NAVSEA relevance. We used the ensemble of supporting activities for the detailed product descriptions. Our final assessments are based on our own expertise and on commentary during our site visits.

Corporate-level decisions on which products and associated activities will be considered of higher or lower importance will depend on the characteristics of product-market interactions evaluated at the planning time horizon. In the commercial world, these interactions involve positioning a product with respect to current or emerging customer needs and preferences and also with respect to competing products. In our analysis, we adopted five measures, or *observables,* of product-market interactions that facilitate management decisions on actions to be taken that will affect organizational structure:

- Specific Product Importance: The importance of a product to a specific market, where *importance* measures the extent to which the product satisfies customer needs and preferences in that market.

- Relative Product Importance: The specific importance of a product summed across all markets to which that product contributes.

- Market Breadth: The total number of markets to which a product contributes.

- Relative Product-Importance Growth: The importance of a product in markets of growing emphasis, calculated by multiplying the market-emphasis-growth factor of a specific market by the specific product importance (6, 3, 1, or 0; see discussion below) of a given NAVSEA product and summing the results across all markets. The market-emphasis-growth factor is the strategy-weighted emphasis-growth factor discussed earlier in this chapter. It assigns 3 to those markets in the High emphasis-growth category; 2 to markets in the Medium category; 1 to markets in the Low category; and 0 to markets in the Very Low category. See Appendix C for a sample spreadsheet and calculation.

- Market-Breadth Growth: The breadth of products in markets of growing emphasis, calculated by summing the market-emphasis-growth factors for all the markets in which the product contributes. Market-breadth growth enters the analysis to determine the corporate centrality of products and is plotted against relative product-importance growth in Figure 3.15 (see Corporate Centrality section).

Specific Product Importance—NAVSEA Market Structure. The specific product importance observable enables us to scan down all products in a specific market, gleaning insights into which markets are preferred—have the highest percentage of High importance products—and how best to reposition products in that market.

We took several passes through the products to determine various rankings. We sought to determine, first, a simple binary property—Yes or No?—of whether a product is of value, or *importance,* in a market. Next, if a product has importance in a market, then how important is it? We did not rank-order the 108 products to identify which product is of the most importance, which is of the least importance, and where the other products fit in between, because importance comes in the relationship between certain aspects of a product or the product and the market or a process. Instead, we combined our two scales into one, asking initially, "On a scale of 0, 1, 2, 3, how important are the products?" (see Table 3.6). We did not use or develop a list of criteria or attributes for each and every product to provide a detailed basis for judgment. Rather, we based our initial assessments on information gained from visits to NAVSEA; on our personal background knowledge of U.S. Navy, management, technology, and science; and on current research. From the first binary pass through the product list, products that did not contribute to a market got a zero.

On the next, more-specific scoring pass through the products, the research team wanted to separate further the products ranked as Very Important from the Important products, as well as the Important products from the Supporting ones. That is, if a product is Important, how important is it?

Table 3.6

**Initial Product-Rating
System**

0	No contribution
1	Supporting
2	Important
3	Very important

RAND*MR1303-T3.6*

Why not just go through a single pass and leave it at whether or not a product is important to a market? We wanted to go further than that because we knew that more than the simple 0, 1 ranking would be revealing and that using that additional knowledge would enrich the research. If we used 0, 1, then all NAVSEA products that contribute to a market have equal importance—a rank of "1"—a uniformity that does not reflect that most of the products in a market will be Supporting or Not Important. Many years of market research justified our sense that, generally, for any market there should be fewer Very Important products than just Important products. We needed to build this bias into the analysis in a consistent and quantifiable way.

We consider here *all* products in the market, not just the ones that NAVSEA supplies. We are assuming that the NAVSEA product-importance structure in a market follows a generalized distribution similar to a Gaussian distribution, with the lowest part of the curve at the High end and the highest at the Low end. If, after the assessment is complete, the NAVSEA product-importance distribution is markedly different from these generalized functions, the market is very important and the NAVSEA strategy for presence in that market demands special emphasis. The details of the derivation of the rating system for this assessment are presented in Appendix C.

To discourage inflation of ratings and a bias on the high side, and to achieve a better balance of product importance in a market, we adopted a system that is nonlinear, with greater spacing between the High and Medium scores than between the Medium and Low scores. Such a system is used in Quality Function Deployment,[10] but with much greater distance between the High (9) and Medium (3) scores. The rating system and the descriptors for each score are as follows:

6 = Market Defining. An essential product in the market and an essential definer of the market. The market would not exist or function at all without this product.

3 = Important. A major contributor to the market. The market depends on this product, but the product does not define the market.

---

[10]Originally developed by a Japanese shipbuilding firm in the early 1970s, "Quality Function Deployment (QFD), also known as The House of Quality, . . . tie[s] product and service design decisions directly to customer wants and needs, ... QFD is designed to deploy customer input throughout the design, production, marketing, and delivery facets of a given product or service. In a typical QFD application, a cross-functional team creates and analyzes a matrix linking customer wants and needs to a set of product and service design metrics that the company can then measure and control" (see www.ams-inc.com/whatwedo/qfd, downloaded December 21, 2001; www.ams-inc.com/whatwedo/qtd.htm, visited August 4, 2002).

1 = Supporting. Contributes to the market, but not a major contributor.

0 = Not Important. Does not contribute to the market.

The results for the distribution of all NAVSEA products for all 15 of the markets are shown in Figure 3.7. We can see that most of the markets have product-importance distributions that are in line with our expectations of general market-emphasis growth illustrated in Figure 3.4.

Several markets have distributions that are strikingly different from the others. The Acquisition Support (ACQ) market, for example, has more High importance products than Low or Medium importance products. Recall that these High importance products are those that define the marketplace. That NAVSEA products define the ACQ market should be no surprise: NAVSEA owns, or dominates, that market. The Operational Availability (OPA) market is similarly very different from the market-emphasis model, but here the NAVSEA products are peaked at the Medium importance bin, with very few Low importance

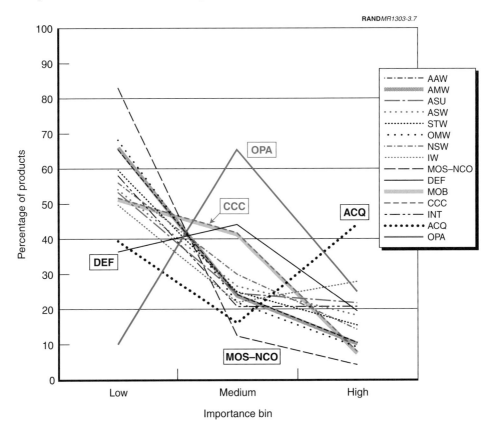

Figure 3.7—Distribution of NAVSEA Products Across All Markets

products. It can be argued that, given the OPNAVINST mandates and mission definitions, NAVSEA should dominate this market just as much as it dominates the ACQ market. This difference indicates that NAVSEA should consider developing a strategy for determining which products will dominate this market.

The DEF and CCC markets also show an abundance of Medium importance products. Here, the recommendation to NAVSEA is that, in the rapidly growing Defensive Systems market, it might be better to seek a larger number of High importance products so that NAVSEA becomes the "owner" of this importance-growth area. Determining which of the products will be suitable for these positions is further refined in the next subsection.

For the Low emphasis-growth CCC market, NAVSEA may want to consider not dominating this market, ensuring instead that the resources needed for creating High importance products are redistributed to markets that NAVSEA seeks to "own."

Relative Product Importance and Market Breadth. The results of the analysis of specific product importance summed across all markets—*relative product importance*—are shown in Figure 3.8. To construct this plot, we summed the importance of a given product across all markets and subsequently placed the results into four bins of the total scores for all products across all markets.

Those products with the highest total importance were binned into the High category, whereas those products with the lowest total importance were binned into the Very Low category. All other product scores were distributed between these two extremes.

The peak of the distribution of relative product importance is roughly in the middle of the Very Low-to-High range, indicating that there is a good balance between a bias toward products at the Very Low end of the spectrum, which would be characteristic of a company with a product portfolio of niche products, and a bias toward products at the High end of the spectrum, which would indicate a company with a portfolio of commodities, or products with broad use. No doubt some of the products in their respective markets are highly specialized niche products, such as specialized services, or are products with broad use, such as managing ships (see Chapter Four for a more detailed discussion); however, in this portfolio analysis of all products across all markets, only the *balance* of the range is relevant (Wong et al., 1998; Saunders et al., 1995). For example, although a product may be Very Important—indeed essential—in one market and one market only, such a product would be of Very Low importance relative to a product of Medium to Low importance in many markets in this portfolio analysis. Nevertheless, products that are High (rightmost bar in the figure) in the spectrum reflect a broad-based importance across many markets.

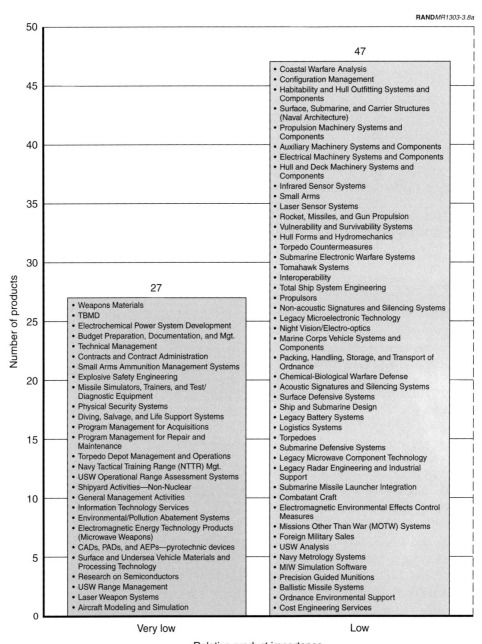

Figure 3.8—Number of Products Falling into Four Bins of Relative Product Importance. Names of products corresponding to each bar are listed, by ranking; total number of products is listed above each bar.

RAND*MR1303-3.8b*

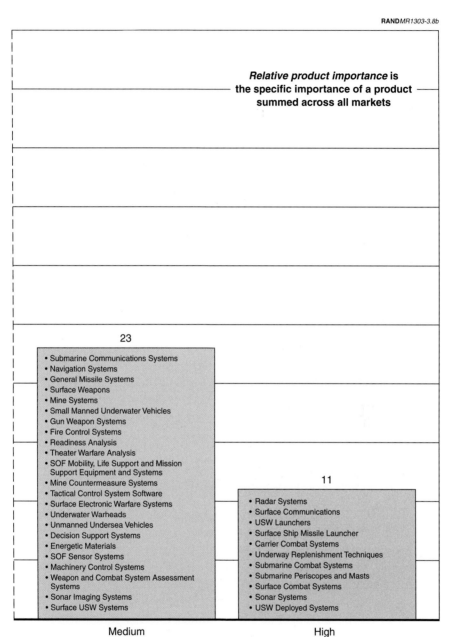

Relative product importance **is the specific importance of a product summed across all markets**

23

- Submarine Communications Systems
- Navigation Systems
- General Missile Systems
- Surface Weapons
- Mine Systems
- Small Manned Underwater Vehicles
- Gun Weapon Systems
- Fire Control Systems
- Readiness Analysis
- Theater Warfare Analysis
- SOF Mobility, Life Support and Mission Support Equipment and Systems
- Mine Countermeasure Systems
- Tactical Control System Software
- Surface Electronic Warfare Systems
- Underwater Warheads
- Unmanned Undersea Vehicles
- Decision Support Systems
- Energetic Materials
- SOF Sensor Systems
- Machinery Control Systems
- Weapon and Combat System Assessment Systems
- Sonar Imaging Systems
- Surface USW Systems

11

- Radar Systems
- Surface Communications
- USW Launchers
- Surface Ship Missile Launcher
- Carrier Combat Systems
- Underway Replenishment Techniques
- Submarine Combat Systems
- Submarine Periscopes and Masts
- Surface Combat Systems
- Sonar Systems
- USW Deployed Systems

Medium   High

Relative product importance

Figure 3.8—Cont'd.

Except for Defensive Systems and Test, Evaluate, Assess, most of the NAVSEA product groups are represented in the High importance bar. Radar Systems and Surface Communications appeal widely to all the markets, as do Sonar Systems and Surface Combat Systems—all of which are warfare-oriented, not defensive. The values of each of these observables was entered in a spreadsheet, a section of which is presented in Table 3.7 (also Table C.7). Examples of the calculations of values for each observable are presented in Appendix C.

Nevertheless, the products also need to be studied in terms of their market breadth, the other important dimension of this product portfolio analysis.

The results of the market-breadth analysis are shown in Figure 3.9. To construct a plot of market breadth, we counted the total number of markets to which a given product contributes, regardless of its importance in that market, then placed that product into one of four bins of the total scores for all products across all markets. Those products with the highest product breadth were binned into the High category; those products with the lowest product breadth were binned into the Very Low category. All other product scores were distributed between these two extremes.

As with relative product importance, the peak of the distribution of products for market breadth is roughly in the middle of the range, between Very Low and High, indicating a good balance between niche products and products with broad use. The likelihood of a niche market's disappearing as the needs and preferences of its customers change is very high; the likelihood of rapid change for a commodity market is very unlikely. Having a wide range of products that spans these possibilities is a sign of a well-designed portfolio strategy at the corporate level. For an organization, a portfolio with a balance of niche products and commodities is designed to offset risk.

Those products in the figure with a High market breadth are mostly from the Engineering Services and Communications Systems and Capabilities product groups, indicating a possible market-breadth emphasis as an overall strategy for these groups. Of such a strategy, Porter (1990, p. 44) notes that "broad scope may lead to competitive advantage if the firm can share activities across industry segments or even when competing in related industries." The Surface Communications product is rated High in both breadth and importance; many other High breadth products are from other parts of the importance spectrum.

To facilitate making decisions about specific products, the interactions of relative importance and market breadth should be considered. We represent this interaction as an intersection of the values from this and the preceding portfolio analyses on a grid, in Figure 3.10, with each observable as a dimension of an opposing axis on a two-dimensional grid. Products get fixed squarely in a cell reflecting both dimensions. The coordinate system is 0 through 3. Products

Table 3.7

Section of Product–Market Observables Rating Sheet

Major Product Groups and Products, with Specific Product-Importance Score by Market	NAVSEA Market (and Market-Emphasis-Growth Factor[a])															Relative Product Importance	Market Breadth	Market-Breadth Growth	Relative Product-Importance Growth
	AAW (0)	AMW (2)	ASU (1)	ASW (2)	CCC (1)	IW (1)	INT (3)	OPA (2)	OMW (0)	MOB (0)	MOS–NCO (0)	ACQ (3)	NSW (0)	STW (2)	DEF (3)				
Test, evaluate, assess																			
USW Operational Range Assessment Systems	0	0	3	3	0	0	0	0	0	0	0	0	0	0	1	7	3	6	12
USW Analysis	0	0	3	3	0	0	0	0	0	0	1	1	3	0	3	14	6	6	21
Missile Simulators, Trainers, and Test/Diagnostic Equipment	3	1	0	0	0	0	0	3	0	0	0	0	0	0	3	10	4	7	17
Weapon and Combat System Assessment Systems	3	3	3	3	0	0	0	0	3	0	1	0	3	3	3	25	9	10	30
Readiness Analysis	3	3	3	3	1	0	0	0	3	3	1	1	3	3	3	29	11	13	33
Navy Metrology Systems	1	1	1	1	1	0	0	3	1	1	1	0	1	1	1	15	12	13	17
MIW Simulation Software	0	1	0	1	0	0	0	0	6	0	1	1	1	0	3	14	7	10	16
Coastal Warfare Analysis	1	3	1	1	0	0	0	0	3	3	1	1	6	1	3	24	11	13	23
Aircraft Modeling and Simulation	0	0	0	0	0	0	0	0	0	0	0	0	0	0	0	0	0	0	0
Theater Warfare Analysis	3	3	3	3	0	0	0	0	3	3	1	1	3	3	3	29	11	13	30
Bullets																			

(Continues to include all product groups and products)

[a] See Figure 3.5 for market-emphasis-growth scores.

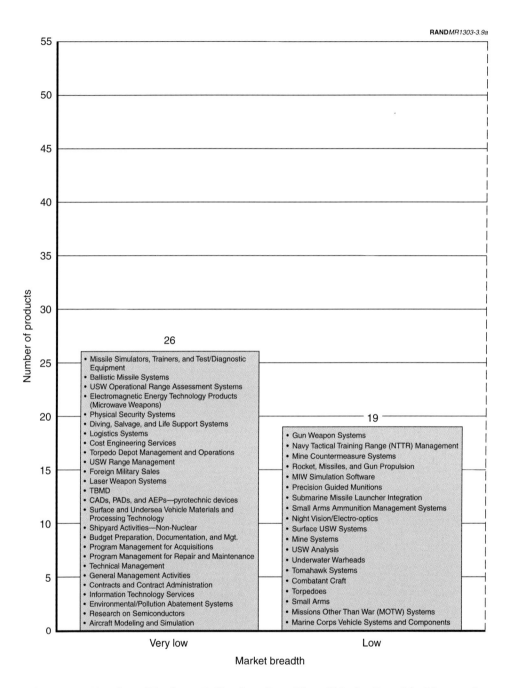

Figure 3.9—Number of Products Falling into Four Bins of Market Breadth. Names of products corresponding to each bar are listed within the bar; total number of products is listed above the bar.

RAND*MR1303-3.9b*

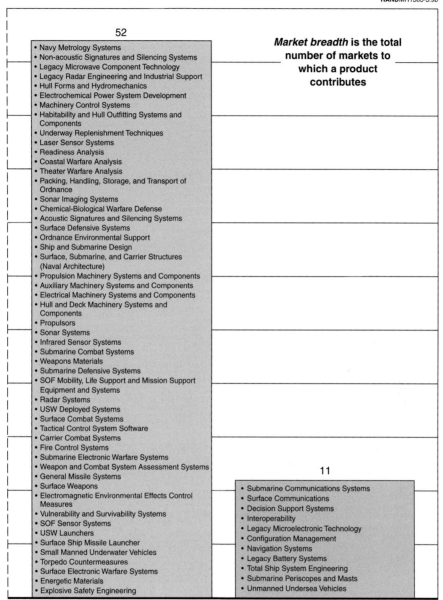

Figure 3.9—Cont'd.

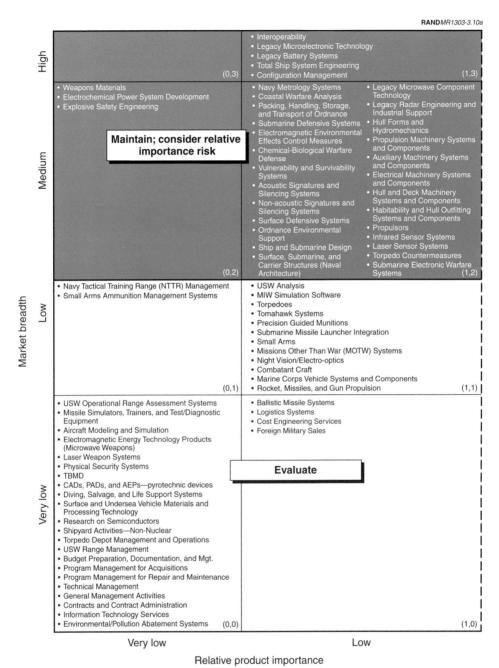

RAND*MR1303-3.10a*

Market breadth (y-axis) vs **Relative product importance** (x-axis)

High (0,3) – (1,3):
- Interoperability
- Legacy Microelectronic Technology
- Legacy Battery Systems
- Total Ship System Engineering
- Configuration Management

Medium – left box (0,2): Maintain; consider relative importance risk
- Weapons Materials
- Electrochemical Power System Development
- Explosive Safety Engineering

Medium – center (0,2):
- Navy Metrology Systems
- Coastal Warfare Analysis
- Packing, Handling, Storage, and Transport of Ordnance
- Submarine Defensive Systems
- Electromagnetic Environmental Effects Control Measures
- Chemical-Biological Warfare Defense
- Vulnerability and Survivability Systems
- Acoustic Signatures and Silencing Systems
- Non-acoustic Signatures and Silencing Systems
- Surface Defensive Systems
- Ordnance Environmental Support
- Ship and Submarine Design
- Surface, Submarine, and Carrier Structures (Naval Architecture)

Medium – right (1,2):
- Legacy Microwave Component Technology
- Legacy Radar Engineering and Industrial Support
- Hull Forms and Hydromechanics
- Propulsion Machinery Systems and Components
- Auxiliary Machinery Systems and Components
- Electrical Machinery Systems and Components
- Hull and Deck Machinery Systems and Components
- Habitability and Hull Outfitting Systems and Components
- Propulsors
- Infrared Sensor Systems
- Laser Sensor Systems
- Torpedo Countermeasures
- Submarine Electronic Warfare Systems

Low – left (0,1):
- Navy Tactical Training Range (NTTR) Management
- Small Arms Ammunition Management Systems

Low – right (1,1):
- USW Analysis
- MIW Simulation Software
- Torpedoes
- Tomahawk Systems
- Precision Guided Munitions
- Submarine Missile Launcher Integration
- Small Arms
- Missions Other Than War (MOTW) Systems
- Night Vision/Electro-optics
- Combatant Craft
- Marine Corps Vehicle Systems and Components
- Rocket, Missiles, and Gun Propulsion

Very low – left (0,0):
- USW Operational Range Assessment Systems
- Missile Simulators, Trainers, and Test/Diagnostic Equipment
- Aircraft Modeling and Simulation
- Electromagnetic Energy Technology Products (Microwave Weapons)
- Laser Weapon Systems
- Physical Security Systems
- TBMD
- CADs, PADs, and AEPs—pyrotechnic devices
- Diving, Salvage, and Life Support Systems
- Surface and Undersea Vehicle Materials and Processing Technology
- Research on Semiconductors
- Shipyard Activities—Non-Nuclear
- Torpedo Depot Management and Operations
- USW Range Management
- Budget Preparation, Documentation, and Mgt.
- Program Management for Acquisitions
- Program Management for Repair and Maintenance
- Technical Management
- General Management Activities
- Contracts and Contract Administration
- Information Technology Services
- Environmental/Pollution Abatement Systems

Very low – right (1,0): Evaluate
- Ballistic Missile Systems
- Logistics Systems
- Cost Engineering Services
- Foreign Military Sales

x-axis: Very low | Low

Relative product importance

NOTE: *Relative product importance* is the importance of a product summed across all markets. *Market breadth* is the total number of markets to which a product contributes.

Figure 3.10—Market Breadth Plotted Against Relative Product Importance for All NAVSEA Products, Overlaid with Possible Management Decisions for Strategies

RAND*MR1303-3.10b*

• Submarine Communications Systems • Navigation Systems • Unmanned Undersea Vehicles • Decision Support Systems (2,3)	• Surface Communications • Submarine Periscopes and Masts (3,3)
• Weapon and Combat System Assessment Systems • Readiness Analysis • Theater Warfare Analysis • General Missile Systems • Surface Weapons • Sonar Imaging Systems • SOF Mobility, Life Support and Mission Support Equipment and Systems • SOF Sensor Systems • Machinery Control Systems • Small Manned Underwater Vehicles • Tactical Control System Software • Fire Control Systems • Surface Electronic Warfare Systems • Energetic Materials **Invest** (2,2)	• USW Launchers • Surface Ship Missile Launcher • Underway Replenishment Techniques • Sonar Systems • Radar Systems • USW Deployed Systems • Submarine Combat Systems • Surface Combat Systems • Carrier Combat Systems (3,2)
• Underwater Warheads • Gun Weapon Systems • Surface USW Systems • Mine Systems • Mine Countermeasure Systems **Maintain; consider breadth risk** (2,1)	 (3,1)
  (2,0)	 (3,0)

      Medium   High

Relative product importance

Figure 3.10—Cont'd.

with Medium scores in both market breadth and relative product importance, for example, get plotted in Medium-Medium grid location (2,2), as shown by the list of products in the cell.

Overlaid on that grid is a straightforward arrangement of decisionmaking categories, which range on one diagonal from outright potential for investment to a need to review how products contribute to the marketplace (Evaluate). On the other diagonal, decisions are not as stark, which suggests maintaining resources.

Possible management decisions on the future appropriate product strategies show that the products categorized as High for both relative product importance and market breadth are candidates for continued or new investment—the products that, from a portfolio perspective, have great appeal to the customers in a wide variety of markets. The products that are candidates for investment are from all NAVSEA product categories except Defensive Systems. Evidently, the products from that category are more focused on specific markets than on appealing broadly to many markets, which is also consistent with the vertical study of products within markets shown in Figure 3.7. In that figure, NAVSEA products in the Defensive Systems market would be considered more in need of repositioning than of investment.

As noted above, this Invest–Evaluate grid could be consulted to refine decisions about products appearing in problematic areas of grids of other observables. For example, a manager may wonder whether to invest in a product when both the process and technology embedded in that product are in a highly unstable environment—i.e., undergoing rapid change (see Figure C.19). In Figure C.19, Navy Metrology Systems, Decision Support Systems, and Propulsion Machinery Systems and Components are in this Unstable region. In Figure 3.10, Decision Support Systems has Medium relative product importance and High market breadth, indicating that a decision to invest in this product would be appropriate. However, the other two products are in the Maintain category. Even though they have Medium market breadth, these products have Low relative product importance and hence lower priority than Decision Support Systems for investment decisions.

Those products plotted in the quadrant closest to the origin in Figure 3.10 are categorized Evaluate, which may signify one of two things.

Some of these products, such as the Program Management for Acquisitions, Program Management for Repair and Maintenance, and Physical Security Systems, have been rated for evaluation but could be of High specific importance in one or two markets. A portfolio analysis is useful for designating these products from the ACQ and OPA markets—markets that NAVSEA defines—as niche products. Their status as niche products means that NAVSEA will not have to make portfolio decisions in their regard because of their importance to these markets and to NAVSEA as an organization. Other products, such as Research on Semiconductors, are not rated highly in any market nor do they have a broad market appeal. These products could be experiments by management to investigate the market appeal of the characteristics of a new product that uses semiconductors. These products are candidates for true repositioning in the market. Of such repositioning, Porter says that "by selecting a narrow target segment, for example, a firm can tailor each activity precisely to the segment's needs and potentially achieve lower cost or differentiation compared to the broader-line competitors" (1990, p. 44).

For a product to keep its current position is acceptable from a portfolio perspective. However, as customer needs and preferences change, the value of that product for that customer is likely to "move" or "slip." Such movement must be monitored. Products in the Maintain categories need to be watched by management for slippage into the Evaluate quadrant.

The above product and portfolio analysis is based on a choice of system for valuing market and portfolio. A valuation system that has all those products located in the upper-right-most cells of the grid as candidates for investment—High in any dimension—is equally valid. Products in the next layer in—the Medium layer—should be held and monitored for slippage. The cells closest to the origin can be considered either the niche products or those products requiring more-detailed questions because market evaluation is required. Such a valuation system would not change too much the results from the analysis developed here.

Relative Product-Importance Growth. An additional measure in the valuation, developed earlier in this section, is growth in market emphasis. Having a portfolio of products of High importance in markets of growing emphasis has a high potential for achieving competitive advantage. Figure 3.11 displays the relative product importance in markets of growing emphasis, or *relative product-importance growth,* which is calculated by weighting (multiplying) the specific product importance in a market by the market-emphasis-growth factor for that market. The total growth in importance is the sum of these scaled importances across all markets. This observable is also referred to as *relative product importance in markets growing in emphasis.*

The results were subsequently placed into four bins of the total scores for all products across all markets. Those products with the highest importance in emphasis-growth markets were binned into the High category; those products with the lowest product breadth were binned into the Very Low category. All other product scores were distributed into the two bins between these two extremes.

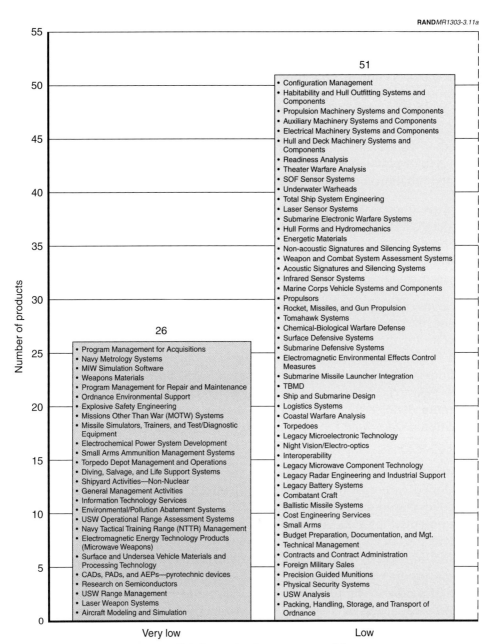

[a]Here, growth is indicated not so much by the increase in the size of a market but by the increase in the emphasis placed on that market.

Figure 3.11—The Four Bins for Relative Product Importance in Markets of Growing Emphasis

RAND*MR1303-3.11b*

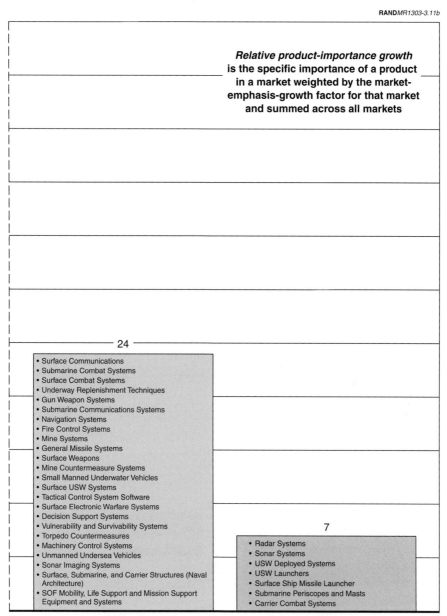

Relative product-importance growth **is the specific importance of a product in a market weighted by the market-emphasis-growth factor for that market and summed across all markets**

24

- Surface Communications
- Submarine Combat Systems
- Surface Combat Systems
- Underway Replenishment Techniques
- Gun Weapon Systems
- Submarine Communications Systems
- Navigation Systems
- Fire Control Systems
- Mine Systems
- General Missile Systems
- Surface Weapons
- Mine Countermeasure Systems
- Small Manned Underwater Vehicles
- Surface USW Systems
- Tactical Control System Software
- Surface Electronic Warfare Systems
- Decision Support Systems
- Vulnerability and Survivability Systems
- Torpedo Countermeasures
- Machinery Control Systems
- Unmanned Undersea Vehicles
- Sonar Imaging Systems
- Surface, Submarine, and Carrier Structures (Naval Architecture)
- SOF Mobility, Life Support and Mission Support Equipment and Systems

7

- Radar Systems
- Sonar Systems
- USW Deployed Systems
- USW Launchers
- Surface Ship Missile Launcher
- Submarine Periscopes and Masts
- Carrier Combat Systems

Medium   High

Relative product-importance growth[a]

[a]Here, growth is indicated not so much by the increase in the size of a market but by the increase in the emphasis placed on that market.

Figure 3.11—Cont'd.

Determining the adequacy of the magnitude of the shift is another component of the valuation system. Comparing the portfolio spectrum in this figure with that in Figure 3.8 for relative product importance unweighted by market-emphasis-growth factors, we see that several products have shifted distinctly to higher importance ratings—e.g., TBMD moves from Very Low to Low, and Torpedo Countermeasures moves from Low to Medium. From a portfolio perspective, therefore, NAVSEA products are already in markets that will be growing in emphasis in 2007.

The idea of centrality combines product-market interactions (such as product importance in markets), market breadth, and market-emphasis-growth determination, with characteristics associated with product-activity interactions. In the next subsection, we look at such interactions at a low-resolution, macro level, through the processes that encompass the organized resources. (The interactions of products and organized resources are described in Appendix C.)

Product-Process Interaction

To facilitate the analysis of centrality, the research team analyzed each product according to how the processes on which it was based would differ in 2007 from those of today (see Figure 3.12). As a component of a product or system, the activity—for example, setting software standards for the Submarine Combat

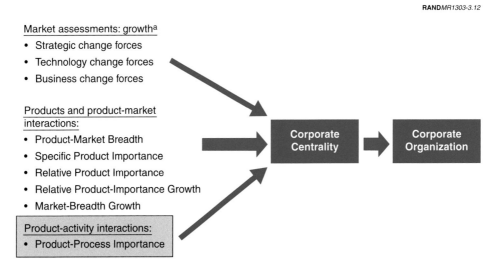

RAND*MR1303-3.12*

aHere, growth is indicated not so much by the increase in the size of a market but by the increase in the emphasis placed on that market.

Figure 3.12—Road Map of Chapter Three, Showing That We Are at the Product-Activity Interactions Stage of the Analysis

System—is going to have the same number/code in 2007 as it has today, but the process itself (organization, personnel, and technologies that make it up) may have changed, as indicated in the discussion of Hull Forms and Hydromechanics in Appendix C, for which the primary equipment/facility for calculating computational fluid dynamics will be done on a computer by a mathematician rather than in a tow tank by a hydromechanical engineer.

To evaluate the products in light of the processes they encompass, the research team took the basic processes associated with main task 4 of the RAND process code, "Execute Agency's Mission" (Table C.3), as shown in Table 3.8, which has direct relevance for evaluating how products are actually produced. (The other main tasks in Table C.3 relate more to how resources are acquired to accomplish the production or are for internal planning purposes. Supporting activities, such as strategic planning, resource acquisition, and human-resource management, are not in the activities database.)

Given the items on Table 3.8 as the major categories by which to evaluate the embedded processes for the product, the basic question becomes:

Will the supporting processes be different in 2007 from what they are today?

To measure the product-process interaction, evaluated by *product-process change,* the research team assessed the processes embedded in NAVSEA products on the basis of our site visits and on the documentation those visits furnished. The team judged some of the products to be provided by world-class

Table 3.8

Processes Used in Rating NAVSEA Products

Execute Agency's Mission

- Designate office of responsibility
- Provide operational information support
- Identify and market customer requirements
- Develop and manage technology
- Design products and/or services
- Market and sell
- Produce and deliver products/services
- Invoice and service customer
- Evaluate program against objectives

RANDMR1303-T3.8

organizations—that is, organizations that had a good business model (i.e., a good way of performing individual activities and of organizing its entire value chain) and that could handle the changes in the future—requiring no adjustment of the processes. Therefore, although the products may change, the embedded processes are robust. For these products, the answer to the above question was, No, the processes would not be different and would get a zero in the ranking system: 0 for not different, 1 for different.

Each of the 108 products was rated according to the aggregate of information just described, with binary scoring across the nine processes listed in Table 3.8. The results of this rating were summed across all processes, resulting in a maximum of 9 and a minimum of 0. If the team was in doubt about the relevance of a process to a product, we used the detailed processes shown in Table 3.9 for clarification. Because the processes do not span a wide numerical range, the research team decided to bin the results according to the system shown in Table 3.10. The minimum—a "hard zero"—was difficult to achieve; the few hard-zero products were placed in the Very Low bin. All other results were distributed uniformly into the other three bins.

The product-process interaction analysis—the final results of this process—is shown in Figure 3.13.

Process change for NAVSEA products peaks roughly in the middle, indicating that most NAVSEA products are in an environment with a level of Low-to-Medium process change. The products that are rated at Very Low were shown by the analysis to be supported by robust processes that would endure through the coming decade or beyond. This is not to say that other parts of the environment, such as technology or strategic need, are not changing, only that the processes embedded in these products can handle such changes.

At the other end of the range are the products that will have processes in place in 2007 that are very different from those in place today. The analysis showed, for example, that the basic manner in which two products—Information Technology Services and Shipyard Activities—are produced will have a different business model (see Chapter Four for a description of such changes) and that the interactions of customers and clients with the product will be different from what they are today, if they in fact occur today. One of the very new products, Decision Support Systems, is in this category because no processes are currently in place to provide it. The other new product, Interoperability, which is already under development, is supported by existing processes and is rated at a Medium process-change level, as shown in the figure.

Table 3.9

Detailed Processes Used in the Product Evaluation

Designate office of responsibility
- Establish the operations structure
- Initiate program documents
- Assess adherence to laws, plans, etc.
- Integrate resources

Provide operational information support
- Collect operational information
- Aggregate and analyze operational information
- Provide situation assessments to decisionmakers
- Provide technical advice to tactical commander

Identify and market customer requirements
- Determine customer needs and wants
- Conduct qualitative assessments
- Conduct quantitative assessments
- Predict customer wants and needs

Develop and manage technology
- Sponsor work on defense-related technology
- Establish parameters for technical feasibility
- Maintain corporate knowledge base
- Set technical standards
- Control technical documentation and configuration management
- Exchange technical information
- Perform basic research
- Perform applied research
- Perform advanced research
- Perform technology scan and identify promising technology
- Evaluate technical feasibility of proposals

Develop and manage technology (cont'd.)
- Develop operational guidelines for technology use
- Transfer technology

Design products and/or services
- Develop product/service concept and plans
- Design, build, evaluate prototype products
- Refine existing products/services, modernize and upgrade
- Test effectiveness of products
- Prepare for production

Market and sell
- Market products and/or services to customer group
- Process customer orders

Produce and deliver products/services
- Acquire material and technology for production
- Convert resources/inputs into products
- Deliver products
- Manage production and delivery processes
- Deliver service to customers

Invoice and service customer
- Bill the customer
- Provide post-delivery service
- Manage customer feedback

Evaluate program against objectives
- Assess technical test results
- Assess deviations and waivers
- Assess program cost, schedule, and performance
- Assess environmental and safety compliance

RAND*MR1303-T3.9*

Table 3.10

**Binning Thresholds for Scoring of
Process Change in Products**

0 – 0 = 0	Very low
1 – 3 = 1	Low
4 – 6 = 2	Medium
7 – 9 = 3	High

RAND*MR1303-T3.10*

COMMERCIAL AVAILABILITY

Just as some products, such as ocean acoustics/sonar, are, according to Gaffney and Saalfeld (1999, p. 15), specific to the Navy, other products have alternatives available in the commercial world. Availability of alternatives will be crucial in the future as part of three decision strategies:

- To develop sources in the private sector for products that are currently without such sources, thereby ensuring a healthy competitive environment

- To encourage a healthy competitive environment in which alternatives are commercial sources

- To determine which products that have not yet been outsourced can be more fully outsourced (i.e., to find a commercial firm that can create a new product line by providing the outsourced product).

A well-defined set of competitors providing products of similar type and quality is a component of the conventional definition of a *market*.

To understand the availability of products similar to the NAVSEA products, the research team defined the nature of the NAVSEA product or service using the detailed activities that gave rise to the product, then searched the U.S. Department of Commerce Standard Industrial Classification (SIC) System (http://www.census.gov/epcd/www.sic.html) to search for commercial sources of that product. To locate a specific product, the team searched the listings in *Thomas' Register of American Manufacturers* (1997), information from discussions with NAVSEA staff during our site visits, and the research team's expertise.

We used the following basic question to determine the commercial availability of a product:

> In 2007, will there exist or could there be made available a credible commercial source for this product?

A *credible commercial source* is an organization or company that can deliver the product in the same time frame, with the same or similar characteristics, and of the same quality as the product provided by NAVSEA. Using a simple binary rating system—0 for not commercially available, 1 for commercially available—we determined which of the NAVSEA products would have availability commercially. Table 3.11 lists the commercially available analogues for NAVSEA products. Organized by their product groups, the 29 products that are listed represent 25 percent of the total NAVSEA product portfolio and nine out of the 13 NAVSEA product groups.

None of the products from the Vehicles, SOF Systems and Capabilities, Explosives RDA&M, and Communications Systems and Capabilities product groups is commercially available. A commercial analogue would have NAVSEA product-group managers for these groups. Those managers would be considering the first decision strategy to ensure commercial sources for products in these groups.

The product-group managers for groups with an abundance of commercially available alternatives—Engineering Services, for which about two-thirds of the products have commercial analogues, and Management Services, for which almost half of the products are available commercially—should be considering the second strategy while maintaining enough in-house work and expertise that the Brilliant-buyer responsibilities for NAVSEA—special arrangements that ensure value to the customer—can be fulfilled.

At the same time, these managers should be considering the third strategy so that new products needed by NAVSEA customers and clients can be developed and added to their portfolio.

Through decisions such as these, and in their plans for restructuring markets and repositioning products, the product group managers become instruments of the strategic intent of the senior NAVSEA leadership.

Commercial availability is yet another element to be factored into the determination of NAVSEA's competitive advantage. The above decision strategies will help to further clarify the centrality of a product to the corporation, the topic of the final section of this chapter.

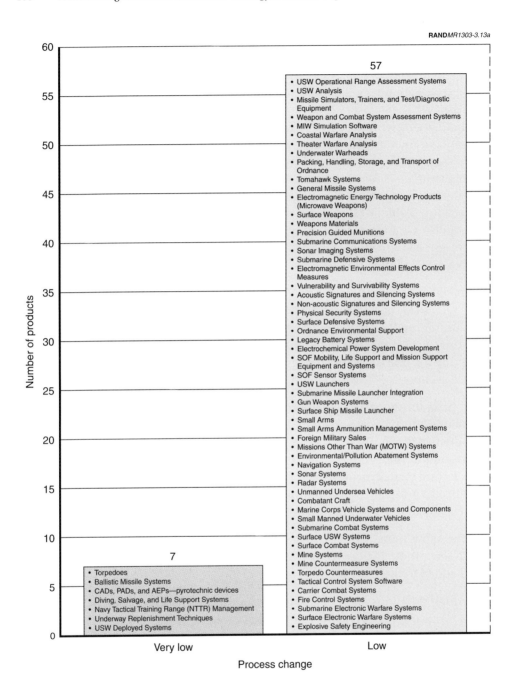

RAND*MR1303-3.13a*

Figure 3.13—Number of Products Falling into One of Four Binned Product–Process Change Evaluation Categories. Products in the High bin are supported by rapidly changing processes.

RAND*MR1303-3.13b*

***Product-process change* is the extent
to which supporting processes
for a given product will be
different in 2007**

33

- Readiness Analysis
- Aircraft Modeling & Simulation
- Laser Weapon Systems
- Interoperability
- Surface Communications
- Chemical-Biological Warfare Defense
- Ship and Submarine Design
- Surface and Undersea Vehicle Materials and
  Processing Technology
- Surface, Submarine, and Carrier Structures (Naval
  Architecture)
- Legacy Microwave Component Technology
- Legacy Microelectronic Technology
- Legacy Radar Engineering and Industrial Support
- Hull Forms and Hydromechanics
- Logistics Systems
- Cost Engineering Services
- Configuration Management
- Torpedo Depot Management and Operations
- USW Range Management
- Budget Preparation, Documentation, and Mgt.
- Research on Semiconductors
- Propulsion Machinery Systems and Components
- Machinery Control Systems
- Auxiliary Machinery Systems and Components
- Electrical Machinery Systems and Components
- Hull and Deck Machinery Systems and Components
- Habitability and Hull Outfitting Systems and
  Components
- Propulsors
- Submarine Periscopes and Masts
- Night Vision/Electro-optics
- Infrared Sensor Systems
- Laser Sensor Systems
- Rocket, Missiles, and Gun Propulsion
- Energetic Materials

11

- Navy Metrology Systems
- TBMD
- Technical Management
- Total Ship System Engineering
- Shipyard Activities—Non-Nuclear
- Program Management for Acquisitions
- Program Management for Repair and Maintenance
- General Management Activities
- Contracts and Contract Administration
- Information Technology Services
- Decision Support Systems

Medium   High

Process change

Figure 3.13—Cont'd.

Table 3.11

Commercially Available NAVSEA Products

Management services • Torpedo Depot Management and Operations • USW Range Management • Navy Tactical Training Range (NTTR) Management • Small Arms Ammunition Management Systems • Information Technology Services **Test, evaluate, and assess** • Missile Simulators, Trainers, and Test/Diagnostic Equipment • Navy Metrology Systems • Aircraft Modeling and Simulation **Bullets** • Packing, Handling, Storage, and Transport of Ordnance **Defensive systems** • Physical Security Systems **Launching systems** • Small Arms **Warfare systems** • Submarine Combat Systems	**Engineering services** • Ordnance Environmental Support • Diving, Salvage, and Life Support Systems • Surface and Undersea Vehicle Materials and Processing Technology • Legacy Microwave Component Technology • Legacy Microelectronic Technology • Legacy Radar Engineering and Industrial Support • Research on Semiconductors • Legacy Battery Systems • Logistics Systems • Shipyard Activities—Non-Nuclear • Electrochemical Power System Development • Cost Engineering Services **Platform systems** • Environmental/Pollution Abatement Systems • Habitability and Hull Outfitting Systems and Components **Sensor systems** • Night Vision/Electro-optics • Infrared Sensor Systems • Radar Sensor Systems

RAND*MR1303-T3.11*

CORPORATE CENTRALITY

Although many commercially available products are also High importance products, the flip side of commercial availability could be considered corporate centrality: the importance of NAVSEA products in the markets and how broadly the products meet the needs and preferences of customers in more than one or a few NAVSEA markets—importance and breadth in markets growing in emphasis. (See Figure 3.14.)

Recall the example that Gaffney and Saalfeld (1999, p. 15) give of the national naval responsibility of ocean acoustics for the Science and Technology portfolio of the Navy. Ocean acoustics is central to the corporation—the Department of the Navy—because it is essential to the Department of the Navy's ability to detect enemy ship and weapon signatures and an area that no other mission agency or private enterprise can reasonably be expected to support.

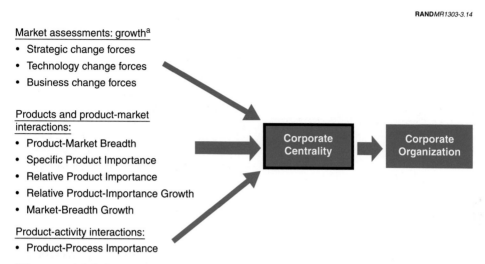

RAND*MR1303-3.14*

Market assessments: growth[a]
- Strategic change forces
- Technology change forces
- Business change forces

Products and product-market interactions:
- Product-Market Breadth
- Specific Product Importance
- Relative Product Importance
- Relative Product-Importance Growth
- Market-Breadth Growth

Product-activity interactions:
- Product-Process Importance

[a]Here, growth is indicated not so much by the increase in the size of a market but by the increase in the emphasis placed on that market.

Figure 3.14—Road Map for Chapter Three, Showing That We Are at the Corporate-Centrality Stage of the Analysis

As we have seen in the figures in this chapter, sonar is essential—rated in the highest category on most measures of value, including breadth. It is central to the portfolio of products and hence central in the corporation.

However, centrality has a two-level hierarchy: portfolio centrality and niche centrality.

Portfolio Centrality

Given the portfolio-analysis perspective of this chapter, we defined product centrality using measures of relative product importance in markets growing in emphasis (see Figure 3.11) and market breadth (see Figure 3.9). Here, we place the NAVSEA products on a two-dimensional grid according to the intersection of importance and breadth in markets growing in emphasis (the intersection of relative product-importance growth and market-breadth growth), in Figure 3.15. The scale on each dimension ranges from Very Low (corresponding to a value of 0) to High (corresponding to a value of 3). The products sharing the coordinates of 16 intersections are listed in the corresponding cells.

RAND*MR1303-3.15a*

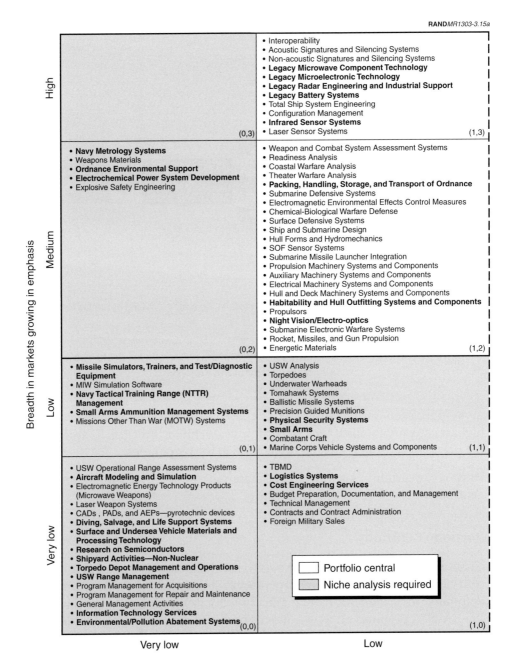

Figure 3.15—Product Centrality, Indicated by the Intersection of Relative Product
Importance and Breadth in Markets Growing in Emphasis in Cells Toward the
Upper Right

RAND*MR1303-3.15b*

• Submarine Communications Systems • Sonar Imaging Systems • Surface Communications • Machinery Control Systems • Navigation Systems • Unmanned Undersea Vehicles • Decision Support Systems (2,3)	• Submarine Periscopes and Masts • Sonar Systems • **Radar Systems** • USW Deployed Systems (3,3)

• General Missile Systems
• Surface Weapons
• Vulnerability and Survivability Systems
• Surface, Submarine, and Carrier Structures
  (Naval Architecture)
• SOF Mobility, Life Support and Mission Support
  Equipment and Systems
• Gun Weapon Systems
• Underway Replenishment Techniques
• Small Manned Underwater Vehicles
• **Submarine Combat Systems**
• Surface USW Systems
• Surface Combat Systems
• Mine Countermeasure Systems
• Torpedo Countermeasures
• Tactical Control System Software
• Fire Control Systems
• Surface Electronic Warfare Systems
 	
(2,2)
	• USW Launchers
	• Surface Ship Missile Launcher
	• Carrier Combat Systems
	
	(3,2)

• Mine Systems (2,1)	(3,1)
(2,0)	☐ Portfolio central ▨ Niche analysis required (3,0)

Medium   High

Relative product importance in markets growing in emphasis

Figure 3.15—Cont'd.

Products that are both broad and important in these markets growing in emphasis—those in the white area—are clearly *central* from the portfolio perspective. Products in the lower fourth and in the left-hand side of the plot are candidates for a more detailed analysis of whether they have niche centrality or can be repositioned—outsourced—because they have commercial analogues.

All product groups are represented in the portfolio-central category of Table 3.12. All the products for the groups Warfare Systems, Sensor Systems, SOF Systems and Capabilities, and Communications Systems and Capabilities are present, implying that those product groups are 100-percent portfolio central.

Niche Centrality

We now need to distinguish the niche products with importance in only a few markets from those products that might have been ranked in the left-hand side of the importance-breadth plot (Figure 3.10) because they were truly unimportant and nonbroad. A niche product may define a market, making that market a *niche market,* a definition common in the high-tech and high-performance product markets in the commercial world. For NAVSEA to meet the needs of very sophisticated customers for highly specialized products, the route to competitive and sustainable advantage may be through differentiation rather than cost leadership or other strategies for market dominance. For example, in its Market Niche Strategy subsection's discussion on sourcing, *Shipbuilding Technology and Education* (NRC, 1996, p. 34) notes that

> U.S. shipbuilders must target niche markets because the yards will find it difficult to compete in high-volume production markets where foreign competitors are well entrenched. . . . They must select shipbuilding market niches in which they can be competitive, adapt the technologies required to develop competitive products, apply the product technologies required to differentiate their products (ship designs) from competitors' products, develop the process technologies required to design and build these products competitively, and last but not least, develop strategies for the procurement of everything the yard cannot make efficiently.

To evaluate in more detail the distribution of relative-importance scores for the products in Figure 3.15 labeled "Niche analysis required," the research team binned the distribution of importance scores for these products, using the scoring system developed in the Specific Product Importance—NAVSEA Market Structure subsection. Products that have an abundance of 6s—Market-Defining scores (see also The RAND Product-Rating System section in Appendix C)—are surely candidates for the niche-market-centrality category. Figure 3.16 displays the rank-ordered products with the characteristic of having at least one importance score in the Market-Defining category.

Table 3.12

Portfolio-Central Products and Associated Product Groups

Test, evaluate, assess
- Weapon and Combat System Assessment Systems
- Readiness Analysis
- Coastal Warfare Analysis
- Theater Warfare Analysis

Bullets
- Packing, Handling, Storage, and Transport of Ordnance
- General Missile Systems
- Surface Weapons

Communications systems and capabilities
- Submarine Communications Systems
- Sonar Imaging Systems
- Interoperability
- Surface Communications

Launching systems
- USW Launchers
- Submarine Missile Launcher Integration
- Gun Weapon Systems
- Surface Ship Missile Launcher

Defensive systems
- Submarine Defensive Systems
- Electromagnetic Environmental Effects Control Measures
- Chemical-Biological Warfare Defense
- Vulnerability and Survivability Systems
- Acoustic Signatures and Silencing Systems
- Non-acoustic Signatures and Silencing Systems
- Surface Defensive Systems
- Mine Countermeasure Systems
- Torpedo Countermeasures

Engineering services
- Ship and Submarine Design
- Surface, Submarine, and Carrier Structures (Naval Architecture)
- Legacy Microwave Component Technology
- Legacy Microelectronic Technology
- Legacy Radar Engineering and Industrial Support
- Legacy Battery Systems
- Total Ship System Engineering
- Hull Forms and Hydromechanics
- Configuration Management

SOF systems and capabilities
- SOF Mobility, Life Support and Mission Support Equipment and Systems
- SOF Sensor Systems

Platform systems
- Propulsion Machinery Systems and Components
- Machinery Control Systems
- Auxiliary Machinery Systems and Components
- Electrical Machinery Systems and Components
- Hull and Deck Machinery Systems and Components
- Habitability and Hull Outfitting Systems and Components
- Propulsors
- Navigation Systems
- Underway Replenishment Techniques
- Submarine Periscopes and Masts

Sensor systems
- Sonar Systems
- Night Vision/Electro-optics
- Infrared Sensor Systems
- Radar Systems
- USW Deployed Systems
- Laser Sensor Systems

Vehicles
- Unmanned Undersea Vehicles
- Small Manned Underwater Vehicles

Warfare systems
- Submarine Combat Systems
- Surface USW Systems
- Surface Combat Systems
- Mine Systems
- Tactical Control System Software
- Decision Support Systems
- Carrier Combat Systems
- Fire Control Systems
- Submarine Electronic Warfare Systems
- Surface Electronic Warfare Systems

Explosives RDA&M
- Rocket, Missiles, and Gun Propulsion
- Energetic Materials

| | Products with commercially available sources |

RAND*MR1303-T3.12*

RAND*MR1303-3.16*

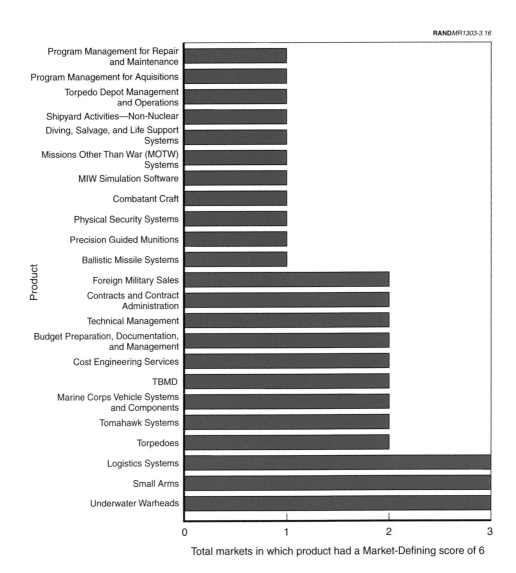

Figure 3.16—Market-Defining Niche Products

From the figure, the Logistics Systems product is a Market-Defining product in three markets and surely should be considered a niche-central product (as should Small Arms and Underwater Warheads). Likewise, the products Torpedoes through Foreign Military Sales, which contribute to the definition of two markets, should also be considered niche central. Any product that receives a rating of Market-Defining should be considered niche central.

What of the products that are rated Important in some or many markets but not Market-Defining in any markets? These are the products the research team designated as 3s. Similarly to the rating system described in Appendix C, this score indicates a greater distance from the center of the niche than for Market-Defining products, as well as a greater distance from the portfolio-central products. The Important niche products are rank-ordered in Figure 3.17.

The spectrum of Important products is broad, with more in the less-important than more-important scores, indicating a continuous transition to noncentrality. The USW Analysis and Missile Simulators, Trainers, and Test/Diagnostic Equipment products are far closer to the corporate center than are the products at the other end of the spectrum, such as Surface and Undersea Vehicle Materials and Processing Technology, which have only one Important score.

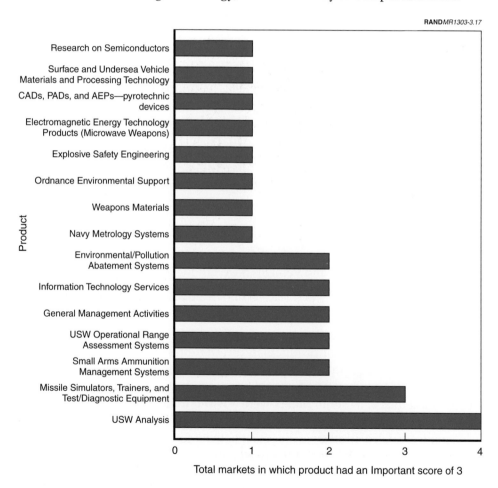

Figure 3.17—Important Niche Products

A representation of a scale of increasing centrality for the niche-central products is shown in Figure 3.18, in which all the products in the "Niche analysis required" sector of the 2-D plot in Figure 3.15 are listed by name and rank in
Figure 3.16 (for niche centrality) and Figure 3.17 (for niche importance). The
bottom-most products in the figure meet neither the Market-Defining nor
Important criterion; they are ranked Supporting to all or any products. In fact,
for the last product listed, Aircraft Modeling and Simulation, there are no markets or matching customers in the Market-Product-Activity analysis. For this
product, the research team concluded that, although activities were listed in the
internal NAVSEA efforts and available from other sources, none of the NAVSEA
markets benefited from these efforts.

Product-Group Centrality

We have presented important and central products individually. Now, we look
at the centrality of the groups themselves. The products in these groups were
binned into the four categories of centrality: Central, Defining, Important, and
Supporting. We calculated the percentage of products in each of these
categories for each of the product groups and display them in Figure 3.19.

In this figure, the product groups whose individual products are listed as
portfolio central in Figure 3.15 and Table 3.12 are shown here to be 100-percent
Central: Warfare Systems, Sensor Systems, SOF Systems and Capabilities, and
Communications Systems and Capabilities. The other product groups contain
a mix of categories, indicating those in which niche products preponderate
(Management Services) or may have niche markets (Vehicles). The product
groups Defensive Systems and Vehicles have products either in the Central or in
the Defining categories, indicating a high level of corporate centrality from both
a portfolio and a niche perspective.

The Management Services product group has no products in the Central category and an abundance of products in the Defining category—more than for
any other product group. In the for-profit/commercial world, the general
manager for this product group would be said to have adopted a *niche strategy*
in the marketplace, as shipbuilders were advised to do in the quotation above.
As was emphasized earlier in this chapter in the discussion of repositioning, the
advantage of such a strategy is that each activity for this product group can be
tailored precisely to the segment's needs and has the potential for achieving
lower cost or greater differentiation than the broader-line competitors. The
manager for the Sensor Systems product group would be said to have adopted a
central strategy, in which the firm can share activities across its various
segments (called *business units* in Chapter Four). These strategies are in-
trinsically neither good nor bad—only different in regard to how they interact

RAND*MR1303-3.18*

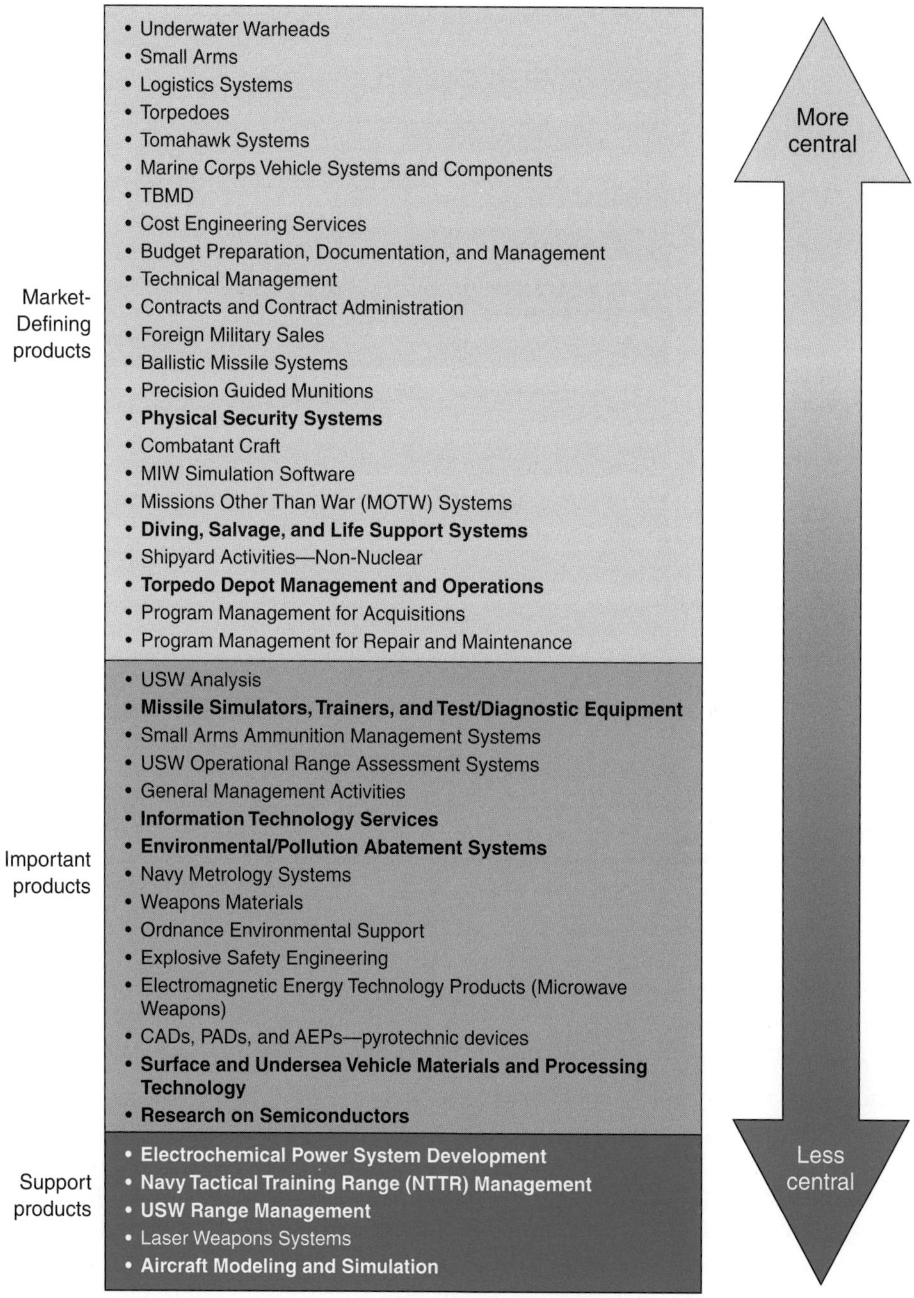

Market-Defining products

- Underwater Warheads
- Small Arms
- Logistics Systems
- Torpedoes
- Tomahawk Systems
- Marine Corps Vehicle Systems and Components
- TBMD
- Cost Engineering Services
- Budget Preparation, Documentation, and Management
- Technical Management
- Contracts and Contract Administration
- Foreign Military Sales
- Ballistic Missile Systems
- Precision Guided Munitions
- **Physical Security Systems**
- Combatant Craft
- MIW Simulation Software
- Missions Other Than War (MOTW) Systems
- **Diving, Salvage, and Life Support Systems**
- Shipyard Activities—Non-Nuclear
- **Torpedo Depot Management and Operations**
- Program Management for Acquisitions
- Program Management for Repair and Maintenance

Important products

- USW Analysis
- **Missile Simulators, Trainers, and Test/Diagnostic Equipment**
- Small Arms Ammunition Management Systems
- USW Operational Range Assessment Systems
- General Management Activities
- **Information Technology Services**
- **Environmental/Pollution Abatement Systems**
- Navy Metrology Systems
- Weapons Materials
- Ordnance Environmental Support
- Explosive Safety Engineering
- Electromagnetic Energy Technology Products (Microwave Weapons)
- CADs, PADs, and AEPs—pyrotechnic devices
- **Surface and Undersea Vehicle Materials and Processing Technology**
- **Research on Semiconductors**

Support products

- **Electrochemical Power System Development**
- **Navy Tactical Training Range (NTTR) Management**
- **USW Range Management**
- Laser Weapons Systems
- **Aircraft Modeling and Simulation**

More central

Less central

NOTE: Bold text indicates commercial-source availability.

Figure 3.18—Increasing Scale for Niche Product Centrality

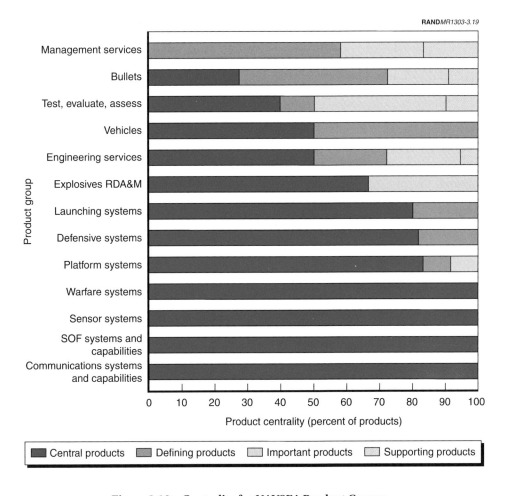

RAND*MR1303-3.19*

Product group

Central products   Defining products   Important products   Supporting products

Figure 3.19—Centrality for NAVSEA Product Groups

with the marketplace and how they fit into the overall corporate strategy for creating value for customers and clients (see Chapter Four).

Centrality and the Organization

If NAVSEA were organized along the lines of product-group managers, then the manager for Management Services could be asking herself about the wisdom of being a niche player if the emphasis in corporate NAVSEA is on centrality and coreness. She might consider divesting or outsourcing some of the less central products and repositioning some of her Market-Defining products so that a better mix of corporate centrality results. Similarly, the manager for Warfare Systems might ask himself if he is being too conservative by being solely in the Corporate-Central category if the increasing emphasis in the NAVSEA corporation is on being agile and innovative. He might consider experimenting with some new products that start in the Important category, repositioning them to higher-centrality categories as the products mature in the marketplace or abandoning them if they do not create the intended value.

Growth in Market Emphasis and Centrality

Finally, we consider the level of centrality for corporate NAVSEA with regard to specific markets (rather than with regard to specific products or product groups) in relation to the forecasts of growth in market emphasis. To do so, we revisit the total product importance for all NAVSEA products in the various markets. This characteristic of growth in market importance for NAVSEA products is shown in Figure 3.20. All histogram bars sum to 100 percent.

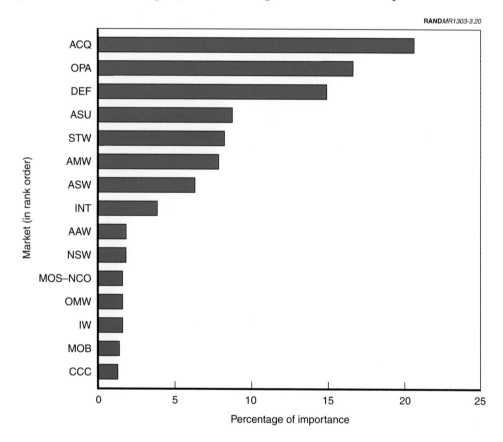

Figure 3.20—Total Importance of Products for All NAVSEA Markets, Scaled by the Market-Emphasis-Growth Forecasts

The market groupings are evident. The Acquisition Support, Operational Availability, and Defense Systems markets are clearly in a group by themselves, capturing more than half of the total importance for all products across all markets. These markets and the products in these markets deserve the highest of management attention, because so much of the market perception of value for NAVSEA comes from them. Moreover, these are the markets that will be growing the fastest in emphasis in 2007.

A second grouping of markets is evident for the Anti–Surface Ship Warfare market to the Intelligence market. Almost one-third of the total perceived importance in the marketplace comes from the products in these markets, and these products, too, should receive a commensurate degree of management attention. The other markets are not significant sources of perceived value for NAVSEA products, although they deserve to be monitored for signposts. Recall that in the Signposts for Changes in Market-Emphasis Growth subsection of this chapter, a number of signposts of change were indicated and could herald a change in emphasis for the Navy and NAVSEA, depending on the external situation. Attention to such signposts and their regular review is a key to business planning in the coming decade for NAVSEA.

These examples demonstrate that the concept of growth in market emphasis can be projected onto both products *and* markets and can be used to gain insights into market centrality and portfolio centrality. This information can be projected onto the supporting activities to gain more insight into the centrality of these components of the Market-Product-Activity Model. Moreover, the various aspects of centrality discussed in this section can be used as an entry point for consideration of organizational design. Understanding NAVSEA markets, products, and activities will be essential to understanding the core businesses and the vertical and horizontal linkages for NAVSEA in the twenty-first century.

Chapter Four

ORGANIZATION

The changing of activities and the expression of a new *strategic intent*—the shifting of *enterprises,* or primary purposeful activities of the organization, what Porter (1990, p. 37) calls positioning for competitive advantage—create a need for change in NAVSEA's organizational structure. To accommodate changes in the enterprise so that the organization can focus on the activities that are central to the enterprise at a given time, NAVSEA must realign its organizational structure. Failing to achieve alignment, the organization will be ineffective in meeting its mission through its new enterprise. Inflexibility and rigidity—failure and inability to change—are the primary causes of an organization's death (Katz and Kahn, 1978).

The analyses of activities and product centrality in Chapter Three can be used as the entry points for considering organizational design. They are particularly important for the size stage (not included in this report). Understanding NAVSEA markets, products, and activities is crucial to understanding the core businesses, the vertical and horizontal linkages, and the size for NAVSEA in 2007.

INTRODUCTION

We approached the third task in the project—the organizational design task—from the perspective of NAVSEA as a single, diverse "corporation" composed of all the organizational elements needed to design, acquire, produce, support, and dispose of naval platforms and systems in 2007. The underlying premise is that, in the role of corporate headquarters for this mega-organization, NAVSEA can add substantial value by managing the portfolio of these interrelated elements, or businesses, to achieve outcomes of importance, such as high levels of customer service or efficiency for customers and stakeholders, that could not be achieved by each separate business alone. We focused not on evolving the present organization to the planning time horizon, the year 2007 but, rather, on determining an appropriate organization matched effectively to markets, products, and activities of that time period, as identified in Chapter Three.

With this in mind, we segmented this corporation into business units that can be employed to carry out the enterprise of the corporation, what Carl Builder in his essay "The American Military Enterprise in the Information Age" (1999, p. 28) clarified as "a deliberately different idea from the . . . objective, mission, role, or purpose of an institution. *Enterprise* tells us about the activities that preoccupy an organization." The essay makes a distinction between an organization's primary purpose and how it fulfills that purpose—its enterprise.

We use the term *purpose* in this section to describe an organization's reason for existence and the essence of its objective. To show how these concepts work together, Builder provides IBM, a business organization, as an example. IBM's purpose—to make a profit for its owners—has remained constant over time, but its enterprise has changed: from making office machines, primarily typewriters; to making large computers (Builder, 1999, p. 28); to making personal computers; to providing services. We borrow Builder's conception of enterprise because it fits closely with the activities analysis described in Chapter Three and with the concept of strategic intent (industry structure and positioning) introduced in Chapter Three and elaborated below.

Because they are key to the achievement of NAVSEA's mission and strategy, some businesses in this portfolio should be managed more intensively. We refer to these as *core businesses.* Core businesses serve as a primary focus of senior leadership attention.

Although we believe that NAVSEA's *purpose* will remain unchanged in 2007 from what it is now—to ensure that the Department of the Navy has superior and operational ships and ship systems—some of the *activities* it undertakes to accomplish that purpose will change, as will centrality of those activities to the enterprise. Some activities are new, some disappear, some are higher in importance in 2007 than in 2000, and some are lower in importance than in 2000. Through our measures of importance and centrality, we capture how closely the activities align with NAVSEA 2007's enterprise: The scorings tell us in which activities NAVSEA should be most engaged in 2007.

It is the changing of activities and the shifting of enterprise that expresses a new strategic intent—how NAVSEA deploys corporate resources to accomplish its mission and provide value to its stakeholders—and that creates a need for change in NAVSEA's organizational structure. To accommodate changes in the enterprise so that the organization can focus on the activities that are central to the enterprise at a given time, NAVSEA must realign the organizational structure.

All organizations face the challenges of shifting enterprises. For example, in an interview with *Sea Power* (April 2000, p. 61), H. Lee Buchanan II, Assistant Secretary of the Navy (RD&A), expressed in the vision he calls "Keeping America's Navy Number One in the World," how the enterprise of the Naval Research Laboratory is shifting and how, as a result, the organization's structure needs to be realigned:

> Our job now is to learn how to adopt and adapt the results of others rather than to generate the results ourselves. So what we must do is learn how to bring technologies from outside the Navy to the inside. This is very different from what we've had to do before. The military, up until 10 to 15 years ago, was always in the forefront of every modern technology. . . . We are not set up right—organizationally or psychically—to go out and be more a consumer of technology rather than a producer of technology.

The Naval Sea Systems Command exists within, and serves, a larger organization—the Department of the Navy. Given NAVSEA's consistent purpose, it is not surprising that we can trace the roots of a NAVSEA-like organization back to the creation of the Navy Department in 1798. When Benjamin Stoddert, Secretary of the Navy, designated Joshua Humphreys Principal Naval Constructor of the United States in May of that year, the concept of having an organization responsible for providing technical support for ships emerged (Wright, 1959).

Since 1798, the Navy has structured a number of organizations to fulfill the basic purpose that NAVSEA accomplishes today: ensuring that the Department of the Navy has superior and operational ships and ship systems. The primary responsibility for ensuring that the Department of the Navy has superior and operational ships and ship systems has been given to such organizations as the Board of Navy Commissioners, established in 1815; the Bureau of Construction, Equipment, and Repair, established in 1841; three bureaus—Engineering, Equipment and Recruiting, and Construction and Repair, established in 1861; the Bureau of Ships, established in 1940; and, finally, NAVSEA, established in 1974. Since 1974, various research and engineering functions and organizations have been added to NAVSEA. At present, NAVSEA has the organizational look and feel of a private-sector conglomerateur—a collection of related but separate (and often competing) enterprises that have accreted over time.

How the purpose was fulfilled—the enterprises undertaken by these various organizations—has changed over time, shifting from sails to steam engines, from wooden to steel ships, adding submarines, then adding nuclear-powered submarines. With the advent of automatic and computerized weapon systems, the enterprise of ship systems has also shifted dramatically. These examples depict how changes in technology influenced the enterprise, as what the Navy considered to be "superior" ships and ship systems changed. Moreover, the activities of the enterprise as well as its technologies have also changed as, over time, the organization has transitioned from designing and building ships itself to contracting for these products and services.

Established on July 1, 1974, the Naval Sea Systems Command encompassed the existing functions of the Naval Ship Systems Command and the Naval Ordnance Systems Command, which were simultaneously disestablished. The two systems commands were merged to simplify and consolidate parts of the organizational structure within the Naval Material Command, which involved design, acquisition, and life-cycle support of total ships and ship systems. The merged activities are visible in Figure 4.1. Further, it was believed that the merger would improve the ability to deliver fully integrated and cost-effective ships in a timely manner (OPNAVNOTE 5450, Department of the Navy, June 11, 1974). The accumulation of these functions and organizations is seen in Figure 4.2, as is the emergence of acquisition support, which we discuss below.

Such enterprise shifts since NAVSEA's establishment (even while NAVSEA's purpose has remained constant) can be seen by examining NAVSEA's 1974 mission statement and its most recent mission statement, for 2000:

> To provide material support to the Navy and Marine Corps for ships and crafts, shipboard weapons systems and components thereof, ammunition, guided missiles, mines, torpedoes, and all other surface and underwater ordnance expendables. Coordinator of shipbuilding, conversion, and repair for DoD. Material support encompasses the complete life cycle—from research and design through test and evaluation to modification, maintenance, and fleet support (Department of the Navy, 1974).

> We develop, acquire, modernize, and maintain affordable ships, ordnance, and systems that are operationally superior so our Sailors and Marines can protect and defend our national interests and, if necessary, fight and win (NAVSEA mission, 2000).

These mission statements reflect how NAVSEA's purpose is being fulfilled; they reflect NAVSEA's primary, purposeful activities. The various organization charts reflect the enterprises that encapsulate that purpose in various periods.

One major shift in enterprise emerges from these mission statements. In 1974, acquisition is not mentioned; in 2000, acquisition and acquisition support have become a major enterprise. NAVSEA certainly acquired items in 1974, but acquisition was not considered to be a primary enterprise of NAVSEA. Perhaps the most salient feature of Figure 4.1 is its product focus, with all activities relevant to those products located completely within the organizational boundaries of NAVSEA. Further, in these enterprises, the organization fostered a production mentality—"You can have any ship you want as long as it is now

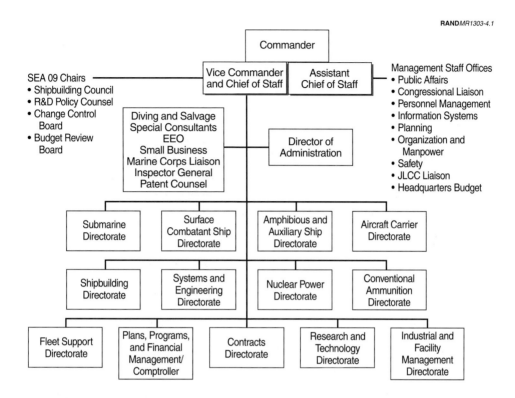

RAND*MR1303-4.1*

Figure 4.1—Organizational Chart for Naval Sea Systems Command, Circa 1974

available"—and an ownership mentality—"Our ships that you use." Today, however, NAVSEA supports over 100 acquisition programs, which are assigned to the command's seven affiliated Program Executive Officers (PEOs) and various Headquarters elements, as seen on the left-hand side of Figure 4.2. We refer to Figure 4.2 later to illustrate where important activities such as research, engineering, and logistics are located.

This shift in enterprise from *make* to *buy,* highlighted by Figure 4.2, predates DoD implementation of the Goldwater-Nichols Defense Reorganization Act of 1986 (Goldwater-Nichols, 1986).[1] Before Goldwater-Nichols, NAVSEA and the organizations that preceded it

---

[1]In July 1989, the Defense Management Review (DMR) directed certain DoD organizational changes to implement the Goldwater-Nichols DoD Reorganization Act of 1986 (Public Law 99-433), to streamline the acquisition process, and to enhance acquisition accountability. The DMR mandated designation of a single civilian official at the Assistant Secretary level within each military department as the Component Acquisition Executive (CAE). Within each service, the CAE manages all major acquisition programs through PEOs.

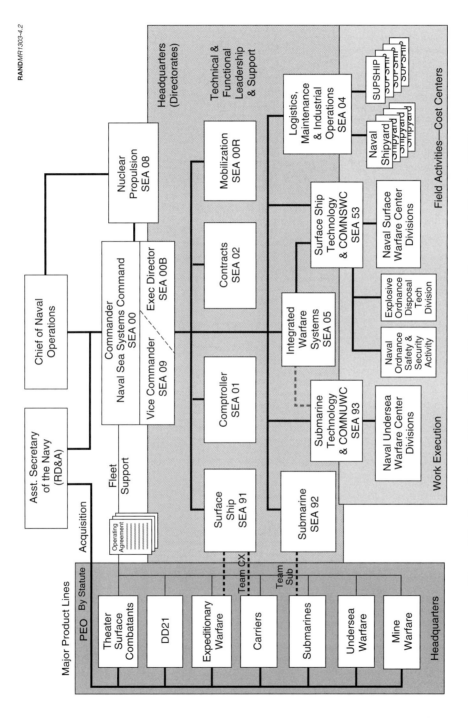

Figure 4.2—Organizational Chart for Naval Sea Systems Command, October 1999

- designed ships

- constructed ships (although this responsibility was shared with private entities)

- maintained, repaired, overhauled, and modernized ships

- disposed of ships.

This is the "life-cycle" referred to in OPNAVNOTE 5450.

Since 1989, the Assistant Secretary of the Navy for Research, Development and Acquisition (ASN [RDA]) has been the Navy Component Acquisition Executive and, as such, is responsible for all research, development, and acquisition. The PEOs,[2] in the leftmost column of Figure 4.2, act for and exercise the authority of the ASN (RDA) to supervise directly the management of assigned programs. The Commander of NAVSEA (COMNAVSEA) acts for and exercises the authority of the ASN (RDA) to supervise directly the management of acquisition programs not assigned to PEOs. PEOs and COMNAVSEA are responsible for all aspects of life-cycle management for their assigned programs. The PEOs and COMNAVSEA report directly to the ASN (RDA) for all matters pertaining to research, development, and acquisition. For the execution of in-service support responsibilities, COMNAVSEA reports directly to the Chief of Naval Operations; PEOs report directly to the Chief of Naval Operations, through COMNAVSEA.

In this context, NAVSEA had shifted by 1999 from a manufacturing (goods-producing) set of enterprises to enterprises focused on services. In contrast to the product organization of Figure 4.1, Figure 4.2 presents an organization focused on customers and service activities.

COMNAVSEA has three roles in this latter organization:

- Managing acquisition programs other than those assigned to PEOs

- Providing for in-service support

- Providing support services to PEOs without duplicating their management functions.

A formal operating agreement elaborates COMNAVSEA's role in providing support services for its affiliated PEOs. This operating agreement highlights the special relationship existing between NAVSEA and the PEOs. The PEOs are physically collocated with NAVSEA and are considered part of NAVSEA for the purposes of administrative space utilization. NAVSEA provides engineering,

---

[2]The reference to PEOs in this section should be read to include a reference to Direct Reporting Program Managers (DRPMs), as well.

logistics, comptroller, contracting, legal, and small-business and disadvantaged-business utilization support through the various organizations shown in Figure 4.2. Such support, particularly research and engineering, is not readily observable in that figure. In addition, NAVSEA provides customary administrative and office support services, as well as communications support.

Thus, NAVSEA fulfills much of its purpose through support of the PEOs. NAVSEA ensures that the Department of the Navy has superior and operational ships and ship systems by

- ensuring that the PEOs and Fleet have access to the institutional knowledge of naval engineering needed to design, construct, modernize, and repair ships and ship systems

- ensuring that the total ship and shipboard systems are properly designed and developed

- maintaining, repairing, and modernizing ships and ship systems.

NAVSEA must make certain that each item and system works separately and together. This service enterprise requires a marketing mentality—"We will meet your schedules."—and a service mentality—"We will meet your needs." To capitalize on this marketing mentality and the shift in enterprises already under way, we have emphasized a customer perspective in this chapter, treating the PEOs and the Fleet as customers of NAVSEA.

PEOs are, indeed, special customers, stemming in part from the evolution of the enterprise and in part from the beneficial outcomes accruing to the closeness of the affiliation between a customer and its supplier of goods and services. We view the full range of support NAVSEA provides to the PEOs—from engineering and logistics to contracting and legal, from technical to administrative—as the goods and services in the supplier-customer relationship. The implications of this status permeate the perspective described in the remainder of this chapter, beginning with our approach to organizational design.

APPROACH TO ORGANIZATIONAL DESIGN

The organizational design approach we take has four stages, illustrated in Figure 4.3. We describe the content of the first three stages in detail in the following three sections. Importantly, although we describe the individual stages sequentially, we employed an iterative process in practice, moving back and forth between and among stages. The organizational design approach depicted in the figure places NAVSEA not only in the industry context but in the broader

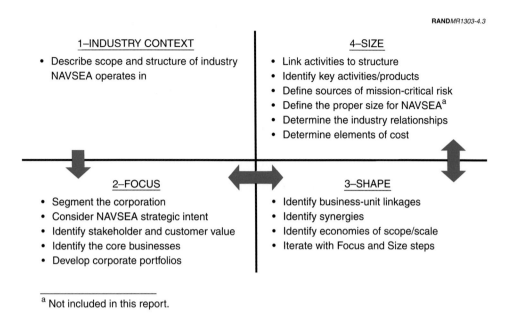

RAND*MR1303-4.3*

1–INDUSTRY CONTEXT

- Describe scope and structure of industry NAVSEA operates in

4–SIZE

- Link activities to structure
- Identify key activities/products
- Define sources of mission-critical risk
- Define the proper size for NAVSEA[a]
- Determine the industry relationships
- Determine elements of cost

2–FOCUS

- Segment the corporation
- Consider NAVSEA strategic intent
- Identify stakeholder and customer value
- Identify the core businesses
- Develop corporate portfolios

3–SHAPE

- Identify business-unit linkages
- Identify synergies
- Identify economies of scope/scale
- Iterate with Focus and Size steps

[a] Not included in this report.

Figure 4.3—Organizational Design Approach

strategic environment described in Chapter Two. We also frequently iterated to the product, activity, and market assessments described in Chapter Three during the course of the research. The research team was the same for all assessments, which facilitated integration of organization with forward-looking (2007) activities and products. Moreover, business units build upon the activity database developed as part of Chapter Three and Appendix C, and central products become part of the framework for determining size.

As we proceed through the stages, the level of detail increases. For example, in the first stage, we employ a very broad classification scheme to characterize the *industry* in which the NAVSEA corporation operates. In the second and third stages, we *focus* on NAVSEA business units and divisions within and between those business units, *shaping* (aggregating) the units into business lines according to a selected strategic intent. Entering the fourth stage, the product perspective developed in Chapter Three would be employed as a basis for the future organizational structure.

INDUSTRY INTEGRATION

To provide the context in which the future NAVSEA corporation is intended to operate, we designed the first stage as a delineation of the scope and the structure of the *overall* industry in which the NAVSEA corporation exists and operates, rather than on specific companies, business units, or command elements.

We approached this stage by asking the question:

What industry is NAVSEA in?

We have already answered this question by looking at the mission/purpose of NAVSEA. Generally, we say the "industry" is in the business of providing, supporting, and disposing of naval platforms. As such, the industry consists of all organizational entities, public or private, that perform significant activities in support of the naval platform life cycle—from the earliest conceptual manifestations of a platform and its component technologies as a requirement to meet a future need through disposal of a vessel that has served the nation long and well. In more-specific terms, the industry is defined by enterprises that perform the activities contributing to the conceptualization, research, design, engineering, construction, in-service support, and disposal of naval vessels and systems. If anything, NAVSEA is unique, because no comparable single industry performing all these activities exists in the United States.

The NAVSEA corporation exists within an even larger sphere of industries in the United States, of which the shipbuilding/ship-repair industry is but one. We employed Standard Industrial Classification codes (SIC; http://www.census. gov/epcd/www.sic.html) as the basis for determining the scope of industrial participation of NAVSEA. The SIC system database delineates the structure of U.S. industry at various levels of aggregation, as well as the size of the industry, as a whole, and that of its participants. To determine the relative importance of the NAVSEA corporation within an industry, we analyzed the funding that flows to and through NAVSEA today. Overall, this funding analysis provided a proxy for the amount of competition available for carrying out the major activities of the corporation; it also identified where the potential for risk was highest, particularly in activities key to NAVSEA corporate operations.

We used several databases to develop the industrial context for NAVSEA. The Department of Defense DD350, or Contractor, database identifies how governmental contract dollars flow to businesses and industries, by product and service. We also used NAVSEA financial data to help relate the size of NAVSEA component organizations to comparable businesses in the private sector. The data available from these different sources were not completely compatible; sometimes, they were drawn from different time periods. Because we were seeking a general description, not specific conclusions, we could accommodate these potential inaccuracies. However, we emphasize that the reader should treat the information presented below cautiously.

Ultimately, we based four assessments on these data:

1. The types of industries within which NAVSEA participates.

2. The percentage of work within each of those industries that supports the Navy, largely through contract dollars that flow through NAVSEA.

3. The percentage of industry output the NAVSEA corporation performs in-house.

4. Competitors for NAVSEA's in-house work (in other words, whether internal NAVSEA products are available in the private sector).

These assessments are summarized below.

Industries Within Which NAVSEA Participates

Money flows from NAVSEA into 46 different industries, identified at the two-digit SIC code level (for example, Transportation Equipment). However, 95 percent of NAVSEA contract dollars go into 10 industries at the four-digit SIC code level (for example, Ship Building and Repairing, a subset of Transportation Equipment). These 10 industries are as follows:

*   Ship building and repairing

*   Engineering services

*   Guided missiles and parts

*   Fabricated structural metal products

*   Ordnance and accessories

*   Research, development, and testing services

*   Computer programming, data processing, services, and repair

*   Engines and turbines

*   Computer and office equipment

*   Special industry machinery.

Navy Share of Work and Role in Industries

The significance of NAVSEA contract dollars varies across these 10 industries. For example, as Figure 4.4 shows, over 60 percent of the dollar value of the ship-building and ship-repairing industry in the United States flows through

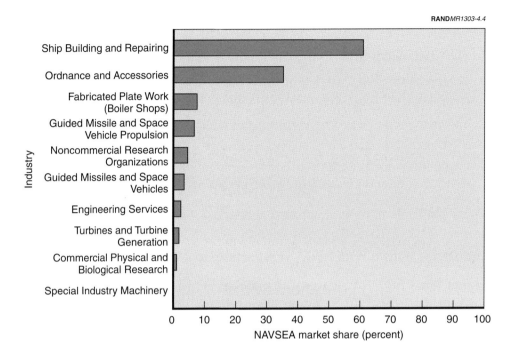

RAND*MR1303-4.4*

Figure 4.4—NAVSEA Contract Dollars as a Share of Industry Shown, with Industries Rank-Ordered by Market Share

NAVSEA. Thus, NAVSEA is a dominant player is some industries, such as shipbuilding and repairing, but not in others, such as engineering services.

NAVSEA's Industry Output

Comparing the percentage of dollars NAVSEA's own enterprises expend in performing tasks in a given industry with the dollars that flow through NAVSEA to the private sector in that industry is one way to view industry dominance. Figure 4.5 portrays the distribution of in-house and private-sector spending for each of the industries receiving the most NAVSEA dollars.

NAVSEA's enterprises that directly build and repair ships are large within NAVSEA, but they are small when compared with the dollars that flow to the overall industry. Conversely, while NAVSEA dollars are a small part of the engineering services industry, about 25 percent of this overall enterprise is performed in-house. Other enterprises for which NAVSEA performs a large share of work internally rather than using contract dollars include research, management services, and computer services.

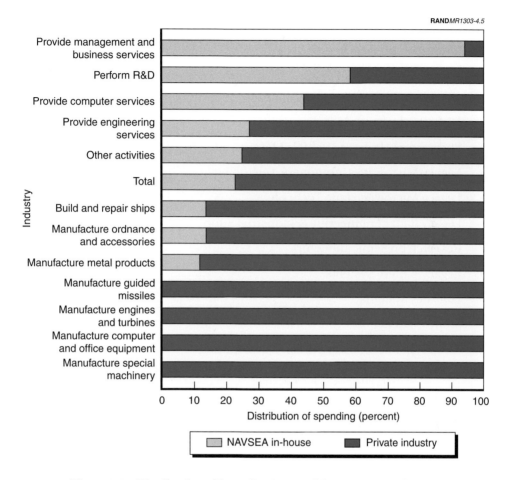

Figure 4.5—Distribution of Spending in Naval Sea Systems Industry

NAVSEA Competitors

We also identified the flow of contract dollars into specific firms in the private sector. Not surprisingly, firms such as Electric Boat, Newport News Shipbuilding, Ingalls Shipbuilding, Bath Iron Works, and Avondale Industries dominate the list. Using these data and data from other sources, we estimated that commercial sources can or could produce, in whole or in part, approximately 25 percent of the NAVSEA products (aggregated activities) identified in Chapter Three:

• Missile Simulators, Trainers, and Test/Diagnostic Equipment

• Navy Metrology Systems

- Aircraft Modeling and Simulation
- Packing, Handling, Storage, and Transport of Ordnance
- Physical Security Systems
- Ordnance Environmental Support
- Diving, Salvage, and Life Support Systems
- Surface and Undersea Vehicle Materials and Processing Technology
- Legacy Microwave Component Technology
- Legacy Microelectronic Technology
- Legacy Radar Engineering & Industrial Support
- Research on Semiconductors
- Legacy Battery Systems
- Logistics Systems
- Shipyard Activities–Non-nuclear
- Electrochemical Power System Development
- Cost Engineering Services
- Small Arms
- Submarine Combat Systems
- Torpedo Depot Management and Operations
- USW Range Management
- Navy Tactical Training Range (NTTR) Management
- Small Arms Ammunition Management Systems
- Information Technology Services
- Environmental/Pollution Abatement Systems
- Habitability and Hull Outfitting Systems and Components
- Night Vision/Electro-optics
- Infrared Sensor Systems
- Radar Sensor Systems

With this as the industrial context in which NAVSEA currently operates, we turn next to considerations of NAVSEA's organizational structure in the future. In the next part of the organizational design task, we identified major business units with common products, competitors, and other linkages to carry out the activities of NAVSEA in 2007—*focus*—then looked across these business units and reconfigured them—*shape*—to take advantage of combined actions and operations (i.e., synergies), economies of scale, and areas of desired emphasis. Practically, we accomplished these two tasks simultaneously. We describe our analysis sequentially.

FOCUS

In an organization as large and as diverse as the NAVSEA corporation, Alfred D. Chandler's time-tested advice from his 1962 *Strategy and Structure: Chapters in the History of the American Industrial Enterprise* continues to hold important sway: structure follows strategy. Consequently, the structural outline is derived from the corporate strategic intent it is designed to execute.

The Core Businesses

In the second stage of the organizational design process, we define the major business units of the corporation by describing the structure that leads to most effectively carrying out their individual missions and strategies, by focusing the organization on the key outcomes it is intended to produce. Our primary objective in this stage is to provide the broad structural outlines of the organization immediately below the NAVSEA corporate headquarters.

In this stage of the analysis, we look at the NAVSEA described in the first stage—a diversified corporation producing a set of related products and services. We emphasize identifying those products and services and arranging the activities that produce them in an organizational structure that contributes best to achieving NAVSEA's mission and overall strategic intent. *Structure*, what Porter (1990, pp. 40–41) calls the *value system* and *value chain,* is the formal allocation and ordering of activities to meet strategic intent.

The Role of Strategic Intent

Strategic intent states how NAVSEA, as a whole, will go about delivering value to its stakeholders. The statement of corporate strategic intent is a blueprint that can clarify organizational direction in different ways:

- How NAVSEA wants to position itself and its business units vis-à-vis the industry in which it exists.

- How the core competencies that set NAVSEA apart from other organizations can be developed and sustained.

- How NAVSEA wants its business units to view the customer.

- How NAVSEA wants to align itself with the structure of the market within which it competes (or how it wants to restructure that market to its own advantage).

We consider each of these perspectives and its implications for NAVSEA structure, in turn.

Strategic intent at the business-unit level is a statement of the value proposition—the competitive advantage—the business unit offers that will cause customers to prefer it to the competition. It may be cost, technological leadership, customer service, or some combination of these and other factors (e.g., innovation, flexibility, productivity, learning, and skill development). What differentiates the business unit from its competition? What do the business unit's customers want? What can the business unit deliver cost-effectively? Working initially from the top down and then from the bottom up, and employing an iterative process, we used the perspective these questions offer, first to suggest the initial structural form of the business units, then to identify how the portfolio of business units can be modified in relation to the corporate strategic intent.

In a corporate context, leaders employ strategic intent as a competitive weapon, and often they are reluctant to share it widely. Frequently, annual reports and other public statements contain a sanitized version, lacking specifics. To gain internal commitment, the chief executive (COMNAVSEA) will be more specific with the senior management team in laying out strategic intent than he will be with the general public. However, it is not uncommon that real strategic intent is not explicitly stated, but exists only in the chief executive's inner thoughts. To design the corporate structure for NAVSEA, we reviewed the most recent statement of corporate strategy and interviewed senior leaders in the Navy, seeking views of NAVSEA strategic intent for 2007.

NAVSEA Corporate Strategic Intent

From our review of the corporate-strategy statement and interviews with top NAVSEA managers, and from our multiple visits to existing NAVSEA business units, we concluded that NAVSEA has several potential manifestations of strategic intent available to it.[3]

---

[3]A number of the business units themselves have an explicit statement of strategic intent for the business unit. These statements helped us identify potential statements of strategic intent in 2007. Integrating these business units' statements with a corporate statement of strategic intent can enhance the synergy among these business units. (See NAVSEA, n.d., 1999b.)

From our interviews, we identified many assertions of what business NAVSEA is in or should be in—in other words, why NAVSEA exists as an organization in the Department of the Navy. NAVSEA leadership and external commentators variously espoused the following reasons for being:

- A high-quality service provider for high-technology products

- A low-cost provider for commodity services (i.e., services in broad use)

- A high-quality provider of complex systems

- The primary provider of leading-edge naval technology and solutions

- Supplier of last resort

- A knowledge repository

- A "Brilliant buyer"

- The Navy's integrator

- Steward of naval technology and knowledge.

NAVSEA will exist, to some extent, for all of these reasons in 2007. However, what it considers most fundamental and how it organizes to execute that emphasis, or centrality, will largely influence how well it satisfies its stakeholders. An organization that chooses to do everything may do everything equally well: mediocrely.

What is the essence of COMNAVSEA Strategic Intent 2007? Given the above variety of strategic intents from which to choose, we propose three variations of strategic intent that are most consistent with the recent corporate strategy and that highlight the impact of that strategy, to suggest how COMNAVSEA Strategic Intent 2007—when formally declared—could shape the NAVSEA organization. Later in this chapter, we outline four variations of strategic intent that lead to four alternative NAVSEA organizations. Here, we focus on components of those organizations.

Today, NAVSEA's strategic intent implies three major missions around which businesses can be organized: technical authority to include science and engineering expertise, acquisition of naval platforms, and in-service support. We used NAVSEA corporate strategic intent to identify specific business units—the first level of division of labor (immediately below the corporate level) within the NAVSEA corporation. We assessed these three businesses and others during the course of our analysis.

Each of the businesses we identified in this stage contributes in important ways; however, NAVSEA corporate headquarters does not necessarily need to view all of them as being *equally* important. Indeed, NAVSEA Headquarters' resources are limited; Headquarters can add the most value by focusing on the key, or core, businesses: those that have the greatest direct impact on the ability of NAVSEA to accomplish its strategic intent and, thereby, add value for NAVSEA stakeholders.

In this stage, we also outlined the structure of the individual business units, which follows from the *business-unit strategy*—how a specific business unit plans to carry out its mission and which leads to the fundamental structure and composition of the business unit. We investigated a variety of organizational templates that diverse businesses have used—product focus, process focus, customer focus, geographic focus, or a combination of two or more focuses, or structures—and assessed their effectiveness in carrying out the individual business-unit strategies. Each has advantages and disadvantages in how well it enables the business unit to carry out its strategy.

Our general approach to organizational design thus has two interdependent perspectives: a corporate perspective and a business-unit perspective. The broader perspective takes the view from corporate headquarters; the more-specific perspective takes the view from individual business units. Neither perspective is the "best" in terms of shaping corporate structure; both are important for a balanced organization. In the remainder of this chapter, we first describe a basic corporate portfolio of business units based on the activities we identified in Chapter Three and Appendix C. We then present four portfolios of business units, each based on a variation of NAVSEA strategic intent.

In this subsection, we first describe the importance of segmenting NAVSEA into business units; we then detail the differences between the corporate/Head-quarters and business-unit perspectives. Finally, we describe different methods for segmenting a diverse organization.

Why Segment into Business Units? The private sector would consider NAVSEA a diversified corporation providing related products. To effectively provide these related, often intertwined, products requires significantly different business models—"ways in which a firm performs various activities and organizes its entire value chain" (Porter, 1990, p. 41). Different parts of NAVSEA face different operating environments. Different driving forces, such as technology and strategy (as discussed in Chapter Three), cause these environments to change in different directions at different rates. Different parts of NAVSEA produce different products, to satisfy different customers who have different kinds of needs. Finally, different parts of NAVSEA compete with alternate sources—competitors—to which customers can go to satisfy those needs. Such an organization in the private sector would organize itself into business units.

Business units provide a coherent framework that allows NAVSEA to respond to and capitalize on these differences. In particular, a *business unit* is an organizational mechanism for focusing attention on those aspects that have the greatest effect on the ability of the organization to satisfy customers; it allows for a tailored strategy that highlights the handful of key factors that determine success. A *strategic business unit* is a conceptual operating unit, or focus for planning, that provides a distinct set of products or services to a *market*—a set of customers with preferences and needs different from those of other customers—while facing a well-defined set of competitors and taking responsibility for fiscal soundness.

If the differences delineated above did not exist, an organization would not require business units; it could design a single effective strategy if it provides similar products to a single set of customers with common needs and preferences facing a well-defined set of competitors. However, faced with the types of differences delineated above, an organization's leadership cannot be expected to create a single strategy that effectively addresses the full range of variability. For example, a strategy/business model for providing repair and maintenance would be expected to be substantially different from a strategy for providing technological innovation; similarly, a strategy for generating innovative technological solutions would be expected to be different from a strategy for managing and applying existing knowledge.

Consequently, by dividing NAVSEA into business units—each of which provides a distinct set of products for customers with similar needs and preferences facing a well-defined set of competitors—each business unit can tailor its particular strategy to its unique needs, rather than attempting to find a single strategy that addresses conflicting visions, missions, or objectives.

To narrow its focus, a business unit looks for the structure of its value chain in products, markets, customers, functions, processes, or geography, although other perspectives or a combination of perspectives may be more effective in some circumstances. The focus chosen establishes the framework for developing a strategy for effective management of the firm's resources. The strategy specifies how the business unit will meet its customers' needs. Business-unit strategy drives business-unit organizational structure.

Corporate Versus Business-Unit Perspective. The corporation as a whole and its business units have different and complementary responsibilities. On the one hand, the corporation is concerned with (1) accountability to its stakeholders, (2) the composition of its portfolio of business units (covered at the end of this chapter), (3) the allocation of resources across those business units (i.e., sizing; not covered in this report), and (4) the source of capital with which to carry out its operations (also not covered in this report). For the purposes of this project, we focus primarily on the first two responsibilities.

A business unit, on the other hand, is concerned with a customer perspective, its *value proposition*—what it offers to its customers more effectively than any other source—the business scope, and the core competencies required to provide the value proposition. It incorporates these considerations in its unique business strategy.

The corporate task is to decide *what* businesses it should be in; the business-unit task is to decide *how* to carry out a particular business.

Importantly, we distinguish between stakeholders and customers. *Stakeholders* are the focus of the corporate leadership; the *customers* are the focus of the individual business units. Markets as defined above are one of the key considerations in segmenting NAVSEA into business units.

Stakeholders. NAVSEA is accountable to stakeholders, in the form of organizational entities, interest groups, and individuals who directly or indirectly accrue the benefits or sustain the costs of the operation of NAVSEA. The interests of the stakeholders are diverse and often conflicting. However, certain stakeholders directly influence whether NAVSEA will continue to exist in the future. To ensure its continued existence by maximizing the satisfaction of its stakeholders, NAVSEA seeks to satisfy the greatest number of interests or the highest-priority interests. One mechanism for doing so is the way it chooses to organize.

Who are NAVSEA's stakeholders, what do these stakeholders value, and what are the implications for the NAVSEA organizational structure?

Who Are They?

Although NAVSEA is accountable in different ways to many interest groups, we identified two major stakeholders for NAVSEA: the Chief of Naval Operations and the Assistant Secretary of the Navy for Research, Development and Acquisition. NAVSEA's ability to provide value to these two officials accounts largely for its continued existence.

In many organizational analyses, managers and workers are also recognized as stakeholders. In public-sector analyses, Congress or the taxpayers are frequently identified as stakeholders. However, we adopt the corporate-governance perspective of delivering value to the providers of ownership capital.

Source of Value

These stakeholders have, to a large extent, codified the nature of their interest in the form of mandates, reflected in Navy directives and instructions. Satisfying these mandates is one means of creating value for the stakeholders. In our description of business units later in this chapter, we indicate that such mandates may need to be revised to enable competition. Most of these mandates take the form of delineating the activities to be performed by NAVSEA. They are primarily inputs for NAVSEA: "Perform these tasks."

Business units organize to carry out these mandates—ideally, as effectively as possible. COMNAVSEA believes that the future of NAVSEA resides on the waterfront, i.e., where the Fleet gets its direct support and services. Business units focused on the waterfront respond to stakeholder interest in Fleet readiness—which is where NAVSEA affects the core of the Navy.

Other senior leaders emphasized that, without an effective *infrastructure*—the larger complex of activities that design, acquire, and deliver materiel (to include systems and technology)—and human assets for the Fleet, the Navy would cease to be. Operating the infrastructure well takes special skills; it cannot be done as a secondary or tertiary duty. If this is a primary role for NAVSEA, a business unit devoted to this role focuses managerial attention and enables consistent and coherent application of resources.

In addition to mandates, the stakeholders are also interested in outcomes over which NAVSEA has influence, although not necessarily complete control. For one such outcome, Fleet readiness, the stakeholder, CNO, acts as the ombudsman for today's Fleet, his interest focusing on such measures as repair and maintenance efficiency, interoperability, and operational availability. His interest also focuses on force structure, particularly on ensuring that platforms and systems reach the Fleet when expected.

Similarly, the Assistant Secretary of the Navy for Research, Development and Acquisition acts as the ombudsman for the future Fleet, his interest focusing on providing the Fleet with the needed systems that meet desired cost, schedule, and performance targets; in addition, as his title highlights, he must also balance the influence of research and development with the efficiency of the acquisition process. During interviews, senior leaders in the Office of the Assistant Secretary raised concerns that the integration between research and development, on the one hand, and acquisition, on the other, was not as robust as desired. They suggested that the acquisition process is driven by the available technology, not by what fits best in the context of mission and threat.

Therefore, leading-edge research and development products focused in the context of the operational environment do not get incorporated effectively in the acquisition process. The two functions need to be better integrated; they cannot be individually entrepreneurial and isolated from each other.

Organizational Implications

The mandates provide business units within NAVSEA with a minimum bound on the scope of activities that they must ensure get carried out (although not necessarily carried out by NAVSEA). As inputs, the mandates directly lead to organizational elements. For example, diving and salvage activities are a mandate, as are activities dealing with explosives safety and technical performance. Organizing around critical work is a generally accepted principle.

Stakeholder interest in a closer link between research and development and acquisition has three organizational implications for NAVSEA:

- NAVSEA provides much of the technology embedded in weapon systems; it must be in this business.

- To enhance the value to the stakeholder, NAVSEA needs to deliver research and development—derived from a deep understanding of the operational environment and naval engineering—to the PEOs in a timely manner.

- NAVSEA also delivers technical services to stakeholders. These services go beyond research and development and include enhanced readiness and technical performance.

Organizational structures provide varying degrees of assurance that Fleet needs are met. For example, a business unit formed around platforms (PEOs) may provide technologies better matched with platform needs than may a business unit formed around types of technologies. The latter could work—and has worked—using formal coordination and other communication mechanisms to supplement the organizational structure. However, to the degree that strengthening the linkage between platform and technology is deemed to be a priority, a platform-oriented organizational structure would be better suited to the objective. Alignment of organizational structure with the business units simplifies communication. That structure could be supplemented with mechanisms for ensuring that the requisite depth of technical capabilities is achieved: possibly a matrixed organization using types of technology as the organizing variable.

Several senior leaders averred that a primary NAVSEA role in the future is engineering discipline, review, and oversight. The Navy relies on interoperable systems; support cannot remain stovepiped in each system. If the concept of technical authority is essential, as with operating the infrastructure, a single organizational entity within NAVSEA should provide it. Products that ensure interoperability and applications of systems engineering provide value to both stakeholders.

Customers. Individual business units focus on customers. Customers are one of the means of segmenting NAVSEA into business units. Today, NAVSEA has elements that can be categorized as business units—for example, the warfare centers and the shipyards—which provide a distinct set of products or services to sets of customers with specific needs and preferences. However, without necessarily being codified as an identifiable business unit,[4] parts of NAVSEA Headquarters—the logistics activities of SEA 04, the research activities of the warfare centers, or the engineering activity of SEA 05, shown in Figure 4.2—also provide products and services to customers external to NAVSEA. Although clearly feasible as a means of conducting the activities required, this structure potentially defuses customer focus and, consequently, the ability to develop a value proposition and strategy to meet the needs and preferences of a set of customers and the competencies to carry them out.

To enhance the ability to meet customer needs and preferences using the approach this chapter describes, we seek to assign to business units almost all those activities directed at providing products to external customers. Consequently, customers help to define business units.

Who Are They?

We identified three primary categories of NAVSEA external customers: PEOs, Type Commanders, and the Fleet. (Other U.S. government organizations and foreign nations are also customers.) These categories are not necessarily mutually exclusive. However, they receive different types of products and services, and they have different needs and preferences. The value NAVSEA provides to each type of customer differs.

Source of Value

One of the primary advantages NAVSEA has over competitors is its ability to enhance its products and services with detailed knowledge of the Fleet, the context in which its offerings will be used, and the effect of these offerings in an operational environment. NAVSEA also provides constancy—of people, skills, and relationships—which few, if any, external organizations can match. Knowledge of the Fleet benefits all three categories of customers.

The PEOs value innovation, particularly in the form of translation of basic and applied research into naval capabilities. Knowledge of the customer is essential

---

[4]However, recent reorganizations have had the effect of moving many of these activities into the existing business-unit structure of warfare centers and shipyards shown in Figure 4.2.

for ensuring that innovation is targeted appropriately. Moreover, NAVSEA provides a range of support services to its affiliated PEOs, including comptroller, contracting, and legal services. In this context, PEOs represent a special kind of customer, one with whom the supplier (NAVSEA) has established a close and trusted relationship.

Type Commanders value efficiency, which contributes to increased operational availability. This focus suggests a business unit that provides on-time, quality service: repairs and maintenance, modernization, and upgrades that are done right, on time, the first time, within budget.

The Fleet values outstanding customer service. Although all customers seek this product characteristic, the Fleet values it the most. Effective solutions, particularly while ships are under way, maintain Fleet capabilities and readiness.

Organizational Implications

NAVSEA provides different kinds of knowledge. Different customers value different subsets of the different kinds of knowledge NAVSEA provides. Therefore, NAVSEA can be segmented into business units organized around customers, and business units can be structured to ensure that the right data are available to the right parts of the business unit. We focus here on business units organized around customers.

- Providing value to the PEOs requires that NAVSEA have a complete understanding of the future environment, the threats, and the concepts of operations. To be most effective, this type of knowledge should permeate the business unit, informing all activities, to ensure that the technology being developed has the best chance of satisfying Fleet needs in the future.

- However, providing value to the Type Commanders and the Fleet requires a different kind of knowledge, largely related to the existing platforms.

    — For the Type Commanders, the required knowledge supports decisions regarding the scheduling and efficient completion of major maintenance availabilities in the face of uncertain operational requirements. Such knowledge leads to a business unit that can adapt to a changing customer demand while ensuring expeditious incorporation of upgrades and modifications, full interoperability, and increased operational availability.

    — For the Fleet, the required knowledge supports the ability to solve, rapidly and effectively, problems that arise while under way or during a scheduled maintenance availability.

Innovation, experimentation, adaptability, and creativity can be inhibited when near-term and long-term activities are mixed together. The tyranny of immediate needs drives out the ability to focus on new and unique means of accomplishing ends. Organizations often create and isolate "skunk works"— that part of the organization from which innovative ideas are sought—from other parts whose activities are more directly concerned with operations. This suggests that NAVSEA should locate activities directed at innovative outcomes in business units separate from activities directed at operations. If both kinds of activities are located in the same overall business unit, then NAVSEA should create separate divisions within the business unit to insulate the two kinds of activities.

Both efficiency and world-class customer service require organizations that are linked closely to the customer. A business unit responsible for a single type of customer can focus more effectively on meeting that customer's needs than can one with many or diverse customers.

Potential Means of Segmenting. From the above considerations, we derived a variety of means for segmenting NAVSEA into business units. There is no one best way; each means has advantages and disadvantages. Below, we describe several means.

Organizing by Function. Most business entities organize themselves—create linkages—around functions first. Doing so has plentiful advantages: Workers in similar occupations or professions work together, sharing knowledge, practices, and contacts, creating synergies not available in other organizational structures. Having a larger number of workers among whom to spread the work means that specialization can increase. Similarly, the sharing of equipment, facilities, and other resources occurs more readily. Functional organizations also promote standardization and reduce the need to reinvent policies and practices in different parts of the organization. Historically, NAVSEA has been structured functionally (although not necessarily as business units), and, as we note below, NAVSEA continues to be influenced by this design.

NAVSEA's activities cluster into functional categories related to the life cycle of an acquisition program: R&D, design, engineering, construction, operational test and evaluation, delivery and certification, maintenance and repair, and disposal, as discussed in Chapter Three. This is not unlike the segmentation seen in Figure 4.1. In addition, this structure is congruent with the value chain for the industry in which NAVSEA participates. Interestingly, the recent reorganization of the Naval Air Systems Command (NAVAIR) reflects a functional structure: program management, contracts, logistics, research and engineering, test and evaluation, industrial, corporate operations, and shore station management.

Synergy—combined action or operation—is captured within the function (which may be valuable to stakeholders and customers). However, the functional organization operates inefficiently when the organization offers a variety of products, through different channels, to different customers. Customer focus—the ability to remain focused on the customer—in particular, is difficult to establish and maintain. In addition, structuring by function tends to erect barriers between the functions, inhibiting cross-functional processes, such as new-product development. Rapid product development overwhelms a functional structure. The functional structure is declining in popularity because speed and innovation are becoming more important than scale.

In summary, NAVSEA would consider structuring around functions to support a strategy capitalizing on the need for

- common standards

- high levels of expertise

- economies of scale for products with long product-development times and life cycles in an undifferentiated market.

If NAVSEA overall is not a likely candidate for a functional structure, parts of NAVSEA (the shipyards, for example), to remain competitive, may require the advantage of economies of scale that a functional structure brings.

Organizing Around Customers. Partly because of shifts in power from the supplier to the buyer, service organizations have structured themselves around their customers or markets. Increased fiscal pressures and increased willingness to use other suppliers mean that NAVSEA's customers have, in effect, captured more power: PEOs have internalized or outsourced many of the activities provided solely by NAVSEA in the past, and the Fleets have alternatives to public shipyards. To remain the provider, NAVSEA business units must offer superior value to their customers.

One means of providing this value is to capitalize on their knowledge of the customer—its needs and preferences—thereby enabling the organization to tailor activities to each type of customer rather than offering a more generalized, functional structure. In addition, the value of a functional structure (particularly one that captures economies of scale) has waned, because these economies can often be secured from other organizations who specialize in the function (FedEx in shipping, and IBM or EDS in computer services are good examples); economies of scale no longer provide a significant competitive advantage. NAVSEA has many unique capabilities. The trend toward contracting out non-unique capabilities and the willingness to do so have removed the need to organize functionally, allowing NAVSEA to more easily align its unique capabilities with customers.

The three NAVSEA customer clusters—PEOs, Type Commanders, and operating Fleets—reside in different segments of the 15 separate market areas described in Chapter Three (Table 3.3), sometimes alone, sometimes sharing a market area. Depending on their mission, the PEOs make up a set of customers in the market area of Acquisition Support, Operational Availability, and one or more others. The Type Commanders make up a set of customers in the market areas of Operational Availability and Mobility. The operating Fleets make up a set of customers in all markets except for Acquisition Support.

Structuring around markets or customers is not without the disadvantage of duplicating activities across business units if the organization lacks (or fails to take advantage of) appropriate outsourcing or horizontal-integration opportunities. The business units may also find sharing common services across markets difficult.

In summary, NAVSEA should consider structuring around customers to support those strategies focused primarily on important market segments, particularly when

- a product or service is unique to the segment

- the customer exhibits significant buyer strength

- knowledge of the customer and rapid customer service and product cycles are particularly important

- the offerings can be produced efficiently in supporting functional areas or functions can be outsourced to capture the necessary scale. (The functional structure is declining in popularity because speed and innovation are becoming more important than scale.)

Organizing Around Products. Forming business units or divisions/departments around products can compress the product-development cycle. It is particularly useful for supporting strategies of product diversification and new-product development.

NAVSEA offers a wide range of products for 2007, listed in Table 3.5. To form product-related business units for NAVSEA, we attempted to aggregate those products into five to seven broad categories here by associating all NAVSEA products with the categories contained in the DD350 contractor database, a source already grouped by major product categories. This exercise produced a significantly larger number of business units than seven. We then aggregated to reflect certain linkages—common products, common competitors, similar responses to price changes, and a standard set of basic business-unit properties: type of strategy, importance of quality, type of workforce, etc. From these considerations, we identified seven basic business units aligned along major end products: submarines, surface ships, expeditionary platforms, weapons and energetics, management services, assessments, and analytic services. This represents a more macro-level aggregation of the product taxonomy used in Chapter Three.

Although focusing attention on the product, this method of segmentation poses risks of duplicating resources and not being able to recognize the opportunity for sharing those resources across business units that are similar to the risks in organizing by customer. In addition, dividing functional areas along product lines risks the loss of economies of scale. Centralizing and sharing some or most of the functional services can minimize this loss. Customers that rely on more than one business unit lose the ability to deal with a single organization. However, organizations in this situation can benefit from a front-end-oriented—outward-looking and market-driven—organization that is focused on customers and a back-end-oriented—inward-looking and production-driven—organization that is structured to focus on products. The interface between the two would be handled within the organization.

The front-end/back-end organization is a hybrid of the product and market structures. The front end focuses on customers/markets; the back end focuses on products and technologies. The products are organized as multifunctional businesses (generally including product marketing, but excluding sales); system integration, sales, and servicing are organized around markets. The front end is adding more value than in the past, through establishing closer ties to customers and more-intimate understanding of their needs.

In summary, NAVSEA should consider structuring around products to support those strategies focused primarily on product diversification and rapid development, particularly when

- the organization chooses to produce separate offerings for separate customers

- the offerings can be produced efficiently in functional areas or functions can be outsourced to capture the necessary scale.

Organizing by Product-Function. In a product-function organization, the products produced are the outputs of the separate functions. We view NAVSEA today as being organized along four major product-function areas—research, development, test, and evaluation (RDT&E), acquisition support professional services, in-service engineering, and repair and maintenance—an organization that is congruent with a generic life cycle.

Organizing by Process. A process structure is based on a complete flow of work. If NAVSEA produced only one product, functions organized in line with the product's life cycle could also be viewed as a process structure—for example, all the activities associated with the repair and maintenance of a ship (the planning, scheduling, actual repair and maintenance, testing, delivery, etc.) would constitute a *process,* since the product moves through each stage. However, not all products move through all stages of the life cycle; in fact, products within NAVSEA are produced using significantly different processes. In a *process structure,* the organization forms around the process, bringing together the people from the necessary functional areas to work in a process team. This structure enables process improvements, because it identifies and highlights the elements of the process and relationships; it also allows greater accountability as individuals and groups focus on self-contained units of work. Cost reductions come about through reduced cycle times and improved quality.

The process structure creates its own barriers—between processes. If processes interface, the organization must manage that boundary as carefully as it does the boundaries between functions in an organization structured functionally. A process perspective appears to be more useful in structuring the business units themselves than in determining the portfolio of business units to begin with.

In summary, NAVSEA would consider structuring around processes to support a strategy of reducing cycle times, particularly in areas in which there is substantial potential for improving processes.

Organizing by Work Activities. Another means of segmenting into business units that is closely related to organizing by processes, and that shares its advantages and disadvantages, is to start with the work activities from Chapter Three and aggregate them. This is called *generalizing the work activities.* We developed and applied a work activity hierarchy to encompass all work that must be performed in a large organization such as NAVSEA.

We chose initially to segment on work activities. We judged that such a basis would be more in line with the time frame we are focused on: 2007. Businesses are moving from a focus on capital assets to a focus on the use of those assets—from a command and control functional hierarchy to a more modern activity concept. Other bases for organizing business units could have been chosen. It is our judgment that this activity focus is a useful starting point for understanding NAVSEA businesses in 2007 and, ultimately, their corporate structuring. We associated each NAVSEA activity with a cluster of work activities. Seven business units resulted, each centered on similar categories of activities:

- Managing ships

- Providing program-management and project-management services

- Resourcing science, engineering, and acquisition professionals
- Managing infrastructure
- Organizing and managing existing knowledge
- Creating and managing new knowledge
- Providing top-level systems engineering services.

Using a work activity structure, rather than the current NAVSEA functional structure, as the basis for the initial design of the NAVSEA organization of the future, affords the most flexibility in the design process itself.

We purposely avoided identifying and characterizing the existing NAVSEA business units. Some readers are likely to infer comparisons between the business units we identify and the existing organizational structure of NAVSEA, but that is not our intent. The extant NAVSEA business structure is a Headquarters-focused, command and control hierarchy that has evolved from the early part of the Industrial Revolution into an organization that can handle complexity and multiple business lines. While it is now flatter, larger, and more far-flung than the model in Figure 4.1, this traditional organization has been pushed to the extent of its useful life, especially as time becomes a critical factor, given the pace of operations in many areas: that pace accelerating beyond the hierarchy's ability to adjust.

Now that we have described the potential/theoretical segmenting considerations for business units, we choose one, and describe the resulting business units in detail.

The Basic Corporate Portfolio

The following subsections describe each of these work-activity-structured business units in detail. For each business unit, we define its offering, its market, and its competitors; describe its *value proposition*—the set of benefits a business offers to convince customers to buy from it and to differentiate itself from its competitors; propose an appropriate business-unit strategy; and suggest the relevant business model—how a business sustains itself over time. We also suggest a private-sector business model to emulate.

In the private sector, a business must generate sufficient operating income (cash flow) to attract periodic infusions of long-term capital (equity and debt). To the extent that the business exceeds all costs, to include those of capital, it is creating value for shareholders. In the public sector, a business unit must also sustain itself over time, either through operating income—*working capital fund*—or through annual infusions of public resources—*budget*. In either case, value must be provided to customers or stakeholders to prevent the sources of cash from drying up over time.

Managing Ships.   This business unit provides two categories of services: (1) planning and scheduling of repairs, maintenance, and modernization, and (2) the actual repairs, maintenance, and modernization. Currently, its customers are the Type Commander and the Fleet. In the future, as total-life-cycle contracts receive greater emphasis, the business unit may see the weapon system platform contractor as the customer, establishing a partnership during the acquisition process that will carry over throughout the life of the platform or having to continually compete to provide repair and maintenance through the contractor. Private shipyards compete, today, with the public yards; in the future, foreign yards could enter the competition.

Value Proposition. The business unit competes primarily on the basis of cost and better understanding of the customer's preferences. Customer service is a key component of the strategy.

Business-Unit Strategy. This business unit bases its strategy on being the least-cost provider of maintenance and repair services. To enhance the value it adds to the end consumer (the Fleet), the business unit could modify its market by vertically integrating the Type Commanders (its current customers), providing in the business unit the value currently provided by the Type Commanders, and dealing directly with the Fleet. To grow and sustain itself, this business unit in 2007 would be integrated backward toward the prime contractor and forward toward the Fleet. "Rolling up the water front"—disintermediation of all other waterfront competitors—would be the goal of this business unit.

Business Model. Manufacturer is the appropriate business model. The unit seeks cost savings through consolidations and vertical integration. The business operates as a working capital fund in that the customer has the resources and can choose to whom they go.

Notional Business-Unit Structure. The business unit divides into two major components along product lines: planning and scheduling, and repair and maintenance (Figure 4.6). Within planning and scheduling, the structure divides along product lines, focusing on the type of maintenance: organizational, intermediate, or depot. Within repair and maintenance, the structure divides geographically, reflecting the costs of moving ships far from home ports. Within the geographical areas, a functional structure to capture economies of scale or a process structure to implement a strategy of continuous process improvement is appropriate.

RAND*MR1303-4.6*

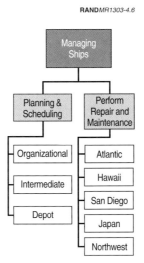

**Figure 4.6—Notional
Business-Unit Structure
of Managing Ships**

Providing Program- and Project-Management Services. This business unit provides program- and project-management services in the form of packaged expertise, including contract management, legal, financial, program-management, and administrative services (see Figure 4.7). This business unit sells these services to the PEOs and program managers, rather than providing the personnel to carry them out. SECNAV Instruction 5400.15A (see Appendix B) designates comptroller, legal, contracting, and administrative support services (among many others) as core processes and requires COMNAVSEA to provide these services to the PEOs. It also designates COMNAVSEA as the Head of Contracting Activity, both for assigned programs and for programs assigned to PEOs.

Numerous professional-services firms (e.g., temporary manpower firms, contracting agencies) provide many of these types of services. Potential competitors for comptroller, legal, and contracting services, in particular, include other Navy and Department of Defense organizations. Clearly, these kinds of services are inherently governmental. Of course, for these competitors to be effective, the mandates in the SECNAV Instruction would need to be revised.

Value Proposition. This business unit competes primarily on the bases of cost and a deep understanding of customer preferences. Therefore, regardless of organizational location, the people providing the services are collocated, working daily with the customer. For legal and contracting services, a balance of customer service and a high degree of autonomy is key to this strategy.

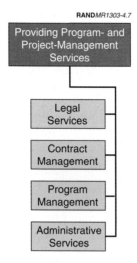

**Figure 4.7—Notional
Business-Unit Structure
of Providing Program-
and Project-Management
Services**

Business-Unit Strategy. This business unit bases its strategy on being the least-cost provider of these services. It seeks to capitalize on its niche of specialized experience, developing customer loyalty in a low-volume, well-defined customer base.

Business Model. *Professional services* is the appropriate business model: Focusing on transaction services, to include quality assurance, it may base its price on performance and offer price and other incentives to long-term customers. The administrative-services segment operates as a working capital fund; the other services are mission-funded.

Notional Business-Unit Structure. The business unit divides along product lines: legal services, contract management, program management, and administrative services. To achieve reduced cycle times and responsiveness to customer needs within the product lines, the divisions organize around process. Figure 4.7 portrays the notional structure of this business unit.

Resourcing Scientific, Engineering, Acquisition Professionals. In essence, this business unit is a human resource department profit center that focuses only on the core resources of NAVSEA; these resources are hired into, assigned, and developed within NAVSEA, as well as being managed by NAVSEA. It acquires, develops, and provides trained professionals—individual human capital—for temporary (although often lengthy) assignments to other organizations. Given the complexity of contracting for naval ships and weapons, this business unit could include contracting professionals. (See Figure 4.8.)

The primary customer is the PEO and the program managers. The business unit identifies current and future needs and ensures that professionals with the right competencies are available. The market could also expand to include other business units within NAVSEA—for example, the business unit for managing ships described above or the business units focused on creating, organizing, and managing knowledge, described below. Other Navy and other government organizations requiring these trained professionals are potential customers. Competitors include professional-services firms that provide the services (not the people), much as for the preceding business unit; independent contractors/consultants (many with previous NAVSEA experience); and, potentially, temporary manpower firms that specialize in professionals.

Value Proposition. The business unit competes on the basis of developing and providing professional resources tailored to the needs of the customer. In particular, the professional resources possess a combination of naval expertise and technical competencies available from no other centralized source, and developed and tailored to the unique needs of the customer.

Figure 4.8—Notional Business-Unit Structure of Resourcing Scientific, Engineering, and Acquisition Professionals

Business-Unit Strategy. With a deep understanding of the requirements of the customer and the capability to dynamically align existing assets with changing customer needs, this business unit bases its strategy on providing a distinctive product. The business unit seeks to gain advantage through affiliation with the customer to assess future needs, develop the necessary competencies through education and assignments in other NAVSEA and naval organizations, and amortize the development costs over these assignments.

Business Model. *Broker* is part of the appropriate business model: The business unit brings the buyer of professional services together with the provider of professional services. *Developer* is another part of this business model: The supplied professional must constantly update/upgrade his or her technical skills to be easily brokered and periodically upgraded in skills to be re-marketed over time. The business operates as a working capital fund (although it could be partially mission-funded).

This is a difficult business to sustain. The customer is most likely to be willing to pay the going budget rate for a professional, but not the long-term cost of acquisition, development, and separation. Moreover, to achieve public funding for these long-term costs of human capital requires stakeholder understanding of and commitment to such workforce planning for the long term. "Who funds the needed annual investment in human capital for future capability?" is one of the critical questions public organizations are striving to answer. If customers do not pay full cost or if stakeholders do not make the needed sustained public investment, product inferiority will cause this business to fail.

Notional Business-Unit Structure. The business unit divides into two major divisions: marketing of the resources and managing of the assets. Marketing is a key function within the business unit; this division is responsible for identifying future needs, working with the other division to ensure that the resource is available, and convincing the customers that these resources are superior to those from any other source. Marketing divides further along functional lines: recruiting/selecting, developing/educating/experiencing, assigning, and rewarding. Figure 4.8 portrays the notional structure of this business unit.

Managing Infrastructure. This business unit provides services for managing the physical assets and material capabilities of NAVSEA. It provides for the acquisition, development, construction, and reuse or disposal of property, plant, and equipment, and for management of the properties. (See Figure 4.9.)

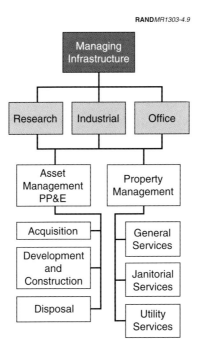

RAND*MR1303-4.9*

**Figure 4.9—Notional Business-
Unit Structure of Managing
Infrastructure**

This business unit services all the other business units of NAVSEA. It could expand its reach into the other systems commands and even into other government organizations. Primary competitors include Real Estate Investment Trusts (REITs), the Naval Facilities Command, and private-sector property-management firms.

Value Proposition. This business unit competes on the basis of least-cost provision of its services, with a primary objective of fully utilizing capacity.

Business-Unit Strategy. The business unit follows a least-cost strategy. It employs a portfolio-management approach to the acquisition, development, and divestment of property, plant, and equipment. It leverages assets across markets so that even competitors may use them. *Dynamic alignment*—matching assets to market needs—is a core competency. In its pricing to customers, the business must also amortize investments or ensure that they are publicly funded.

Business Model. Utility or *REIT* is the appropriate business model: If operated as a utility, pricing is regulated and customers pay set rates; if operated under a REIT model, the business unit would charge users to amortize the cost of the property, plant, and equipment, seeking premium prices for the best plant and equipment. It will use a revenue-management approach for property management, charging customers on a pay-as-you-go basis. The business operates as a working capital fund (although it could be partially mission-funded).

As with the Resourcing Scientific, Engineering, and Acquisition Professionals business unit, this is another difficult business because of its investment needs. Removing ownership of a facility from its users should allow for greater efficiencies, particularly in partnering with other governmental entities or the private sector, or in disposal of legacy or outmoded plant property and equipment. For example, the Air Force is in the process of transferring seven wind tunnels at Wright Patterson AFB to Ohio State University. Expected to save about $500,000 per year, the transfer is opening the facilities to other universities, as well as to nonmilitary, commercial industries that need to do aerodynamic research.

Notional Business-Unit Structure. The business unit divides along type of infrastructure: research, industrial, and office. Each of these divisions has a product-oriented subdivision that focuses on asset management and a division that focuses on property management. Figure 4.9 portrays the notional business-unit structure.

Organizing and Managing Existing Knowledge. This business unit provides engineering information and solutions in a form most useful to a diverse set of users, and it sets and enforces standards for ships and systems. Customers include the Fleet, the Type Commanders, and the PEOs; the other NAVSEA business units, particularly Managing Ships; contractors; other Navy organizations; and other government organizations. (See Figure 4.10.)

Value Proposition. This business unit competes by differentiation: It is the single comprehensive source of knowledge to its customers—knowledge ranging from information on legacy systems to information on the latest systems in the Fleet. The key elements of value are the depth of knowledge and the speed with which the business unit provides information in a form that meets the unique needs of the customer. In terms of setting and enforcing standards, the business unit provides the balance between maximum safety standards and minimum performance standards.

Business-Unit Strategy. The business unit bases its strategy on providing a distinctive product—immediate access to information in user-friendly form—available from no other source. It is the linchpin of naval engineering.

Business Model. Selling codification of knowledge, and sharing and use of knowledge, the engineering-solutions side of the business unit follows an *infomediary* business model: The best of such businesses enhance client-customer

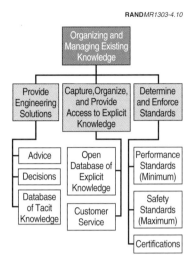

RAND*MR1303-4.10*

Figure 4.10—Notional Business-
Unit Structure of Organizing and
Managing Existing Knowledge

relations through an electronic push strategy focused on customer needs. The business unit forms a knowledge network based on professional expertise and specialized knowledge of the users and their needs. The business operates as a working capital fund (although it could be partially mission-funded).

In the private sector, an infomediary sustains itself through advertising that exists side by side with apparently free information. "Eyeballs" or traffic—keeping track of who has made use of the service—becomes critical to success. The high demand for this knowledge beyond the Navy indicates that a conscious decision could be made to provide the knowledge as a public service, with public budget. The standard-setting and -enforcing side follows a Federal Aviation Administration (FAA) business model. This part of the business unit is mission-funded.

Notional Business-Unit Structure. The business unit comprises three divisions: engineering solutions; standard setting and standard enforcement; and the capture, organization, and provision of access to explicit knowledge (Figure 4.10). The first two divisions are front-end, dealing directly with customers. Engineering solutions subdivides along product lines: one element that provides advice; one that assumes more risk and specializes in decisions; and one that provides the means of accessing and using tacit knowledge—knowledge about relationships and processes. Standard determination and enforcement subdivides along product lines, as well: one element that sets minimum performance standards, one that sets maximum safety standards, and one that conducts certification inspections. The third division is largely a back-end organization, providing a user-friendly interface for customers to access explicit knowledge—facts or information about things. One subdivision focuses on the development and sustainment of an open database; the other subdivision provides the front-end component by focusing on customer service.

Creating and Managing New Knowledge. The business unit creates and sells new knowledge that is tailored to meet naval requirements—for example, knowledge about systems that are yet to be acquired or are still being developed. The PEOs are the primary customers; the Type Commanders and the Fleet are secondary customers. A multitude of competitors include the defense community, independent research institutions, and universities. (See Figure 4.11.)

Value Proposition. The business unit competes through differentiation: It provides knowledge unavailable from other sources, based on sustained expertise and on intimate understanding of a customer's current and future needs.

Business-Unit Strategy. The business unit bases its competitive advantage on providing a distinctive product, particularly one that can deliver cutting-edge innovation and technological know-how in a timely manner. The business unit provides high value-added content on a regular basis. It seeks to establish and maintain high levels of customer loyalty.

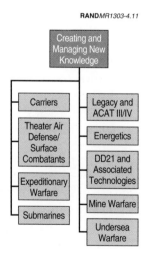

RAND*MR1303-4.11*

**Figure 4.11—Notional
Business-Unit Structure
of Creating and Managing
New Knowledge**

Business Model. Professional services is the relevant business model: This business unit embraces a network, or consortium, of professional expertise. The business operates as a working capital fund (although it could be partially mission-funded).

Notional Business-Unit Structure. This business unit organizes along customer lines (see Figure 4.11) that reflect the composition of the PEO structure in Figure 4.2. This structure should change as its customers change (for example, a change from DD21 as a customer to surface strike as a customer has implications for the business unit's organization). Alternatively, this business unit might organize along the lines of technologies—sensors, computers, etc.—to foster communication among technical specialists. More so than any of the other business units, this business unit would operate as flexible, somewhat temporary (although long-lived) teams. The ability of the business unit to respond to customer needs is critical.

Providing Systems-Engineering Services. This business unit provides systems engineering services. The primary customer for these services is the CNO. Other customers include the PEOs, commanders in chief and/or Joint Chiefs of Staff (CINCs/JCS), the Department of Defense, and other government organizations. (See Figure 4.12.)

Defense contractors, particularly prime contractors, provide these services for platforms. Other potential competitors include professional-services firms, and other Navy and Department of Defense organizations.

Value Proposition. This business unit competes by differentiation: It is the single, comprehensive repository of knowledge and professional expertise on

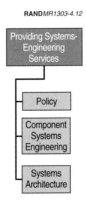

RAND*MR1303-4.12*

**Figure 4.12—Notional
Business-Unit Structure
of Providing Systems-
Engineering Services**

naval systems engineering, spanning both platforms and missions. This business unit provides realism and candor across platforms, missions, and services. The core expertise is sustainable because it can be expanded beyond ships/platforms and missions to battle-group and joint activities.

Business-Unit Strategy. The business unit bases its competitive advantage on providing a unique service by developing, demonstrating, and sustaining unequaled knowledge of naval systems and of the discipline of systems engineering.

Business Model. Professional services is the business model. The business operates as a working capital fund (although it could be partially mission-funded).

Notional Business-Unit Structure. The business unit divides along product lines: systems engineering policy, systems architecture, and component systems engineering products that work on or with ships—gun systems, sonars, etc. Figure 4.12 portrays the notional business-unit structure.

Table 4.1 summarizes the elements of the seven business units described above.

From the perspective of the generalized work activities that make up NAVSEA, the complete corporate structure comprises all of the business units described above, with no organizational strategic priority/hierarchy. Figure 4.13 portrays this overall business-unit structure, aligned simply under a NAVSEA Headquarters.

SHAPE—THE ROAD TO EFFECTIVE CORPORATE OPERATION

Unfortunately, designing the business units independently can lead to suboptimization. In the third stage, we identify major *leverage points*—potential areas of synergy and areas in which NAVSEA can achieve economies of scope and scale by restructuring the business units or by centralizing processes, functions, and/or activities that are common across business units—for increasing the effectiveness of the NAVSEA corporation. We then use those leverage points to modify the design of the organization suggested in the second stage. Similarly, we identify critical interrelationships—linkages—among business units that require leadership attention to ensure that transactions between them are smooth and effective. Understanding these interrelationships is especially important if the business units span the boundary of the NAVSEA organization proper—relying on outsourced activities as well as in-house activities—an assessment that would be addressed during the fourth stage of our organizational design process.

Table 4.1

Summary Description of Business Units

Element of Business Unit	Business Unit						
	Manage Ships	Provide Services	Resource Professional People	Provide Facilities	Organize and Manage Existing Knowledge	Create and Manage New Knowledge	Provide Systems Engineering
Product	Maintenance Repair Modernization	Packaged functional expertise	Individual human capital	Physical infrastructure	Information Solutions Standards	Ideas Innovation Technology	Integration
Customers	Type Commander (TYCOM) Fleet	PEOs	PEOs Other NAVSEA Other Navy Other government	Other NAVSEA Private sector Other Navy Other government	PEOs, TYCOM, Fleet, Other NAVSEA, Private sector	PEOs TYCOM Fleet	CNO CINCs/JCS PEOs, DoD Other government
Competitors	Private and foreign yards	Professional-services firm PEOs Other Navy Other DoD	Professional-services firm Temporary-manpower firm Other NAVSEA	NAVFAC Private sector	Prime contractor Associations	Other Navy, defense Private sector	Prime contractor Professional-services firm Other Navy Other DoD
Value	Low cost Customer service	Low cost Customer service	Naval expertise & technical competency	Low cost High utilization	Deep, timely knowledge Balance safety and performance	Sustained expertise Customer loyalty	Complete, consistent for platform and mission
Strategy	Least cost Vertically integrate	Niche experience Customer loyalty	Dynamically align Amortize or subsidize costs	Dynamically align Amortize or subsidize costs	Differentiate Linchpin of naval engineering	Timely, cutting-edge know-how High value-added	Unique service High value-added Pre 0
Business Model	Manufacturer Working capital	Professional-services firm Working capital	Broker Working Capital/ Navy funded	Utility or REIT Working Capital/ Navy funded	Distributor Infomediary FAA Working Capital/ Navy funded	Linked interests Consortium Working Capital/ Navy funded	Professional-services firm Working Capital/ Navy funded
Structure	Product Functional Geographical	Functional	Marketing and managing	Ownership Management Property type	Functional	Product	Functional

RAND*MR1303-T4.1*

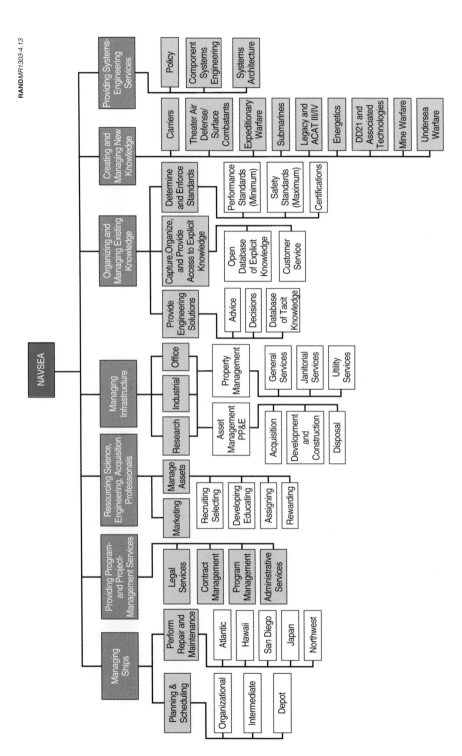

RAND*MR1303-4.13*

Figure 4.13—Corporate Structure of NAVSEA for the Activities Portfolio

We reviewed best business practices (Hax and Majluf, 1996; Porter, 1990; Sethi and King, 1998; Levine and Luck, 1994; and Quinn, 1992) to highlight the relationships among important organizational elements and to suggest promising areas in which economies of scope and scale can be found. The result of this stage of our analysis is to improve the effectiveness of the operation of NAVSEA as a whole, perhaps—but not necessarily—at the expense of the effectiveness of the individual business units.

We now examine four portfolios reflecting four variations of strategic intent for competitive advantage: an industry-positioning portfolio, a market/customer portfolio, a competency portfolio, and a product-life-cycle portfolio. In these portfolios, the business units are regrouped from a purely lateral structure under NAVSEA Headquarters to under business lines under or within Headquarters. What is now a business unit or an activity within a business unit may itself become a business line. Each of the several forms of strategic intent we suggest is relatively narrow. Indeed, the scope of strategic intent should be focused to maintain attention to the key aspects. A strategic intent should serve to focus leaders' attention, not to spread that attention evenly over a vast array of good things to do. (Strategic intent must come from the leaders of the organization—NAVSEA, in this case. It is an inherent function that cannot be delegated or imposed from outside the organization.)

As with the business units, the discussion of each business line begins with a general description, then gives value proposition and business-line strategy.

Industry-Positioning Portfolio

By definition, each business unit faces unique markets or competitors. Consequently, each business unit benefits from a strategy tailored to its particular environment. We first examine dimensions of size, cost, and product/service differentiation for each of the business units as they were derived from the analysis of generalized work activities, to determine whether a common strategy emerges for the NAVSEA corporation.

Figure 4.14 portrays a strategic map of NAVSEA as we characterized the initial business units along the three dimensions of size, cost, and product/service differentiation. Space near the bottom of the box denotes business units with lower unit costs; space near the top of the box denotes business units with higher unit costs. Space toward the left of the box represents commodity-like offerings that are not otherwise differentiated from competitors' offerings. Space toward the right of the box represents products and services that can be differentiated according to qualities important to the customer, such as product

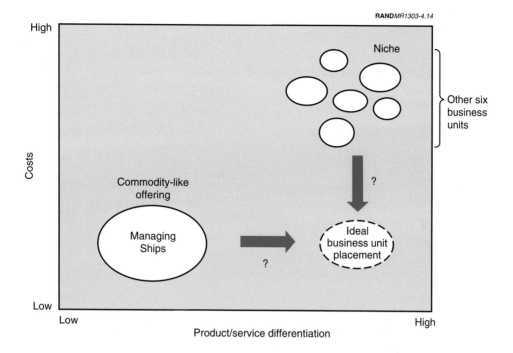

Figure 4.14—NAVSEA Strategic Map

innovation, remarkable customer service, or extraordinary quality. Relative size of the business unit is denoted by the size of the oval.

The lower-left-hand corner contains the business unit focused on managing ships; the upper-right-hand corner contains the six smaller business units focused on the other major types of activities in which NAVSEA engages. An ideal corporate portfolio for the future would contain business units that compete on the basis of low-cost, highly differentiated products and services, all located in the lower-right-hand corner. However, such a portfolio appears unlikely, for two reasons.

First, the overall industry for the commodity service of managing ships operates well below capacity today—a situation that is likely to continue. As a result, competition will continue on cost and other dimensions, such as time to complete maintenance and repair, and modernization availabilities. NAVSEA has been in this position for a number of years, and has seen both public- and private-sector shipyard contractions, consolidations, and closures. Continuing competition will require successful execution of a least-cost strategy for survival. Differentiation along other dimensions (for example, time to complete scheduled availabilities) may be possible, but such efforts would tend to drive up the costs (through capital investment in technology and automation) without a significantly commensurate increase in value to the customer to offset them.[5] Consolidation or closure in favor of a lower-cost competitor could result from erosion of quality or responsiveness and, particularly, from increases in cost.

Second, the smaller business units—which represent small niches of expertise and appeal to specialized markets—will strive to differentiate themselves from the private sector and from each other. Providing these specialized services drives up costs but leads to narrowly branded products and services. If the business unit cannot differentiate itself sufficiently (that is, if it moves to the left side of the box) and fails to provide valued specialized services, absent any other compelling rationale (for example, the need to preserve one or more government suppliers in order to foster competition), the business unit should compete with the private sector on a cost basis or merge with other business units.

It appears unlikely that *all* business units can move toward the ideal corporate strategy of being low cost and highly differentiated. However, by viewing NAVSEA from an industry perspective, we can suggest three fundamental business lines for NAVSEA: Enhancing Readiness, Managing [Naval] Knowledge, and Managing [Critical] Resources. The synergy among the units (sometimes many units) within a business line derives from grouping together business units that employ a particular linkage, such as a common form of strategy—for example, least cost or unique service. Enhancing Readiness provides stakeholder value to the CNO; Managing [Naval] Knowledge provides stakeholder value to the ASN (RDA); Managing [Critical] Resources provides to the other two lines of business or key customer groups (in this case, the PEOs) resources that are unique or too critical to rely on from other sources.

Enhancing Readiness. This business line comprises the Managing Ships business unit, which is composed of a division for planning and scheduling and a division for repair and maintenance.

Value Proposition. It offers its customers (Type Commanders and the Fleet) a unique understanding and appreciation for their needs and preferences. It is also uniquely positioned to establish guaranteed long-term relationships.

---

[5]A related question is whether higher-value services (for example, planning and scheduling) now bundled within the Managing Ships business unit could be separated from the lower-value activities and merged with other, more-differentiated business units. We address this question below in the Managing Resources business-line section.

Business-Line Strategy. The business line and its divisions employ a strategy of least cost.

Managing Knowledge. This business line comprises three business units: Creating and Managing New Knowledge, Organizing and Managing Existing Knowledge, and Providing Systems-Engineering Services.

Value Proposition. This business line adds unique value by being able to offer and leverage the largest, most comprehensive, central repository of explicit and tacit knowledge relevant to its customers' needs. As with the Enhancing Readiness business line, it is also uniquely positioned to establish guaranteed long-term relationships.

Business-Line Strategy. The strategy of this business line and its business units is *customer specialization*—providing high-value, well-differentiated knowledge-based services; and identifying and satisfying customer needs and preferences for data, information, and knowledge—for the Navy: specifically, for the PEO, the Type Commander, and the operating Fleet. Each business unit serves different customers and meets different customer needs and preferences; consequently, each should remain a separate business unit.

Managing Resources. This business line comprises three separate business units: Resourcing Science, Engineering, and Acquisition Professionals; Providing [general] Program- and Project-Management Services; and Managing Infrastructure. The customers of the first two business units are the PEOs; the customers of the third business unit are the other two business lines.

Value Proposition. This business line ensures the efficient and effective availability of critical resources necessary to provide value to both major stakeholders. It requires strong mechanisms for forecasting future requirements and the capability to develop resources and products that meet those requirements in a timely manner.

Business-Line Strategy. These individual business units can differentiate themselves somewhat on the basis of intimate customer knowledge; however, by itself, such a strategy will not be sufficient to ensure viability in the future. Many competitors provide the basic kinds of services offered by these business units; differentiation occurs at the margin. Consequently, the business units employ a strategy balanced between customer specialization and least cost.

Further inspection of the business units can identify differences, particularly among divisions, that suggest further realignments of the structure. Within the Managing Ships business unit, for example, the planning and scheduling division conducts high-value activities different in type (i.e., business model) from the activities of the division for repair and maintenance. The planning and scheduling division, in fact, has much in common with the business units in the Managing Resources business line and could benefit from the balanced strategy (customer specialization and least cost) being employed in that line. An alternative corporate structure would include this division as a separate business unit in the Managing Resources business line.

A possible focal point/structuring mechanism for evaluating component parts of the organization is the decision on whether to outsource activities to other government or private-sector organizations. This corporate structure, for example, permits the continual review of the viability of the business units associated with the Managing Resources business line. A separate business unit facing well-defined and numerous competitors can be the focus of NAVSEA corporate headquarters, which can maintain the pressure on the business unit (or its divisions) to perform. When the activities of business units are distributed throughout the greater organization, it is much more difficult, if not impossible, to evaluate the situation effectively. The balanced strategy (i.e., customer specialization and low cost) highlights the necessity for these business units to look for cost savings (through process improvements, quality-control programs, creative sourcing arrangements, etc.).

We reconfigured the initial seven business units, arranged in Figure 4.13 according to the type of strategy appropriate to a business unit, into a NAVSEA corporation of three major business lines. We illustrate these business lines in this and succeeding figures; however, we are not suggesting that this layer of management needs to be operationalized. If it is added, it needs to be kept thin. Figure 4.15 portrays this corporate structure.

Market/Customer Portfolio

The customer—important to the continued viability of NAVSEA—can be viewed as the second structuring mechanism for business lines. Organizing business units around the customer is a growing trend, reflecting the success of this mechanism in creating stakeholder value.

NAVSEA can provide stakeholder value by structuring business lines to focus on what matters to the stakeholders. In particular, the CNO is interested in meeting *current needs*—which center on readiness—and the ASN (RDA) is interested in supplying *future capabilities*—which center on the efficient and effective acquisition of weapon systems. Through various business units, NAVSEA provides the Type Commanders and the Fleets with services for keeping the Fleet operational; through various business units, NAVSEA provides the PEOs with services critical to the acquisition process. Consequently, the interests of NAVSEA's stakeholders and the business-unit customers are highly congruent: A strong relationship exists between customer value and stakeholder value.

RAND*MR1303-4.15*

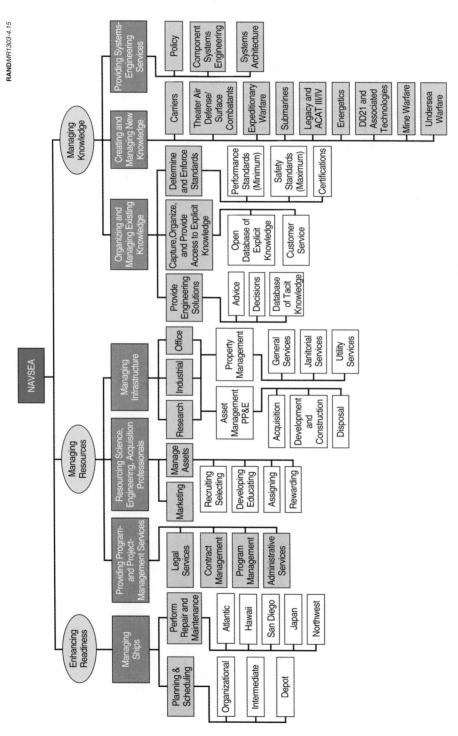

Figure 4.15—Industry-Positioning Portfolio

Structuring business lines around stakeholders sets the stage for holding NAVSEA business units accountable for providing customer—and, therefore, stakeholder—value.

From this perspective, the answer to the corporate question, "What businesses should NAVSEA be in?" is, "NAVSEA is in the business of meeting current and future naval needs." Two NAVSEA business lines are needed: Enhancing Readiness and Developing Future Capabilities.

Enhancing Readiness. This business line includes the Managing Ships business unit, and the Organizing and Managing Existing Knowledge business unit. Its divisions capture, organize, and provide access to explicit knowledge; provide engineering solutions; and set and enforce standards.

Value Proposition. This business line, with a complete set of offerings to meet the complete readiness needs of the Fleet, focuses on being the full-service provider of readiness.

Business-Line Strategy. Customer service is the overall strategy, with a heavy emphasis on a least-cost strategy for the Perform Repair and Maintenance business unit.

Developing Future Capabilities. The Developing Future Capabilities business line comprises four business units: Providing [general] Program- and Project-Management Services; Resourcing Science, Engineering, and Acquisition Professionals;[6] Creating and Managing New Knowledge; and Providing [top-level] Systems-Engineering Services. Therefore, it is in four separate but related businesses of providing the PEO with management services, professional people, knowledge management, and integration services.

Value Proposition. The business line captures the value of a full-service provider having long-term relationships with affiliated organizations and deep understanding of the PEO's needs. This portfolio preserves the special relationship existing today between the PEOs and NAVSEA. However, that relationship is made even more explicit in this portfolio by placing all elements of NAVSEA that meet PEO needs under a single line of business—PEO Support—unlike the dispersed and intermingled placement today.

---

[6]The business unit responsible for resourcing science, engineering, and acquisition professionals takes on the form of a functional integrator in several corporate structures described in this section. Lateral processes (holding functions together) facilitate a move from a functional structure to a product or market structure. These processes, in turn, can be structured into the form of a functional integrator. Then, near-term operating decisions move to the product or market segments; long-term capability-building activities move to the functional integrators.

Business-Line Strategy. The business line employs an overall strategy of customer service. As well, in the Creating and Managing New Knowledge and the Providing Systems-Engineering Services business units, there is heavy emphasis on innovation.

Each business line is integrated vertically, gathering together the critical activities in a chain that produces products and services of value to its customers. To ensure seamless, one-stop shopping for the Type Commanders and the Fleet, on the one hand, and for the PEOs, on the other hand, both business lines will benefit from organizing as a front-end/back-end structure, with customer-service teams assigned to all major customer groupings.

The Managing Infrastructure business unit becomes a Headquarters function, managing the critical infrastructure resources needed by the two lines of business. It has no customers external to NAVSEA and, consequently, is best considered a cost center. It employs a least-cost strategy and can be continually evaluated for outsourcing.[7]

Given the customer aggregation, we reconfigured the initial seven business units into a NAVSEA corporation comprising two major business lines and a separate Headquarters function, portrayed in Figure 4.16.

Competency Portfolio

An important role for NAVSEA corporate headquarters is to identify, develop, and sustain *core organizational competencies*—the collections of skills, knowledge, and technology that provide a key benefit to customers. The core competencies, which set NAVSEA apart from other organizations, are the primary reason customers choose the offerings of NAVSEA. If these competencies are viewed as a critical element of strategic intent, the organization can be structured to develop and sustain them. We formulate such a structure here.

Engineering is the competency that has commonality in the value NAVSEA's stakeholders assign to NAVSEA's products and services. Historically, although NAVSEA's role has changed, engineering and engineering support have been the mainstay of NAVSEA and its predecessors. Some NAVSEA leaders view engineering as the key to the future.

---

[7]Alternatively, this unit could take the form of a *distributed organization,* which moves corporate-wide activities to an operating unit; the operating unit then provides products or services to the whole corporation. This form is a compromise between a centralized headquarters structure and a decentralized fragmented structure (conducted independently by each business unit). This form allows the maintenance of core competencies supporting core products, even though the activities cross business units. Placing the activities in an operating unit moves them closer to the action/customer.

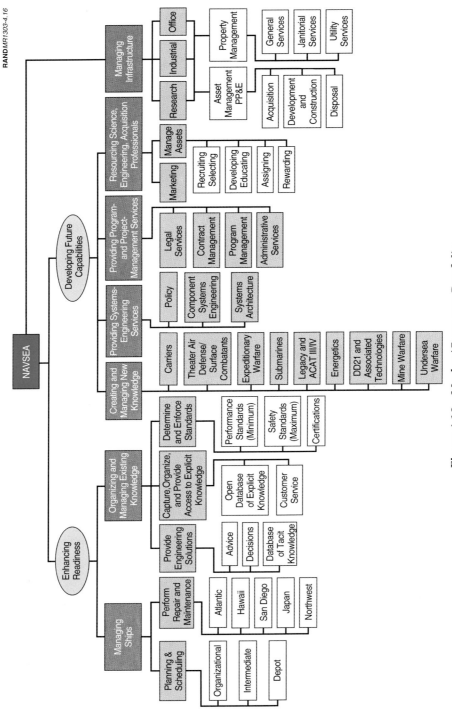

Figure 4.16—Market/Customer Portfolio

From this perspective, the answer to the corporate question, "What businesses should NAVSEA be in?" is, "NAVSEA should be in the business it is in— providing world-class naval engineering and in-service engineering support. Two NAVSEA business lines are needed: Providing Engineering Services and Managing Ships. The first provides stakeholder value to both the ASN (RDA) and CNO; the second provides stakeholder value to the CNO.

Providing Engineering Services. This business line comprises five business units: Engineering New Products (formerly Creating and Managing New Knowledge); Providing Systems-Engineering Services; Providing Engineering Solutions; Determining and Enforcing Standards; and Resourcing Science, Engineering, and Acquisition Professionals. The Providing Engineering Solutions activity and the Determining and Enforcing Standards activity are elevated from divisions of the Organizing and Managing Existing Knowledge business unit to become separate business units in this business line.

Value Proposition. This business line adds particular value by specializing in naval engineering, thereby developing and sustaining unparalleled depth compared with its competitors.

Business-Line Strategy. This business line employs an overall strategy of functional excellence, which is achieved, in part, by structuring the organization so that all the engineering resources (including the management of the engineering professionals themselves) are located together.

Managing Ships. This business line is composed of three business units: Planning and Scheduling; Performing Repair and Maintenance; and Capturing, Organizing, and Providing Access to Explicit Knowledge. The third business unit was the remaining activity of the Organizing and Managing Existing Knowledge business unit, now elevated to the business-unit level.

Value Proposition. This business line affords learning opportunities for the professional resources being developed in the other business line. However, if this business line provides little in the way of value in the context of the overarching strategic intent—engineering excellence—and becomes uncompetitive in cost, it should be divested.

Business-Line Strategy. This business line employs an overall strategy of customer service. For the Performing Repair and Maintenance business unit, it places heavy emphasis on a least-cost strategy.

As with the previous portfolio, the Managing Infrastructure business unit becomes a Headquarters function and cost center. It employs a least-cost strategy and can be continually evaluated for outsourcing.

The Providing [general] Program- and Project-Management Services business unit can be retained as a business unit (it serves customers external to NAVSEA); however, as with Managing Ships, it is an unrelated business unit and unnecessary, given the focus of the strategic intent. Consequently, it also employs a least-cost strategy and can be continually evaluated for outsourcing to another government entity or to the private sector.

Given the premise that engineering is a core competency for NAVSEA, we reconfigured the initial seven business units into a NAVSEA corporation consisting of two major business lines, an unrelated business unit, and a separate Headquarters function, portrayed in Figure 4.17.

Product-Life-Cycle Portfolio

Product life cycle is the paradigm that most influences the structure of the overall market within which NAVSEA competes: From this perspective, the answer to the corporate question, "What businesses should NAVSEA be in?" is, "NAVSEA should be in the business of providing full-spectrum life-cycle support." Strategically, NAVSEA can choose to participate in those areas in which it can have the greatest influence on the outcomes of particular interest to its stakeholders.

Three NAVSEA business lines are needed: Creating and Managing New Knowledge; Supporting Acquisition; and Providing In-Service Support. The first two business lines provide stakeholder value to the ASN (RDA); the third business line provides stakeholder value to the CNO. Value is derived specifically from the understanding of the overall life-cycle process and NAVSEA's ability to leverage its capabilities in that context.

Creating and Managing New Knowledge. This business line is organized around the PEOs as customers, as in the previous portfolios. Here, however, it stands alone as a separate business line.

Value Proposition. Customers of this business line attach particular value to the Navy-specific expertise and the depth of understanding of the Fleet's future needs.

Business-Line Strategy. The business line employs an overall strategy of innovation.

Supporting Acquisition. This business line comprises four business units: Providing [top-level] Systems-Engineering Services; Determining and Enforcing Standards (formerly an activity within the Organizing and Managing Existing Knowledge business unit); Providing [general] Program- and Project-

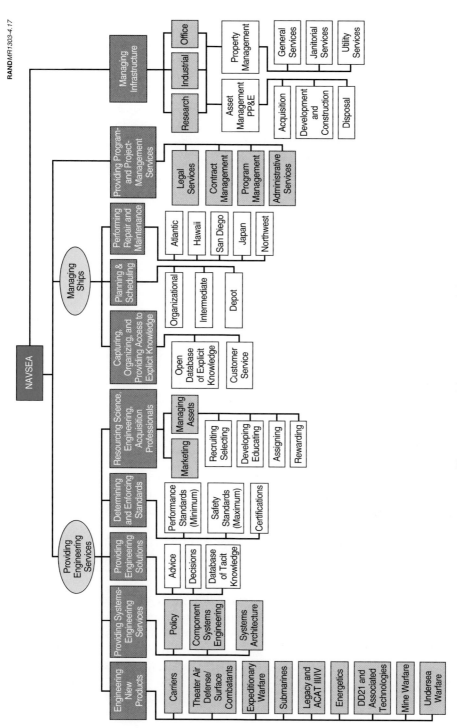

RANDMR1303-4.17

Figure 4.17—Competency Portfolio

Management Services; and Resourcing Science, Engineering, and Acquisition Professionals. *The first and fourth business units do not produce products or services that are part of the product life cycle; however, they do provide resources that are critical to the success of the life-cycle process.*

Value Proposition. The value proposition of this business line centers on specialized knowledge of the life-cycle process and the unique Navy context within which it operates.

Business-Line Strategy. This business line and its business units employ a strategy of customer service.

Providing In-Service Support. This business line is made up of three business units: Planning and Scheduling; Performing Repair and Maintenance; and Organizing and Managing Existing Knowledge. The third, an activity of the Capturing, Organizing, and Providing Access to Explicit Knowledge business unit and of the Providing Engineering Solutions business unit, is now a business unit in its own right.

Value Proposition. This business line offers particular value as a full-service provider of in-service support.

Business-Line Strategy. This business line employs an overall strategy of customer service. For the Performing Repair and Maintenance business unit, it places heavy emphasis on a least-cost strategy.

As with the previous two portfolios, the Managing Infrastructure business unit becomes a Headquarters function and a cost center. It employs a least-cost strategy and can be continually evaluated for outsourcing.

Looking for congruity in the core process that pervades the industry within which NAVSEA operates, we have reconfigured the initial seven business units into a NAVSEA corporation of three major business lines and a separate Headquarters function, portrayed in Figure 4.18.

Selecting the Portfolio of Businesses

Each of the four portfolios of business units described above—four variations of strategic intent manifested in NAVSEA corporate structure—has advantages. It would be convenient if a single structure captured all or most of these advantages. However, not all the advantages are equally important. The choice of organizational design should be based on what best accomplishes the desired organizational strategic intent.

RAND*MR1303-4.18*

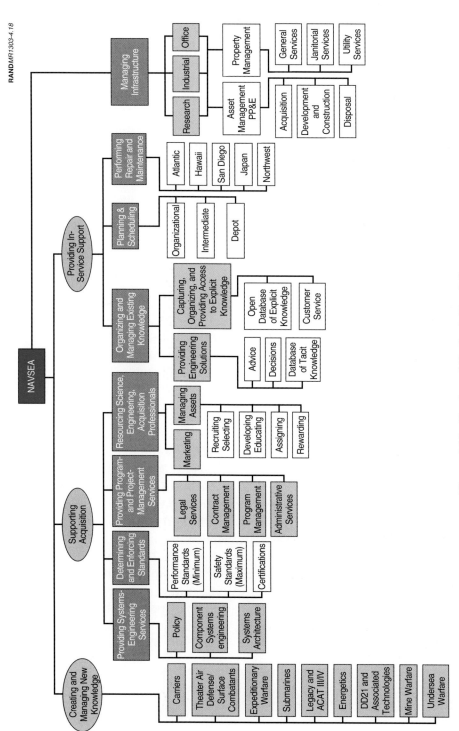

Figure 4.18—Product-Life-Cycle Portfolio

THE PROPER SIZE FOR NAVSEA

In the fourth and concluding stage of our organizational design process, NAVSEA can identify an efficient organization to achieve the NAVSEA strategic intent. This organization, which does not exist today, is not something we can supply in this report. It will be the target for NAVSEA action in the future.

To this point, we have talked in terms of those general functions that the parts of the organization perform but not to particular activities executed within these organizations. The objective of the fourth stage, sizing NAVSEA for efficiency, is to link activities to a specific organizational structure, to further refine the corporate structure according to the importance of the activities, and to delineate what might be inside and what might be outside the formal boundaries of the Department of the Navy organization called NAVSEA. Here, we describe a framework NAVSEA can use to carry out the fourth stage.

Sizing Framework

This stage begins by linking activities and products to the corporate structure suggested in stage three, Shape. It then identifies those activities and products that are central to the accomplishment of the NAVSEA mission and overall strategic intent for competitive advantage and/or that can substantially improve corporate effectiveness if managed specifically toward that end. It also identifies and evaluates those activities and products that cut across multiple business units.

The suggested framework assumes the perspective that NAVSEA does not necessarily need to produce every product that is important to NAVSEA customers and stakeholders, nor to perform internally every activity making up such products. Either other organizations (inside or outside of government) may be able to provide products more efficiently than can NAVSEA or having NAVSEA develop and/or sustain the requisite capabilities to be the best provider may not be cost-effective. However, even if there are organizations that can better provide products currently provided by NAVSEA, NAVSEA's responsibility includes recommending governing arrangements for ensuring value to the customers and stakeholders—i.e., NAVSEA must remain a smart buyer. Therefore, the Size stage also asks the question, "For those business units or parts of business units outside of NAVSEA, what is the most appropriate level of NAVSEA involvement?"

The results of our current research provide the basis for NAVSEA to proceed with the organizational sizing analysis. Products, activities, personnel, facilities, and technologies can be linked to NAVSEA organizational elements. In addition, NAVSEA business units have been described and evaluated individually and within a corporate-portfolio context.

We suggest approaching the above task by assessing the NAVSEA organization at three levels. Although described sequentially, it is expected that the planner will move back and forth among the levels of analysis:

First, that NAVSEA view the decision from the perspective of the overall corporation by asking the question, "What is the appropriate set of business units to retain in the corporate portfolio?" This consideration was addressed in the second and third stages of the organizational design approach, through the use of NAVSEA strategic intent.

Second, that NAVSEA view the decision from the perspective of the business unit by asking the question, "Which business units or parts of business units can be provided efficiently elsewhere while maintaining control and meeting customer needs?" In addition to the business units' contribution to corporate strategic intent, we recommend that NAVSEA evaluate business units on the basis of their sustainability (as public or private entities), the cost of divesting or acquiring the capability, the ability to provide world-class products or services, the basis of control, and the nature of the work required to be performed.

Third, that NAVSEA view the decision from the perspective of the products by asking the question, "Which business units have high concentrations of central products such that they should reside within NAVSEA?" We recommend that NAVSEA consider the effect on management's ability to focus on business-unit success, access to world-class capabilities, risk sharing, surge capacity, smart buyers' expertise, freeing resources for other purposes, and controlling operating costs.

Of particular importance for the Size stage is the product-centrality analysis described in Chapter Three. That analysis can be used as the entry point for considering organizational design. Understanding NAVSEA's markets, products, and activities will be crucial to understanding the core businesses, the vertical and horizontal linkages, and the proper size for NAVSEA in 2007.

RAND would be pleased to work with NAVSEA to implement this framework or a modified version of it.

PROJECT VISITS AND BRIEFINGS

During this project, we drew on numerous sources inside and outside the Navy and NAVSEA to provide us with a broad understanding of the responsibilities, mandates, capabilities, and organizational relationships that define the Naval Sea System Command (NAVSEA) within the broader Navy, Department of Defense (DoD), and industry context. One of the important sources of information has been site visits to NAVSEA Headquarters, Program Executive Officers (PEOs), and field activities, as well as discussions with Naval War College faculty, the Chief of Naval Operation's (CNO's) Strategic Studies Group, and representatives from the Fleet. We benefited greatly by having the opportunity of attending NAVSEA Commander's Forums (CF's) VI, VII, VIII, and IX, as well as the Supervisor of Shipbuilding's (SUPSHIP's)/Navy Shipyard Joint Board of Directors' meeting during the course of this project. We also participated as a member of the Red Team Review for NAVSEA's internal Core Equities Initiative.

These activities broadened our perspective of the issues, difficulties, and challenges that NAVSEA deals with on a continuing basis. Further, they provided the opportunity to meet the NAVSEA leaders who manage the Warfare Centers and their respective Divisions; the Naval Shipyard Commanders; the SUPSHIP leaders; PEOs; and Type Commanders; as well as NAVSEA Headquarters' leaders and staff. Our discussions with them of the issues and problems facing NAVSEA in carrying out its responsibilities for the U.S. Navy enriched the context of our subsequent site visits and meetings with individuals. As a result, we benefited from a broader understanding of NAVSEA as a corporation.

Table A.1 lists the primary visits and types of discussions that took place during the course of this study. Following the table is a survey that we used to elicit comprehensive information during our site visits.

Table A.1

NAVSEA Project Visits and Briefings

Time Period	Activity, Organization, or Office	Visit	Briefing
January–March 1999	• NAVSEA Core Equities Red Team Review	√	
	• NAVSEA Comptroller, CAPT Ackley	√	
	• VADM Nanos and Staff	√	√
April–June 1999	• RADM Balisle, Vice Commander NAVSEA, and staff	√	√
	• PEO DD21, RADM Carnevale and staff	√	√
	• NAVSEA POC meeting, VADM Nanos, Pete Brown, et al.		√
	• SUPSHIPS, Stanley Sachs & Len Thompson	√	
	• Representatives of NAVSEA Corporate Ops, Naval Underwater Warfare Center (NUWC) Headquarters and Naval Surface Warfare Center (NSWC) Headquarters	√	√
	• Naval War College	√	
	• National Defense University	√	
	• Naval Studies Board	√	
	• CNO's Strategic Studies Group	√	
	• Navy Warfare Development Center	√	
	• Atlantic Command, 2nd Fleet	√	
July–September 1999	• SEA 08 Staff	√	
	• NAVSEA CF VI, Norfolk Naval Shipyard (NNSY)	√	
	• RADM Young, Acting Deputy Commander NAVSEA	√	√
	• Deputy PEO, Carriers, Brian Persons	√	√
	• VADM(R) Bowes, Vice President, Litton	√	√
	• NSWC Headquarters, Bill Cocimano and staff	√	√
	• NUWC Headquarters and Newport Division, RADM Young, Dr. Sirmalis, and staff	√	
	• Carderock Division, NSWC, CAPT Preisel, Mr. Metrey, and staff	√	√
	• Port Hueneme Division, NSWC, CAPT Phillips, Mr. Giacchi, and staff	√	√
	• Naval Warfare Assessment Station, NSWC, CDR Lang, Dr. Meeks, and staff	√	√
October–December 1999	• Indian Head Division, NSWC, CAPT Walsh, Philip Anderson, and staff	√	√
	• Dahlgren Division, NSWC, CAPT Mahaffey and staff	√	√
	• Panama City Station, NSWC, CAPT Covert and staff	√	√
	• SUPSHIPS/NNSY Joint Board of Directors' Meeting, RADM Baugh, Bernie Clark, et al.	√	√
	• NAVSEA CF VII, Port Hueneme Division, NSWC	√	√
	• Puget Sound Naval Shipyard, CAPT Bryant and staff	√	√
	• Submarine Force, U.S. Atlantic Fleet (SUBLANT) Headquarters, VADM Giambastiani and staff	√	√
	• 7th Fleet Headquarters, VADM Doran and staff	√	√
	• Norfolk Naval Shipyard, CAPT Scheib and staff	√	
	• SUPSHIP, NNSY, Brian McAvoy	√	

Table A.1—Cont'd.

Time Period	Activity, Organization , or Office	Visit	Briefing
January–March 2000	• NAVSEA Corp. Ops. Staff, Craig McKay, Jeanie Woods, Michael Allman, et al.	√	√
	• VADM Nanos, RADM Etnyre, RADM Yount, Pete Brown, et al.	√	√
	• PEO TSC, RADM Cobb	√	√
	• PEO CXW, RADM Morral	√	√
	• SEA 03, RADM Yount and Gregg Hagedorn	√	√
	• VADM(R) Bowes, Vice President, Litton		√
	• NAVSEA CF VIII, SUPSHIP, Jacksonville, FL	√	√
April–June 2000	• VADM Nanos, RADM Etnyre, RADM Yount, Pete Brown, Gregg Hagedorn, Bonnie Flynn, Craig McKay, Jeanie Woods, et al.	√	√
	• NAVSEA CFIX, Portsmouth, NH	√	√
July–September 2000	• VADM Nanos, NEC & BTET		√
	• Core Equities Working Group		√
	• SEA 91, PEO EXW		√
	• SEA 01, SEA 02 and Staff Codes		√
	• LOG, SEA 04		√
	• NUWC Newport		√
	• NSWC Working Group, Day-Long Symposium		√
	• SEA 09B, SEA 05		√
October–December 2000	• NSWC Board of Directors Meeting		√
	• PEO TSC and (S)		√
	• Team SUB, PEO SUB, SEA 92, SEA 93, PEO CV, Others		√

SURVEY FOR RAND SITE VISITS

The RAND study team plans to meet with each of the major organizational elements in NAVSEA. Given that scheduling will allow, we expect to meet first with the Headquarters element and then proceed with visits with the various associated field activities. During each visit we would generally prefer to start with an overview presentation of the host organizational element, followed by a more detailed discussion of the organization's principal clients and customers and what products and services are provided to them. The general topics we would like to cover are:

•   What basic missions and mandates are being satisfied?

•   Who are the customers and clients?

•   What products and services are provided?

- What unique qualities and requirements are necessary to satisfy the customer needs?

- What personnel and facility support is needed to satisfy the customer needs?

- What kinds of authority and responsibility are exercised by your organization?

- What is the flow of obligation and expenditure funding in your organization?

We would like to interact with several levels of management and staff in the organization and to allow sufficient time during the site visit to take a detailed tour of the physical plant and real property holdings of the organization. In particular we would like to see the major technical facilities and discuss their unique capabilities with the members of technical staff involved.

The internal equities effort that the NAVSEA organizational units conducted represents an enormous undertaking and an important source of information and insight for our study. We would like to meet with the team leaders and members of this effort to discuss the process and the criteria they used in their study and the data sources used for assigning work years and facility utilization.

There follows a more detailed list of areas and questions we would like to address during an initial or a subsequent visit to an organizational element. These more detailed questions fall into the following categories:

- Organizational Questions

- Programs, Products, and Services

- Internal Equities Initiative

- Financial Questions

- Research and Technology

- Publications, Reports, Presentations, Awards, and Patents.

We would prefer scheduling a subsequent visit rather than trying to cram too much into a single visit. Our first priority is to gain an overall knowledge of the organization, its missions and mandates, principal customers, and salient products and services. Discussing these areas with several levels of staff and management and visiting the important associated facilities are highest on our list of initial interactions. If time allows during an initial visit, we can go into the detailed questions.

Although we would like to cover these subject areas and questions, we would also like to allow time during our visit to learn and discuss issues your organization believes to be important which are not reflected in our discussion topics.

The RAND study team very much appreciates the time and effort of the staff and management at host organizations to arrange for a site visit. We would like to conduct the visit in as informal and relaxed a manner as possible.

DETAILED QUESTIONS FOR SITE VISITS

Organizational Questions:

1.   What is the overall mission and vision for your organization?

2.   Does your organization have a strategic plan or business plan?

3.   For what corporate-level goals is your organization responsible?

4.   Is there a detailed organizational chart available?

5.   How are the lines of authority, responsibility, and accountability indicated?

6.   Has there been a recent business process re-engineering effort and what were the results?

7.   What interactions have you had with the Defense Acquisition Reform Initiative?

8.   What organization do you report to?

9.   What organizations report to you?

10. Do you have the authority to reorganize?

11. What are the legal or regulatory impediments to reorganization?

12. In round numbers how many personnel, military and civilian?

13. What mix of occupations is represented by your staff?

14. What is the mix of military and civilian staff in terms of officers and enlisted and white-collar and blue-collar?

15. What is the experience level of your staff in the major skill areas?

16. How many advanced-degreed staff are there and what is the technician-to-scientist-and-engineer ratio?

17. How many individuals have taken advanced training courses in the last several years?

18. What is the turnover rate of staff?

19. Who directs the assets of your site on a daily basis—Headquarters, Subordinate elements, or organizations outside of your own?

20. Does your organization direct the assets of some other organization—subcontractors, for example?—If so, what organizations?

21. Do you have reprogramming authority or must you secure approval from your supervising headquarters?

22. Are all personnel on site or are some located with clients and customers?

23. Are there any contractors located on site?

24. What is the 5–10 year trend in manpower and budget for your organization?

Programs, Products, and Services:

1. What basic mission and mandates does your organization fulfill?

2. What NAVSEAINST, OPNAVINST, and SECNAVINST guide and direct your organization's activities?

3. Who are your customers and clients?

4. In what sense are they your clients and customers?

5. Have you recently conducted a survey of your customers and clients?— What did you measure and what were the results?

6. What is your relationship with the PEOs?—What services do you supply?

7. What are the final products and services that you provide to them?

8. What unique qualities and requirements are necessary to satisfy the customer needs?

9. What are the major programs underway in your organization?

10. Does your organization provide a service entitled "smart buyer" for your clients or customers?—If so, what is the basic job description of this service and what is your view of the qualifications of a "smart buyer"?

11. What are the basic raw materials that you use as inputs for these final products and services?

12. What are the basic processes that are used to transform these input materials into final products and services?

13. Are there other credible sources for the final products and services?

14. If your organization were rendered ineffective by a natural disaster or other catastrophic event, what organization might step in to perform your functions?

Internal Equities Initiative:

1. What are considered the equities of your organization?

2. What were the criteria used in determining these equities?

3. What is the key feature of features that distinguish core equities from other equities?

4. Who were the leaders of the equities effort in your organization?

5. What has been your recent organizational thinking on the kinds of activities that must be done within NAVSEA and more generally within DoD or the US Government?

Financial Questions:

1. What is the operating budget for your organization?

2. What are the funding sources for your organization?

3. How much of the funding is mission related and how much is NWCF, or other?

4. What are your overhead rates and how are they set?

5. What is the average small purchase rate?

6. Are there any GIS-based databases available and what information do they contain? Were any prepared by NAVSEA for the BRAC a few years ago for example?

7. Is there a database for facilities containing associated historical costs, replacement costs, and depreciation information?

8. Are there any valuations for the PP&E on site?

9. Are there any environmental liabilities associated with the PP&E?

10. Are there other liabilities?

11. What software tools are used to manage finances in your organization?

12. How is funding distributed in your organization?

13. Do you have a database that provides time charges by Task/project or equity area?

14. What is the investment in new capital equipment for the last several years?

15. What is the investment in new or updated facilities for the last several years?

Research and Technology:

1. Is there an internal R&D Program and how does a project qualify for it?

2. How is the internal R&D program funded?

3. Are there CRADAs in place and how is the utility of these programs viewed in the organization?

4. What are the major facilities in your organization?—What are the products or services they deliver?—Who are their customers?—What is the historical facility utilization rate?—What staff is involved in operating the facility?

5. Is there a list of Science and Technology Objectives, which guide the course of the research?—What are these STOs?—How many have been achieved?

6. To what extent is your research agenda linked to and influenced by broad Navy strategy developments?

7. How many researchers from other institutions are visiting your organization to conduct research?

8. What involvement do you have with universities and other research organizations?

9. Is there a post-doc program in your organization?

10. What is your involvement with the National Research Council?

11. What has been your experience with outside contractors providing R&D services?

12. During previous downsizing actions, what activities were outsourced?—What was the selection criteria?

Publications, Reports, Presentations, Awards, and Patents:[1]

1. How many technical reports have been published?

2. What is the number of refereed journal articles published?

3. What is the number of test reports published?

4. How many books or book chapters published?

---

[1] Round numbers and estimates only.

5.   How many patent disclosures have been filed?

6.   How many patents have been granted?

7.   How many invited talks have been delivered at professional meetings?

8.   How many awards have been received and for what reasons?

9.   How many professional society fellowships are held by staff researchers?

10. How many patent licensing agreements have been placed most recently?

OFFICE OF THE CHIEF OF NAVAL OPERATIONS (OPNAV) AND SECRETARY OF THE NAVY (SECNAV) INSTRUCTIONS

Table B.1

OPNAV Instructions

Document Number	Subject
OPNAVINST 1151.9C	Acoustic Sensor Training Aids Program (ASTAP)
OPNAVINST 1500.61	Intermediate Maintenance Activity (IMA) Journeyman Navy Enlisted Classification (JNEC) Program
OPNAVINST 1540.51c	Submarine On Board Training (SOBT) Program
OPNAVINST 1540.54	Naval Reserve Force (NFR) Innovative Naval Reserve Concept (INRC) Implementation Plan
OPNAVINST 1640.8	Brigs Afloat
OPNAVINST 2710.1	DON Standards for Commercial (Non-Tactical) LAN on Navy Ships
OPNAVINST 2720.2G	Fleet Modernization Program (FMP) Policy
OPNAVINST 3000.12	Operational Availability of Equipments and Weapons Systems
OPNAVINST 3100.8	Deck Landing Operations by Civilian Helicopters with Civilian Pilots on U.S. Navy Vessels
OPNAVINST 3120.28B	Certification of the Aviation Capability of Ships Operating Aircraft
OPNAVINST 3120.33B	Submarine Extended Operating Cycle (SEOC) Program
OPNAVINST 3120.42A	Safe Engineering and Operations Program for Landing Craft, Air Cushion
OPNAVINST 3120.42B	Safe Engineering and Operations Program for Landing Craft, Air Cushion
OPNAVINST 3150.27A	Navy Diving Program
OPNAVINST C3501.2J	Naval Warfare Mission Areas and Required Operational Capability/Projected Operational Environment (ROC/POE)
OPNAVINST 3501.225	Navy Premeditated Personnel Parachuting (P3) Program
OPNAVINST 3502.5	Policy for Managing the Life Cycle Support of the TRIDENT Engineering and Operations Training (EOT) Program
OPNAVINST 3540.4J	Propulsion Examining Boards for Conventionally Powered Ships
OPNAVINST 3960.16	Navy Test and Monitoring Systems (TAMS)
OPNAVINST 4000.57F	Logistic Support of the Trident System
OPNAVINST 4080.11C	Navy War Reserve Material Management
OPNAVINST 4400.10B	Policies for Integrated Logistics Overhauls (ILO) and Reviews (ILR)
OPNAVINST 4700.3	Trials, Acceptance, Commissioning, Fitting Out, Test and Evaluation, Shakedown and Post-Shakedown Availability of Guided Missile Frigate *Oliver Hazard Perry* (FFG-7); Responsibilities for
OPNAVINST 4700.7J	Maintenance Policy for Naval Ships

Table B.1—Cont'd.

Document Number	Subject
OPNAVINST 4710.31	TRIDENT Planned Equipment Replacement (TRIPER) Program
OPNAVINST 4720.2F	Salvage and Recovery Program
OPNAVINST 4770.5F	General Instructions for Inactive Ship and Craft
OPNAVINST 4780.6C	Procedures for Administering Service Craft and Boats in the U.S. Navy
OPNAVINST 4790.11	Policy and Responsibility for Detection, Action, and Response Technique (DART) Program
OPNAVINST 4790.15B	The Aircraft Launch and Recovery Equipment Maintenance Program
OPNAVINST 4790.4C	Ships' Maintenance and Material Management (3-M) Manual
OPNAVINST 5090.1B	Environmental and Natural Resource Program Manual
OPNAVINST 5100.21B	Afloat Mishap Investigation and Reporting
OPNAVINST 5200.29	Participation in Government-Industry Data Exchange Program
OPNAVINST 5239.1A	DON Automatic Data Processing Security Program
OPNAVINST 5510.1H	Department of the Navy Information and Personnel Security Program Regulation
OPNAVINST 5530.13B	Department of the Navy Physical Security Instruction for Conventional Arms, Ammunition, and Explosives (AA&E)
OPNAVINST 7130.8	Guidance for the Execution of Program Funds at Naval Shipyards
OPNAVINST 8011.9A	Non-Nuclear Ordnance Requirements (NNOR) Process
OPNAVINST 8020.8J	Responsibilities of the DON Commands with Respect to the DoD Explosives Safety Board
OPNAVINST 8023.20E	Waivers of and Exemptions from Explosives Safety Requirements; Policies and Procedures for Requesting
OPNAVINST 8023.21C	Explosives Safety Standards for U.S. Navy Combatant Ships and Tenders at U.S. Naval Stations and Similar Support Activities
OPNAVINST 8023.2C	U.S. Navy Explosives Safety Policies, Requirements, and Procedures
OPNAVINST 8027.6D	Naval Responsibilities for Explosive Ordnance Disposal
OPNAVINST 9010.300A	Development of Naval Ship Characteristics
OPNAVINST 9010.335	Warfighting Improvement Plan (WIP) Development
OPNAVINST 9027.6D	Naval Responsibilities for Explosive Ordnance Disposal
OPNAVINST 9070.1	Survivability Policy for Surface Ships of the U.S. Navy
OPNAVINST 9070.2	Signature Control Policy for Ships and Craft of the U.S. Navy
OPNAVINST 9072.2	Shock Hardening of Surface Ships
OPNAVINST 9080.4B	Relationships Between the Naval Inspector General and the President, Board of Inspection and Survey
OPNAVINST 9094.1B	Full Power and Economy Trial Requirements for Non-Nuclear Surface Ship Classes
OPNAVINST 9096.1	Weight and Stability Limits for Naval Surface Ships
OPNAVINST 9110.1B	Submarine Test and Operating Depths; Policy Concerning
OPNAVINST 9200.3	Engineering Operational Sequencing System (EOSS)
OPNAVINST 9220.2	U.S. Navy Boiler Water and Feedwater Test and Treatment Program (Nuclear Excluded)
OPNAVINST 9221.1B	U.S. Navy Steam Generating Plant Inspection and Inspector Training and Certification Program
OPNAVINST 9233.1A	U.S. Navy Diesel Engine Inspection and Inspector Training and Certification Program
OPNAVINST 9233.2A	U.S. Navy Automated Diesel Engine Trend Analysis Program
OPNAVINST 9234.1A	Marine Gas Turbine Inspector (MGTI) Program
OPNAVINST 9410.1A	Interoperability of Tactical Command, Control and Communications Systems
OPNAVINST 9410.5	Data Base and Communication Standards Interoperability Requirements for Tactical Naval Warfare Systems
OPNAVINST 9640.1A	Shipboard Habitability Program

Table B.2

SECNAV Instructions

Document Number	Subject
SECNAVINST 400.85	Navy Logistics System
SECNAVINST 4000.36	Technical Representation at Contractors' Facilities
SECNAVINST 4855.3	Product Deficiency Reporting and Evaluation Program (PDREP)
SECNAVINST 4900.48	Transfer of U.S. Naval Vessels to Foreign Governments and International Organizations
SECNAVINST 4950.4	Security Assistance and International Logistics Joint Security Assistance Training
SECNAVINST 5200.39	Participation in the Government-Industry Data Exchange Program (GIDEP)
SECNAVINST 5400.15A	Department of the Navy Research, Development and Acquisition, and Associated Life Cycle Management Responsibilities
SECNAVINST 5400.16	Department of the Navy Warfare Centers and Corporate Laboratory
SECNAVINST 5510.36	DON Information Security Program (ISP) Regulation
SECNAVINST 11420.1	Leasing of Navy-Controlled Floating Drydocks

TECHNICAL APPENDIX

The analysis presented in Chapter Three is based on an extensive data-collection effort occurring during the 38 site visits (listed in Appendix A) to gain as much information on all elements of the Naval Sea Systems Command (NAVSEA), then to assemble that data in numerical form in databases. Chapter Three presents an overview of the databases and analyses, as well as the most salient results for products, processes, and market structure in 2007.

Here, we provide more background on the data-analysis effort, beginning with that related to the market-emphasis-growth factors and the evolution of strategy drivers and market emphasis. Next, we derive the product-rating system for relating importance and breadth of products to markets. We then describe how information on activities was classified and assembled into databases on activities, technologies, facilities, and personnel. We then provide more-detailed descriptions of the observables for product-market interactions, including calculations with simple math, along with samples of the various scorecards on which the results were entered.[1] Interactions for determining resource-allocation decisions were not covered in Chapter Three. This appendix presents the observables for interactions between and among processes, technologies, facilities, personnel, and products.

ANALYSES RELATED TO GROWTH IN MARKET-EMPHASIS FACTORS

Our analyses of markets and products occurred concurrently with our analyses of the strategy and organization phases of the study, evolving over the course of our study and meetings with NAVSEA, the Navy, contractors, and Program Executive Officers (PEOs); information gained from printed documents; and our own expertise. In this section of the appendix, we look at the analyses

---

[1]Most of the scorecards-databases provide only a small portion of the total databases used in this project. The primary purposes of including the database portions here are to illustrate how the databases were constructed and how the scoring and calculations were done.

underpinning our discussion of market-emphasis-growth factors at the beginning of Chapter Three, starting with the next subsection, Strategic Drivers, to illustrate that the Market-Product-Activity Model is an iterative approach that relies on information about an organization that is as complete as possible and that may change dramatically in the course of data gathering.

Strategic Drivers

From the Strategy phase of the research, we first culled four major strategy drivers that will influence the NAVSEA markets in 2007. These drivers grew to 10 by the end or our study. We focus on the 10-driver case here, presenting charts and tables of the 4-driver case primarily for comparison.

We considered the impact of each of the drivers on changes in emphasis in the markets by national security directives (deter, shape, prepare, respond) from Chapter Two, by strategic driver, according to inputs from many Navy individuals consulted in the Strategy phase of our research plan as reviewed by the RAND project research team. The results of this assessment are shown in Figure C.1, under the acronyms shown in Table 3.3 for the NAVSEA markets.

The score assessed for each market—each cell of the matrix of markets—is a 1 (for Yes, has an impact) or 0 (for No, has no impact) in answer to the question,

> In 2007, will the respective strategy driver still be forcing emphasis on a certain NAVSEA market to grow or increase as a response?

The total driver impact is shown in the far-right-hand column and is the sum of impacts across all markets. It is greatest for network-centric warfare, followed closely by information dominance and effective engagement. Forward presence has the least impact.

Technology Drivers

In our discussions with Navy personnel and in our review of Naval Studies Board–National Research Council (NSB–NRC, 1997a), National Research Council (NRC, 1996), and Office of Naval Intelligence (ONI; 1998) documents, and Gaffney and Saalfeld (1999) of the Office of Naval Research, we found a number of technological developments that determined the emphasis on many of the NAVSEA markets. These are cross-cutting technological developments that are most appropriately scored as a market driver rather than a technology embedded in a specific product. The information environment is an example of such a driver, because all naval force elements must be designed to operate within that environment (NSB–NRC, 1997a, p. 54). We considered the impact of each of these technological drivers across the NAVSEA markets on the basis of

RAND*MR1303-C.1*

Strategy drivers for 2007	Impact on NAVSEA markets															Total driver impact
	AAW	AMW	ASU	ASW	CCC	IW	INT	OPA	OMW	MOB	MOS–NCO	ACQ	NSW	STW	DEF	
Deter																
Information dominance	1	1	1	1	0	1	1	0	0	0	1	0	0	1	0	8
Potent forces	0	1	0	1	0	1	0	0	1	0	0	0	0	0	0	4
Shape																
Forward presence	0	1	0	0	0	0	0	0	0	0	0	0	0	0	0	1
Force protection—allies	0	0	0	0	0	0	1	0	0	0	1	0	0	0	1	3
Prepare																
Effective engagement	0	1	0	1	1	1	1	0	0	0	0	1	0	1	1	8
Complex terrain operations	0	1	0	0	0	0	1	0	0	0	0	0	0	1	1	4
Standoff operations support	0	1	1	1	0	0	1	0	0	0	0	0	0	1	1	6
Respond																
Network-centric warfare	1	1	1	1	1	1	1	0	0	0	0	1	0	1	1	10
Littoral warfare	0	1	1	1	0	0	1	0	0	0	0	1	0	1	1	7
Force protection—U.S.	0	0	0	0	0	0	1	0	0	0	0	1	0	0	1	3
Total strategy impact	2	8	4	6	2	4	8	0	1	0	2	4	0	6	7	

Figure C.1—Scoring Matrix for Strategic Drivers of NAVSEA Markets

discussions with many Navy personnel during our site visits (see Appendix A) and the assessment of RAND analysts. The assessment is again based on the question,

> In 2007, will the respective technology driver still be forcing emphasis on a certain NAVSEA market to grow or increase as a response?

where a 1 is given for a Yes response and a 0 for No. The results of this assessment are shown in Figure C.2.

As with strategy drivers, the total driver impact is shown in the far-right-hand column and is the sum of impacts across all markets. Two technology drivers are affecting the most NAVSEA market emphasis: the advent and continued development of very-high-speed computational tools and very-high-bandwidth networks.

RAND*MR1303-C.2*

Technology drivers for 2007	Impact on NAVSEA markets															Total driver impact
	AAW	AMW	ASU	ASW	CCC	IW	INT	OPA	OMW	MOB	MOS–NCO	ACQ	NSW	STW	DEF	
Hostile smart minefields with networked sensors	0	0	0	0	0	0	0	0	1	0	0	0	0	0	1	2
Hostile smart torpedoes with advanced hunter seeker capabilities	0	0	0	0	0	0	0	0	0	0	0	0	0	0	1	1
Hostile quiet, modern, air-independent submarines[a]	0	0	0	1	0	0	0	0	0	0	0	0	0	0	0	1
Anti-ship cruise missiles with challenging flight characteristics	0	0	0	0	0	0	0	0	0	0	0	0	0	0	1	1
Anti-ship chemical and biological warheads	0	0	0	0	0	0	0	0	0	0	0	0	0	0	1	1
Very-high-speed computational tools	0	0	0	1	1	0	0	0	0	0	0	1	0	1	0	4
Very-high-bandwidth networks	0	0	0	0	1	1	1	0	0	0	0	0	0	1	0	4
Total technology impact	0	0	0	2	2	1	1	0	1	0	0	1	0	2	4	

[a]Such submarines separate oxygen and hydrogen from water and use oxygen for breathing.

Figure C.2—Scoring Matrix for Technology Drivers of NAVSEA Markets

Business Drivers

The final set of forces driving the emphasis on NAVSEA markets for 2007 is business forces. Sources for these drivers are the NSB–NRC (1997a) and NRC (1996) studies and the many discussions we have had with Navy personnel. Again, the scoring is based on the question,

> In 2007, will the respective business driver still be forcing emphasis on a certain NAVSEA market to grow or increase as a response?

where a 1 is given for a Yes response and a 0 for No. These drivers and our assessment are shown in Figure C.3.

RAND*MR1303-C.3*

Business drivers for 2007	Impact on NAVSEA markets															Total driver impact
	AAW	AMW	ASU	ASW	CCC	IW	INT	OPA	OMW	MOB	MOS–NCO	ACQ	NSW	STW	DEF	
Modeling and simulation applied to acquisition	0	0	0	0	0	0	0	1	0	0	0	1	0	0	0	2
Consolidation in the defense industry	0	0	0	0	0	0	0	1	0	0	0	0	0	0	0	1
Acquisition reform	0	0	0	0	0	0	0	1	0	0	0	1	0	0	0	2
Increasing use of commercial firms for maintenance and support functions	0	0	0	0	0	0	0	1	0	1	0	1	0	0	0	3
Total business impact	0	0	0	0	0	0	0	4	0	1	0	3	0	0	0	

Figure C.3—Scoring Matrix for Business Drivers of NAVSEA Markets

The most important business driver for NAVSEA markets is the increasing use of commercial firms for maintenance and support functions. The market most sensitive to changes in the business environment is the Operational Availability (OPA) market. As to acquisition reform, shipyards are the units that are looking for the new processes emerging from acquisition reform to upgrade vessels, improve performance, and reduce the cost of rebuilding ships. Therefore, acquisition reform drives the OPA market. By the same token, systems engineering, which is included in the Developing Future Capabilities business line of Figure 4.16, has Policy as one of its business units, as well as all of the future platforms. It will be profoundly affected by acquisition reform. Therefore, ACQ gets a 1.

Market Emphasis

To arrive at an overall assessment of market emphasis, we combined the results from the three major driver categories, summing the total driver impact for each market for each of the driver categories uniformly, normalizing the driver categories so that each category contributes equally, multiplying the final score, and summing the scaled scores across drivers (the calculations for the case in which strategy is weighted 1.5 times more than the other drivers is shown in Table C.1, later in this section).

We put the final results into four bins corresponding to Very Low, Low, Medium, and High emphasis in 2007. These results are shown in Figure C.4. Weighting the market-emphasis-growth drivers equally, we see that the Operational Availability (OPA), Acquisition Support (ACQ), and Defensive Systems (DEF) markets are expected to grow in emphasis most rapidly; Naval Special Warfare (NSW), Anti-Air Warfare (AAW), Missions of State–Non-combat Operations (MOS–NCO), Offensive Mine Warfare (OMW), and Mobility (MOB) are expected to grow in emphasis the least.

We next wanted to know how the results will alter with changes among the market-emphasis-growth drivers. To test the sensitivity of our results, we evaluated what the market-emphasis-growth factors would be if the technology or strategy drivers were weighted as being 1.5 times more important in

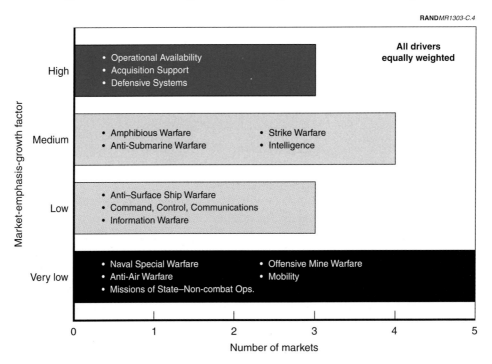

RANDMR1303-C.4

NOTE: The following binning decisions represent thresholds for the total normalized value of all market scoring, based on the apparent separation of percentage bands that came out of the analysis:

     High ~ 13.8–10.6 percent
     Medium ~ 10–8.5 percent
     Low ~ 5.8–4.3 percent
     Very low ~ 2.7–0 percent

Figure C.4—NAVSEA Market-Emphasis-Growth Factors, with Equivalent Weights for All Drivers

forecasting NAVSEA market-emphasis growth. We felt that a 150-percent weighting was a reasonable variation, whereas a factor-of-2 increase for any of the driver categories was not: The importance of one driver category was considered close to that of the others. For a 150-percent weighting of the technology drivers, Figure C.5 shows that, assuming NAVSEA markets to be predominantly technology-driven, the DEF and ACQ markets will be the only markets growing rapidly in emphasis, whereas the NSW, AAW, MOS–NCO, MOB, ASU, and OMW markets will remain very low in growth in emphasis. The OPA market is now at a Medium emphasis-growth level. This sensitivity to technology emphasis reveals that the DEF and ACQ markets have a technology emphasis, whereas the emphasis of the OPA market is only weakly coupled to technology.

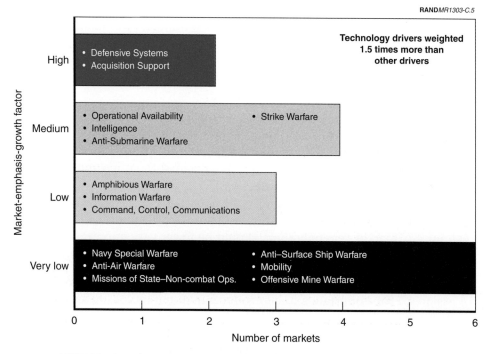

NOTE: The following binning decisions represent thresholds for the total normalized value of all market scoring, based on the apparent separation of percentage bands that came out of the analysis:

      High ~ 15–13.1 percent
      Medium ~ 9.9–9.6 percent
      Low ~ 7.7–5.9 percent
      Very low ~ 3.9–0 percent

Figure C.5—NAVSEA Market-Emphasis-Growth Factors, with Technology Drivers Weighted 1.5 Times Higher Than Other Drivers

Consider next the sensitivity of the results to a 150-percent weighting in emphasis for the strategy drivers, calculated in Table C.1 and shown in Figure C.6. Here, the DEF and ACQ markets have remained High, given a strategic emphasis, and the intelligence (INT) market has moved into the High category as well. The OPA market has moved to the Medium level, whereas NSW, MOS–NCO, OMW, MOB, and AAW have remained Very Low. The Anti-Submarine Warfare (ASW), Strike Warfare (STW), and Amphibious (AMW) markets remain at a Medium growth rate.

The case for four strategy drivers is calculated in Table C.2 and shown in Figure C.7 for comparison with Table C.1 and Figure C.6. We see that Defensive Systems is the only market rated High when there were only four drivers. The Low category is highly populated, and the Very Low category is less populated. The mix of markets in each category is markedly different from that in Figure C.6. The four ranking categories were assigned numbers for quantification of market interactions with product measures: High = 3, Medium = 2, Low =1, Very Low = 0.

THE RAND PRODUCT-RATING SYSTEM

Just as one set of drivers can be identified as having more influence than another on market-emphasis growth in 2007, certain products may be more important to a market than others are. We decided to go beyond the binary ranking, which indicates that those NAVSEA products that contribute to a market have equal importance—a rank of 1. Our many years of market research and the technique known as Quality Function Deployment (QFD)[2] indicate that, for any market generally there should be fewer very important products than those that are just important.

Most of the products in a market will be supporting or not very important at all. To assign a 1 for importance to all products in a market fails to take into account those products the customer values most highly. Therefore, we needed to build into the analysis this imbalance in a consistent and quantifiable way. A rating system that accommodates a "normal distribution" while indicating the outstanding quality of specific products is what we sought.

---

[2]Originally developed by a Japanese shipbuilding firm in the early 1970s, "Quality Function Deployment (QFD), also known as The House of Quality, . . . tie[s] product and service design decisions directly to customer wants and needs, ... QFD is designed to deploy customer input throughout the design, production, marketing, and delivery facets of a given product or service. In a typical QFD application, a cross-functional team creates and analyzes a matrix linking customer wants and needs to a set of product and service design metrics that the company can then measure and control" (see www.ams-inc.com/whatwedo/qfd, downloaded December 21, 2001; www.ams-inc.com/whatwedo/qtd.htm, visited August 4, 2002). QFD uses a scale of 9 for High importance; 3 for Medium importance; 1 for Low importance; and 0 for no importance.

Table C.1

Normalization of Scores for the Case of 10 Strategy Drivers Weighted at 1.5 Times the Other Drivers

Market	Strategy Drivers (10 drivers)			Technology Drivers (7 drivers)		Business Drivers (4 drivers)		Normalized Total, All Drivers	Percent of Total[b] and Rank
	Total Impact	Weighting at 1.5 times	Normalization Factor (2.1)[a]	Total Impact	Normalization Factor (3)[a]	Total Impact	Normalization Factor (5.25)[a]		
AAW	2	3	6.3	0	0	0	0	6.3	2.48 VL
AMW	8	12	25.2	0	0	0	0	25.2	9.92 M
ASU	4	6	12.6	0	0	0	0	12.6	4.96 L
ASW	6	9	18.9	2	6	0	0	24.9	9.80 M
CCC	2	3	6.3	2	6	0	0	12.3	4.85 L
IW	4	6	12.6	1	3	0	0	15.6	6.14 L
INT	8	12	25.2	1	3	0	0	28.2	11.11 H
OPA	0	0	0	0	0	4	21.0	21.0	8.26 M
OMW	1	1.5	3.15	1	3	0	0	6.15	2.42 VL
MOB	0	0	0	0	0	1	5.25	5.25	2.07 VL
MOS–NCO	2	3	6.3	0	0	0	0	6.3	2.48 VL
ACQ	4	6	12.6	1	3	3	15.75	31.35	12.34 H
NSW	0	0	0	0	0	0	0	0	0.0 VL
STW	6	9	18.9	2	6	0	0	24.9	9.80 M
DEF	7	10.5	22.05	4	12	0	0	34.05	13.40 H
TOTAL								254.1	

[a] The normalization factor was calculated as follows: 10 strategy drivers + 7 technology drivers + 4 business drivers = 21 drivers. The total number of drivers was divided by the number of drivers in each category to obtain the factor: 21/10 = 2.1 for strategy; 21/7 = 3 for technology; and 21/4 = 5.25 for business.

[b] The percent of total is the total for the individual market divided by the total for all markets. For example, for DEF, 34.05/254.1 = 13.4 percent, which places it in the High (H) rank.

RAND*MR1303-TC.1*

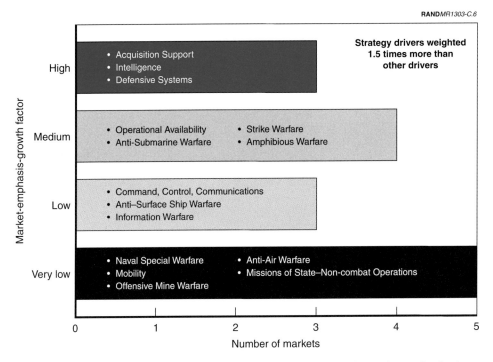

RAND*MR1303-C.6*

NOTE: The following binning decisions represent thresholds for the total normalized value of all market scoring, based on the apparent separation of percentage bands that came out of the analysis:

High ~ 13.4–11.1 percent
Medium ~ 9.9–8.3 percent
Low ~ 6.2–4.9 percent
Very low ~ 2.5–0 percent

Figure C.6—NAVSEA Market-Emphasis-Growth Factors for the Case with 10 Strategy Drivers Weighted 1.5 Times Higher Than Other Drivers

We consider here all products in the market, not just the ones that NAVSEA supplies. Our final assessments are based on our own expertise and on commentary during our NAVSEA site visits.

Agreeing that the very important products are fewer in number than the least important ones, we rejected the notion that the products have a flat frequency distribution across importance, as illustrated in Figure C.8. The figure shows a notional flat distribution normalized for a range of importance between 0 and 3, corresponding to three uniform sections—Low, Medium, and High—all with an equal frequency represented by equal areas. Markets that use products that are not highly differentiated from each other (for example, commodity [products of broad use] markets or some consumer-product markets) could be

Table C.2
Normalization of Scores for Four Strategy Drivers Weighted at 1.5 Times the Other Drivers, for Comparison with Table C.1

Market	Strategy Drivers (4 drivers)			Technology Drivers (7 drivers)		Business Drivers (4 drivers)		Normalized Total, All Drivers	Percent of Total[b] and Rank
	Total Impact	Weighting at 1.5 times	Normalization Factor (3.75)[a]	Total Impact	Normalization Factor (2.143)[a]	Total Impact	Normalization Factor (3.75)[a]		
AAW	0	0	0	0	0	0	0	0	0.0 VL
AMW	2	3	11.25	0	0	0	0	11.25	6.98 L
ASU	0	0	0	0	0	0	0	0	0.0 VL
ASW	0	0	0	2	4.286	0	0	4.286	2.66 L
CCC	1	1.5	5.625	2	4.286	0	0	9.911	6.15 L
IW	1	1.5	5.625	1	2.143	0	0	7.768	4.82 L
INT	2	3	11.25	1	2.143	0	0	13.393	8.31 M
OPA	1	1.5	5.625	0	0	4	15.0	20.625	12.79 M
OMW	1	1.5	5.625	1	2.143	0	0	7.768	4.82 L
MOB	2	3	11.25	0	0	1	3.75	15.0	9.3 M
MOS–NCO	1	1.5	5.625	0	0	0	0	5.625	3.49 VL
ACQ	0	0	0	1	2.143	3	11.25	13.39	8.3 M
NSW	3	4.5	16.875	0	0	0	0	16.875	10.47 M
STW	1	1.5	5.625	2	4.286	0	0	9.911	6.15 L
DEF	3	4.5	16.875	4	8.57	0	0	25.445	15.8 H
TOTAL								161.25	

[a] The normalization factor was calculated as follows: 4 strategy drivers + 7 technology drivers + 4 business drivers = 15 drivers. The total number of drivers was divided by the number of drivers in each category to obtain the factor: 15/4 = 3.75 for strategy; 15/7 = 2.143 for technology; and 15/4 = 3.75 for business.

[b] The percent of total is the total for the individual market divided by the total for all markets. For example, for DEF, 25.445/161.25 = 15.8 percent, which places it in the High (H) category.

RAND*MR1303-TC.2*

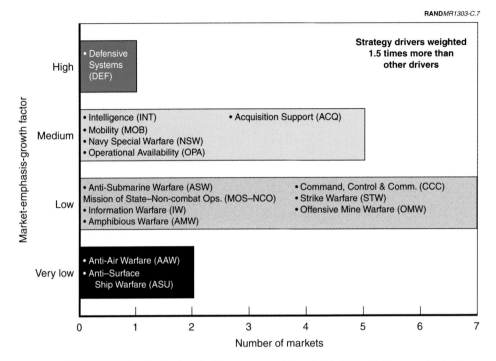

Figure C.7—NAVSEA Market-Emphasis-Growth Factors for the Case with Only Four Strategy Drivers Weighted 1.5 Times Higher Than Other Drivers

structured this way. However, for the high-tech markets, such as Anti-Submarine Warfare (ASW) or Naval Special Warfare (NSW), the products are likely to be very highly differentiated. This reality informs our inclination to make High importance products of lesser frequency than the Low importance products.

We embraced, instead, the notion that the frequency distribution is lower at the High end and higher for the Low end of the importance scale, and considered the next simplest distribution to a flat distribution: the triangle distribution. This distribution has a frequency maximum at the origin and intercepts zero at some maximum-importance value, which we take to be 3 to simplify comparisons with other distributions, in Figure C.9. As for the flat distribution, the

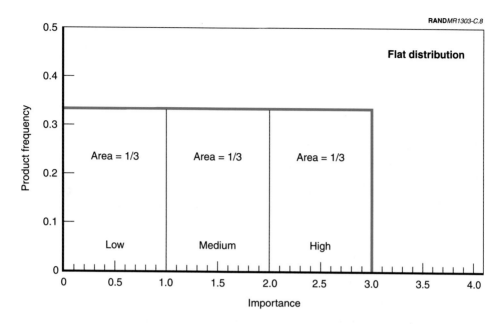

Figure C.8—Product Frequency Versus Importance for a Flat Distribution. Equal thirds of total area correspond to Low, Medium, and High ranks.

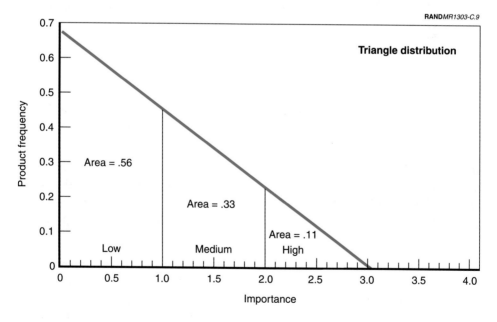

Figure C.9—Product Frequency Versus Importance for a Triangle Distribution. Intervals of equal thirds correspond to Low, Medium, and High ranks.

Low, Medium, and High importance frequency elements have been normalized to 1 and the importance interval is between 0 and 3, which we have divided equally. There is no rationale for doing a nonlinear division. Consequently, areas decline in magnitude with increasing importance—behavior we have sought. From the figure, the normalized area for the Low importance products is 0.56, which means that 56 percent of the products in the market will be in the Low importance category, whereas the High importance category will have 11 percent of the products, and the Medium category will have 33 percent of the products.

We consider next a Gaussian distribution for the product frequency as a function of importance, assuming that, since many groups of things seem to be normally distributed, the importance frequency for products in a market may be as well. In such a distribution, shown in Figure C.10, the normalized frequency of product importance is plotted as a function of importance, with the standard deviation, σ, of the Gaussian equal to 1. As before, the figure shows the Low, Medium, and High importance areas taken to be 1σ, 2σ, and 3σ, since there is no rationale for assigning some nonlinear scaling for these intervals. For the importance ratings in this model, the Low importance products represent 68 percent of the products in the market and the High importance products, only 5 percent.

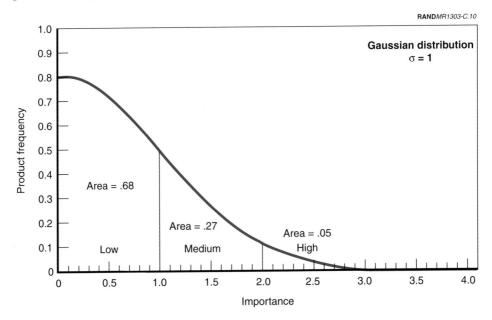

Figure C.10—Product Frequency Versus Importance for a Gaussian Distribution. Intervals of equal thirds correspond to Low, Medium, and High ranks.

Using this distribution, we can see a way in which our bias toward more Low importance products and fewer High importance products in a highly differentiated market can be introduced in a consistent fashion. However, in our rankings of products, we wanted to achieve some additional characteristics in the rating process: first, a large rating for High importance products and a larger distance in rating between High and Medium than between Medium and Low; second, to adjust down the ratings of experts.

To achieve both of these objectives, the research team sought a distribution function for which the inverse of its areas would be the importance rating and for which the sum of the inverses for the three areas would be normalized to 1 for easy comparison among different choices of distribution function.

We can now ask, What distribution and what rating-area sizes correspond to the old 1, 2, 3 system—1 for Low importance, 2 for Medium importance, and 3 for High importance—with which we were dissatisfied initially? The data in Figure C.11 are presented for comparison of normalized rating areas for the four distribution functions considered—flat, triangle, Gaussian, and 1, 2, 3 weights, plotted as a function of the importance bin. Unlike the flat distribution with its 0.33 frequency for all bins, the Gaussian curve shows a very steep transition from the Low bin to the High bin. The simple triangle distribution shows a uniform transition in areas from Low to High importance, and the 1, 2, 3 weights is somewhere between the Gaussian and the triangle distributions.

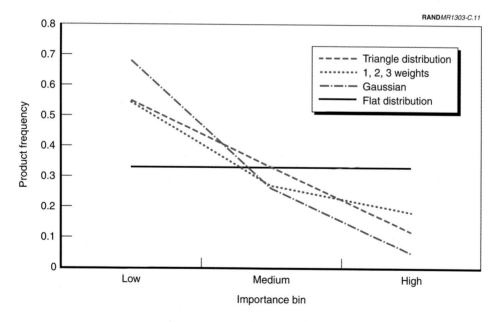

Figure C.11—Comparing Distribution Area with Importance Bin for the Distributions Considered

We next considered what market structure was appropriate for the highly differentiated markets to which the NAVSEA products contribute. After some discussion, we agreed that having about two-thirds of the products in the market in the Low importance bin seemed about right, as did having about 11 or 12 percent of the products in the High importance bin. This leaves about 22 percent for the area of the Medium importance bin. The resulting areas are plotted in Figure C.12, along with the distributions shown in Figure C.11. The area for the Low importance bin (67 percent) for the new distribution—the RAND distribution—is consistent with the Gaussian distribution area for this bin; however, the area for the High importance bin is consistent with that for the triangle distribution. The area for the Medium importance bin is lower than that for all the distributions considered.

Where does all this lead for the importance ratings for the various distributions? Beginning with the basic assumption that the importance rating is proportional to the inverse of the importance-bin area in the frequency-distribution function and keeping all the ratings normalized for easy comparison, we arrived at the results shown in Figure C.13, in which the importance ratings of the RAND distribution weights have a slope steeper than that for the 1, 2, 3 weights, as required by our feel for the market. The RAND distribution is not as steep as is the Gaussian distribution, which we considered too extreme from the outset.

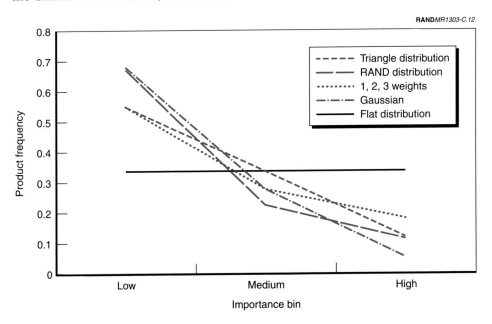

Figure C.12—Adding a New Comparison to the Set: the RAND Distribution

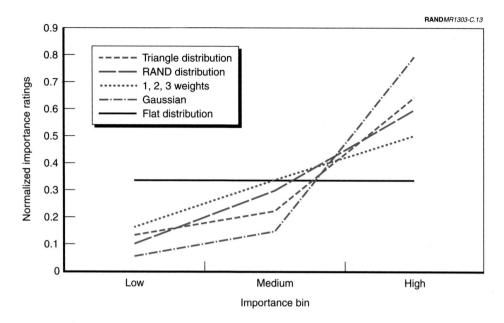

RANDMR1303-C.13

Figure C.13—Normalized Importance Ratings Versus Importance Bin for All Distributions

The resulting importance rates for the NAVSEA products in the various markets are 0.1 for Low importance; 0.3 for Medium importance; and 0.6 for High importance.

To facilitate the rating process for the individuals doing the rating, we multiplied the results by 10: 1, Low importance; 3, Medium importance; 6, High importance. To further emphasize the point of the ratings, we adopted the following operational definitions of what each of the ratings means for the market—different terminology but essentially the same meaning:

6 = Market Defining. An essential product in the market. The market would not exist or function at all without this product. The product is an essential definer of the market.

3 = Important. A major contributor to the market. The market depends on this product, but the product does not define the market.

1 = Support. Contributes to the market, but not a major contributor.

0 = Not Important. Does not contribute to the market.

These are the values given for specific product importance in the Product-Market Interactions section of Chapter Three and this appendix and again in the Corporate Centrality section of Chapter Three.

NAVSEA ACTIVITIES AND CLASSIFICATION SCHEMES FOR THE ACTIVITIES DATABASE

As well as developing rating systems to relate the importance and breadth of products to markets, our analysis of NAVSEA products involved developing classification schemes to relate activities to products.

The Activity portion of Figure 3.1 comprises organized resources, such as technologies, people, and facilities. These resources are set in motion by processes. One of many components of a product or system, an activity is the basis for the creation of products. We needed to compile a database that would contain all activities making up a product for all 108 products in 2007 in Table 3.5.

To build the database of NAVSEA activities, the research team started with the *Core Equities—Red Team Review* (NAVSEA, 1999a) as initial input. How NAVSEA reported its activities varies across units. For this reason, and because the Product-Market-Activity Model focuses not within a center, as does the Core Equities study, but *across* NAVSEA, we reformulated this list of activities in which NAVSEA will have to engage in 2007 iteratively and interactively, with the aid of information gathered from the 38 site visits to NAVSEA units and NAVSEA's customers (see Appendix A) conducted as part of this research. Information on those activities became part of our activities database, described below. In many cases, we were able to connect an activity to the organized resources currently carrying out the tasks associated with that activity, as in Figure C.14.

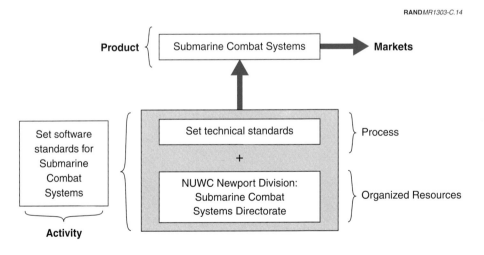

Figure C.14—The Classification Systems for the RAND Market-Product-Activity Model, for the Activity "Set software standards for Submarine Combat Systems"

The *Red Team Review* included little data regarding support activities, such as human resources, facilities management, and administrative support activities, for the majority of NAVSEA units. These important support functions are part of the sizing analysis that was to have been included in Chapter Four.

We developed an activities database for all NAVSEA products, using EXCEL spreadsheets. Every entry in the activities database has associated with it a product, a facility/organization, and a process code. Each activity is linked to the product associated with the output of the activity. As seen below, an activity that produces software standards for a Submarine Combat System is linked to that system rather than to software standards, thereby keeping the entire life cycle of a product under a single code. The research team chose to focus on system-level products (e.g., Submarine Combat Systems) rather than on platforms (e.g., submarines), because, at the system level, the team could separate activities into a manageable set of products while providing enough differences in coding to enable meaningful analysis across activities and avoiding too much detail. Limitations in available data made it impossible to generate accurate subsystem product lists. Therefore, system-level coding was also superior to subsystems coding.

Through activities, the product is linked with technologies, people, and facilities. Thus, all characteristics required to describe and analyze the NAVSEA activities are available and linked. An example of how all these characteristics fit together is shown in Figure C.14, in which the root activity being considered is "Setting software standards for submarine combat systems."

This activity, just one of many that contribute to the product, is characterized by process 4.4.4—"Set technical standards"—performed by the organized resources of the Submarine Combat Systems Directorate of NUWC Newport Division. It is also characterized by the resulting product—Submarine Combat Systems.

Links to the required technology, people, and facilities are created through the process code.

RAND Process Code

The research team developed the RAND process code classification scheme, using several sources (American Productivity & Quality Center, 2000). However, it owes much of its overall structure to the Government Process Classification Scheme (GPCS; Inter-Agency Benchmarking & Best Practices Council, 1996), a coding system developed by the GPCS Consortium, which was created by the National Performance Review, Office of the Vice President, and the Inter-

Agency Benchmarking & Best Practices Council. The GPCS was intended as a tool that government organizations would use to classify their processes, manage their organization's work more effectively, and increase use of best practices through greater inter-agency sharing of lessons learned. We chose this coding scheme to underpin our code primarily because it was designed for use by public-sector organizations, and because of its comprehensiveness and adaptability.

After testing the GPCS on sample NAVSEA activities, the team found that NAVSEA's role as a manager of technology research, provider of ship repair and maintenance, and furnisher of the acquisition support base produced a number of activities that did not fit the original GPCS structure. The code required further adaptation to better reflect the scope and focus of work done by NAVSEA. For example, the GPCS's "Conduct Research and Development" code captured part of those NAVSEA activities that center on developing and managing technology; however, a coding system better able to distinguish between the different types of work being done was needed. Modifying the GPCS by adding process codes gleaned from other Navy documents provided this particularity. Especially helpful was a Naval Surface Warfare Center (NSWC) working draft (NSWC, 1998) created to identify that agency's technical capabilities. It includes an appendix that sets forth the major functions by life cycle. We adopted slightly modified forms of many of those functions as part of the RAND process code.

We also examined process classification systems that were focused primarily on private-sector organizations; however, we adapted those parts of the systems that were applicable to NAVSEA. Arthur Andersen & Co. and the American Productivity & Quality Center's International Benchmarking Clearinghouse (2000) developed a taxonomy of common business processes known as the "Process Classification Framework," an important source for the RAND process code. The Process Classification Framework was particularly helpful in identifying processes that involve interactions with clients, and we incorporated those processes into the RAND process code to enhance the scope of the GPCS code.

As detailed in Table C.3, the RAND process code has several levels of detail that capture what is being accomplished. The following are the major categories of processes considered in our code to cover the complete life cycle of a product:

1. Establish direction.

2. Acquire and manage resources.

3. Develop capabilities.

4. Execute agency's mission.

5. Sustain field operations.

Generally, the structure of this classification system is to plan, gather the needed resources, produce the needed product or service, and, finally, to maintain customer contact and reconsider new planning initiatives.

Application of the RAND process code has two minor limitations:

1. Its level of depth is irregular, varying from one to four levels (see Table C.3). For example, the section of the code dealing with new-product development provides many levels of processes below that of "Design Products and/or Services" (4.5); the part of the code covering budget-related processes does not go deeper than "Budget programs" (1.4). In all cases, the level of detail covered by the RAND process code was adequate for classifying NAVSEA activities relevant to products that are the focus of our analysis.

2. In some cases, two or more codes cover similar types of work. Left unchecked, this anomaly can cause the coding to vary for activities that involve identical types of work. We attempted to overcome this problem by having coders agree to use one code for each type of work. All coding was then reviewed to limit the variance across coders.

RAND NAVSEA Organization Database

Each activity is listed by the current NAVSEA unit responsible for performing that activity: for example, the Naval Undersea Warfare Center (NUWC), Naval Surface Warfare Center, Navstar Operation Center (NOC), Headquarters/PEOs, Supervisor of Shipbuilding (SUPSHIP), Newport News Navy Shipyard, etc., and their units (see Appendix A for a partial list). We attached a numeric code to each unit in the NAVSEA organization chart. When we were unable to identify the unit associated with an activity, we left this field of the database blank. In addition, all new activities fall into this blank category.

DERIVATION OF TECHNOLOGY CLUSTERS AND TECHNOLOGIES FOR THE TECHNOLOGIES DATABASE

The next level of database below the activities database encompasses databases on technology, personnel, and facilities. Part of the process of developing the technology database involved organizing inputs into a manageable form. In its assessment of technologies of value and concern to NAVSEA, the research team

Table C.3

RAND Process Code

1	Establish Direction		3	Develop Capabilities
1.1	Establish Policy		3.1	Provide admin. support services
1.1.1	Assess current macro environment		3.1.1	Inform & advise
1.1.2	Establish priorities		3.1.2	Provide electronic information systems
1.1.3	Establish strategies		3.1.3	Provide financial services
1.1.4	Establish safety specifications		3.1.4	Provide facility services
1.2	Determine Requirements/Needs		3.1.5	Provide community services
1.2.1	Evaluate current performance		3.1.6	Provide personnel services
1.2.2	Develop regulations		3.2	Develop resources into capabilities
1.2.3	Structure the organization		3.2.1	Organize resources
1.2.4	Establish resource requirements		3.2.2	Integrate physical and human resources
1.3	Develop Plans		3.2.3	Train personnel (includes curriculum development)
1.3.1	Identify missions, goals, etc.		3.2.3.1	Approve DAWIA certification
1.3.2	Develop courses of action & schedules		3.2.4	Assess performance readiness of resources
1.3.3	Develop operational & emergency plans		3.2.5	Manage improvement and change
1.3.4	Deploy policy/plans		3.3	Enhance/Upgrade capabilities
1.4	Budget Programs		3.3.1	Measure organizational performance
1.4.1	Develop programs/budgets		3.3.2	Conduct quality assessments
1.4.2	Consolidate and prioritize program requirements		3.3.3	Benchmark performance
1.4.3	Balance programs/budgets & Justify to higher authority		3.3.4	Conduct research to improve capabilities
			3.3.5	Design improved capabilities
2	Acquire & Manage Resources		3.3.6	Improve processes and systems
2.1	Manage Acquisitions of Organization's Resources		3.3.7	Test and evaluate improved capabilities
2.1.1	Develop acquisition guidance		4	Execute Agency's Mission
2.1.2	Define & justify program		4.1	Designate office of responsibility
2.1.3	Administer Acquisition Program		4.1.1	Establish the operations structure
2.1.4	Acquire physical resources that meet acceptance criteria		4.1.2	Initiate program documents
2.1.5	Take delivery		4.1.3	Assess adherence to laws, plans, etc.
2.2	Access labor		4.1.4	Integrate resources
2.2.1	Develop hiring practices guidance and procedures		4.2	Provide operational info. Support
2.2.2	Create and manage human resources strategies		4.2.1	Collect operational information (requirements., environ.)
2.2.3	Plan and forecast workforce requirements		4.2.2	Aggregate and analyze op. information
2.2.4	Recruit, select, & hire workers		4.2.3	Provide situation assessments to decision-makers
2.3	Manage facilities		4.2.4	Provide technical advice to tactical commander
2.3.1	Manage capital planning		4.3	Identify & market customer requirements
2.3.2	Acquire and redeploy fixed assets		4.3.1	Determine customer needs and wants
2.3.3	Construct facilities		4.3.2	Conduct qualitative assessments
2.3.4	Manage physical risk		4.3.3	Conduct quantitative assessments
2.4	Support Resources		4.3.4	Predict Customer wants and needs
2.4.1	Maintain Resources		4.4	Develop & Manage Technology
2.4.2	Transport personnel & material		4.4.1	Sponsor work on defense-related technology
2.4.3	Manage natural resources		4.4.2	Establish parameters for technical feasibility
2.4.4	Release Personnel and assets from government control			

RAND*MR1303-TC.3a*

Table C.3—Cont'd.

4.4.3	Maintain corporate knowledge base		4.5.4.2	Monitor laboratory & field tests
4.4.4	Set technical standards		4.5.4.3	Perform testing
4.4.5	Control technical documentation & configuration management		4.5.4.4	Evaluate test results
			4.5.4.5	Approve processes, material to ensure producilbility
4.4.6	Exchange technical information		4.5.4.6	Assess technical problems that arise
4.4.7	Perform basic research		4.5.5	Prepare for production
4.4.8	Perform applied research		4.5.5.1	Develop and test prototype production process
4.4.9	Perform advanced research			
4.4.10	Perform technology scan & identify promising technology		4.5.5.2	Approve technical problem resolution
4.4.11	Evaluate technical feasibility of proposals		4.5.5.3	Design and obtain necessary material and equipment
4.4.12	Develop operational guidelines for technology use		4.5.5.4	Install and verify processes
			4.6	Market & sell
4.4.13	Transfer technology		4.6.1	Market products and/or services to customer group
4.5	Design Products and/or Services			
4.5.1	Develop product/service concept & plans		4.6.1.1	Define product/service value
4.5.1.1	Translate customer wants into product requirements		4.6.1.2	Develop pricing structure
			4.6.1.3	Develop marketing message
4.5.1.2	Develop ship/system concept		4.6.1.4	Identify target customers
4.5.1.3	Perform feasibility studies to refine system concept		4.6.1.5	Sell product/service
			4.6.1.6	Negotiate terms of sale
4.5.1.4	Evaluate & approve system concept		4.6.2	Process Customer orders
4.5.1.5	Plan and deploy quality targets		4.6.2.1	Accept orders from customers
4.5.1.6	Plan and deploy cost targets; validate estimates		4.6.2.2	Enter orders into production/delivery system
4.5.1.7	Develop product life cycle targets		4.7	Produce & deliver products/services
4.5.1.8	Approve life cycle planning		4.7.1	Acquire material and technology for production
4.5.1.9	Request & Evaluate bids			
4.5.1.10	Award & monitor contracts, Source Selection		4.7.1.1	Select and certify suppliers
			4.7.1.2	Purchase capital goods
4.5.1.11	Integrate leading technology (Tech. Insertion)		4.7.1.3	Purchase materials and supplies
			4.7.1.4	Acquire appropriate technology
4.5.1.12	Manage technical maturity risks		4.7.2	Convert resources/inputs into products
4.5.1.13	Develop product specs with approved trade-offs		4.7.2.1	Develop/adjust production process
4.5.2	Design, build, evaluate prototype products		4.7.2.2	Schedule production
4.5.2.1	Conduct concurrent engineering		4.7.2.3	Move materials and resources
4.5.2.2	Implement value engineering		4.7.2.4	Make product
4.5.2.3	Document design specifications		4.7.2.5	Test & validate system performance
4.5.2.4	Develop prototypes		4.7.2.6	Package product
4.5.2.5	Evaluate prototype		4.7.2.7	Warehouse/store product
4.5.2.6	Apply for patents		4.7.2.8	Stage products for delivery
4.5.3	Refine existing products/services; Modernize & Upgrade		4.7.3	Deliver products
			4.7.3.1	Arrange product delivery
4.5.3.1	Develop product/service enhancements		4.7.3.2	Deliver product to customer
4.5.3.2	Eliminate quality/reliability problems		4.7.3.3	Install product
4.5.3.3	Eliminate outdated products/services		4.7.3.4	Perform system integration
4.5.4	Test effectiveness of products		4.7.4	Manage production & delivery processes
4.5.4.1	Establish testing and acceptance plan		4.7.4.1	Document and monitor order status

Table C.3—Cont'd.

4.7.4.2	Manage inventories		4.8.2.4	Provide the service to customer
4.7.4.3	Ensure product quality		4.8.2.5	Perform system improvements and retrofits
4.7.4.4	Schedule and perform maintenance			
4.7.4.5	Monitor environmental constraints		4.8.2.6	Perform overhauls and rework
4.7.5	Deliver Service to customers		4.8.2.7	Investigate and fix system failures
4.7.5.1	Confirm specific service requirements		4.8.2.8	Document maintenance
4.7.5.2	Design strategy to meet customer requirements		4.8.3	Manage customer feedback
			4.8.3.1	Respond to information requests
4.7.5.3	Identify and schedule resources for service		4.8.3.2	Manage customer complaints
4.7.5.4	Schedule service		4.8.3.3	Monitor satisfaction with product/service
4.7.5.5	Provide the service to customer		4.8.3.4	Monitor satisfaction with complaint resolution
4.7.5.6	Develop and deploy training hardware			
4.7.5.7	Conduct user training		4.8.3.5	Monitor satisfaction with communications
4.8	Invoice and service customer			
4.8.1	Bill the customer		4.9	Evaluate program against objectives
4.8.1.1	Develop, deliver, and maintain customer billing		4.9.1	Assess technical test results
			4.9.2	Assess deviations and waivers
4.8.1.2	Invoice the customer		4.9.3	Assess program cost, schedule, & performance
4.8.1.3	Respond to billing inquiries			
4.8.2	Provide post-delivery service		4.9.4	Assess environmental & safety compliance
4.8.2.1	Confirm service requirements for customer		5	Sustain field operations
			5.1	Maintain material
4.8.2.2	Identify and schedule resources for service		5.2	Sustain people
4.8.2.3	Schedule service		5.3	Resupply operational assets

RAND*MR1303-TC.3c*

used the extensive review of technologies, and the capabilities they enabled, done by the Naval Studies Board of the National Research Council (NSB–NRC, 1997a, pp. 42–51, especially Table 6.1). The NSB considered technologies under development not only by the Navy but also by all branches of the military, by the Defense Advanced Research Projects Agency (DARPA), and by industry. We evaluated over 100 technologies, which we grouped into 10 technology clusters. These technology clusters and the operational capability they enable or influence are shown in Figure C.15.

There is not a one-to-one correspondence between technology clusters and product groups or technologies. Technology clusters are more analogous to activities, a combination of many of which goes into the making of one discrete product and a different combination of which goes into the making of another discrete product. A combination of many of the technologies go into a separate, discrete activity and, in turn, that activity combines with other activities to form different products.

For example, the revolutions in electronics, computation, and information systems contribute significantly to the new capabilities from network-centric

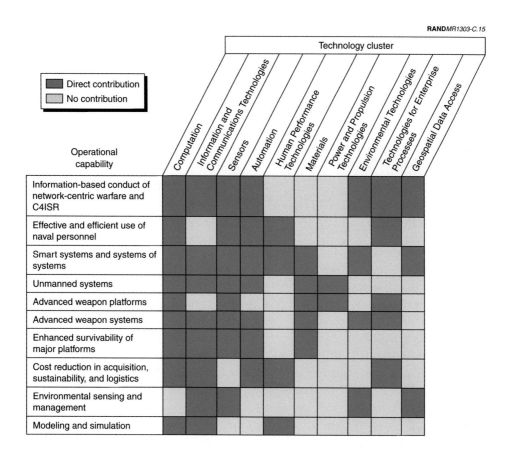

Figure C.15—Technology Clusters That Contribute to Operational Capability

warfare through effective and efficient use of personnel to cost reduction in acquisition. Advances in materials science will enable a new generation of designer materials for naval applications. The advances in power and propulsion technologies will transform the manner in which ships are made mobile, and the revolutions in the enterprise-management technologies will enable a new and more efficient ship-based and shore-based Navy. From the Strategy phase of the research (Chapter Two), we know that many of the capabilities enabled by these technology clusters will be needed in 2007 to respond to the changing geopolitical situation. The enabling technologies for operational capabilities provided detailed guidance to the research team in determining the role of technology in the NAVSEA products.

All technologies associated with Navy nuclear reactors were excluded from this analysis by specific request.[3]

Within each of the 10 technology clusters are about 10 more-specific technologies (see Table C.4) that enable detailed analysis of those NAVSEA products that could use them. Through these more-detailed technologies, we gauged the technology change that could be anticipated for the NAVSEA products. In addition, these technologies can be ranked according to importance to NAVSEA products and are ranked later in this appendix.

DERIVATION OF OCCUPATIONAL CLUSTERS AND JOB TITLES FOR THE PERSONNEL DATABASE

NAVSEA employs almost 45,000 people in 319 occupations. As with technologies, these numbers required aggregation into fewer, more manageable groupings, according to certain commonalities. We refer to such groupings here as *occupational clusters*. We used the occupational clusters derived in prior RAND work (Levy et al., 2001), which combined several occupational systems, including the U.S. Office of Personnel Management (OPM) Occupational Series (General Schedule, GS) and Occupations (Federal Wage Grade, FWG); the Department of Labor Net Occupations, to provide crosswalks to the OPM Occupational Series and Occupations and information about knowledge, skills, abilities, work context, and generalized work activities; and the Military Occupational Training Database System, to include task lists and crosswalks. All OPM Occupational Series and Occupations were reduced to a total of 39 occupational clusters.

OPM Occupations and Occupational Series were assigned to a particular cluster on the basis of commonality (clustering) of knowledge, skill, and ability profiles, across over 100 dimensions (for example, number with advanced degrees, those with knowledge of launchers or life-cycle cost analysis). NAVSEA has employees in 32 of the 39 RAND occupational clusters. Throughout the remainder of this appendix, we refer to *occupational clusters* to reflect the aggregation of NAVSEA personnel into these 32 RAND occupational clusters and to *job titles* to reflect OPM Occupational Series or Occupations.

---

[3]The scope of this study did not include the Navy nuclear program, which is a separate organization that reports to the Chief of Naval Operations and Commander of NAVSEA. Consequently, technologies having to do with Navy nuclear reactors have been omitted. This omission will bias the analysis to de-emphasize job titles such as "Nuclear Engineer" or "Health Physics Services." Although the technology and facilities needed for Navy reactors are rich and varied, none of them is included in this analysis.

Table C.4

NAVSEA Technologies

Computation
- High-performance computing
- Functional low-cost computing
- Micro electronics
- Systems-on-a-chip micro and nano technology
- Data storage
- Digital-analog signal processing
- Air flow modeling
- Water flow modeling

Information and communications technology
- Networking
- Distributed collaboration
- Software engineering
- Communications
- Geospatial information processing
- Information visualization
- Human-centered systems
- Intelligent systems
- Planning and decision aids
- Defensive and offensive information warfare

Sensors
- Electromagnetic—radar; optical (IR VIS, UV)
- Acoustic—sonar, seismic-vibration
- Inertial-gravimetric
- Chemical
- Biological
- Nuclear
- Environmental
- Time

Automation
- UUVs
- UAVs
- Robots
- Navigation
- Guidance
- Automatic target recognition
- Ship subsystems automation

Human performance technologies
- Communications, information processing, health care, biotechnology and genetics, and cognitive processes as applied to education and training
- Operational performance of personnel
- Health and safety
- Quality of life

Materials
- Computer-designed materials
- Materials with specifically designed mechanical and physical properties
- Functionally adaptive materials
- Structural materials
- High-temperature engine materials
- Specialty materials—superconductive, organic coatings, adhesives, energetic materials

Power and propulsion technologies
- Electric power
- Engines and motors
- High-temperature superconductors
- Pulsed and short-duration power—batteries, flywheels, superconducting magnetic energy storage, explosively driven MHD
- Energy storage and recovery systems—rechargeable batteries, fuel cells
- Microelectronic power controls and power electronic building blocks—PEBBs
- Primary propulsion
- Gun-tube projectile propulsion
- Rockets
- Air-breathing missile propulsion
- Ship, aircraft, and ground vehicle engines

Environmental technologies
- Weather modeling and prediction—space, atmosphere, ocean
- Oceanography and oceanographic modeling
- Ship environmental pollution control—waste minimization
- Shipboard waste processing
- Hazardous materials handling
- Noise modification

Technologies for enterprise processes
- Modeling and simulation
- Simulation-based system design and acquisition
- Rapid prototyping
- Agile manufacturing
- Logistics management
- Resource planning
- Dynamic mission planning
- Simulated theater of war
- Systems engineering
- Cognitive process modeling

RAND*MR1303-TC.4*

Of the 32 occupational clusters in which NAVSEA currently has staff, the top 15 clusters represent 99 percent of the total staff—44,046 of 44,511 individuals in all. NAVSEA provided a file for all civilian employees by grade, series or occupation, and organizational assignment. To simplify our analysis, the RAND team used these data to align the NAVSEA personnel with the RAND occupational clusters. The research team focused the analysis on the top 15 occupational clusters in which NAVSEA currently has staff, shown in Figure C.16.

With about 17,000 positions representing almost 40 percent of all of NAVSEA, the Scientists and Engineers cluster is the largest cluster in NAVSEA. After Administrative personnel, most of the remaining staff at NAVSEA are distributed in clusters closely associated with engineering and heavy construction.

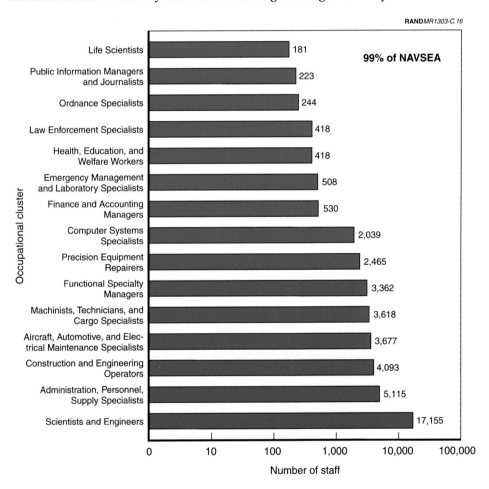

Figure C.16—Number of NAVSEA Staff in the Top 15 RAND Occupational Clusters

In the data that NAVSEA provided to the research team, we found that NAVSEA has a diversity of job titles within each of these clusters. To facilitate the analysis, and to ensure that it will encompass 90 percent of the most-staffed positions at NAVSEA in the most-staffed occupational clusters, we restricted titles to those that represented the top 90 percent of all titles within the cluster. Doing so resulted in about 100 total job titles in 15 occupational clusters (representing 99 percent of NAVSEA) to be analyzed. The research team determined that this was a sufficient sample to demonstrate the analytic method and to provide the necessary input for managerial decisions on actions to be taken at a high level at NAVSEA. The detailed job titles are listed in Table C.5.

For completeness, job titles associated with Navy nuclear reactors have not been excluded from the listing of such titles in the clusters. However, by specific request, the analysis does not include products that need these job titles. No statement as to their importance is made or implied in this work.

DERIVATION OF FACILITIES DATABASE

Aggregation of information for the facilities database was in many ways more straightforward than for the technologies or personnel database. The research team built a facilities list up from the Navy Laboratory–Center Coordinating Group (NLCCG, 1994), from the DoD RDT&E In-House Activities Report (FY97), and from input obtained during the many site visits to NAVSEA field activities. The research team realizes that some facilities on the resulting list used in the analysis may have been part of the closure of Philadelphia and White Oak laboratories in the year 2000, but that eventuality was not evident in the available lists. Some sources indicated that the facilities had been relocated to other active sites. Regardless of these factors and in the interest of erring on the side of inclusion rather than the exclusion, the research team included a facility on the list if it appeared on at least two current lists with no direct reference to closure.

The detailed list of facilities the research team used in the further analysis, in Table C.6, does not distinguish facilities at Carderock, Headquarters for the Navy Surface Warfare Center in Bethesda, Md., from those at Indian Head, a division of Carderock that specializes in energetic materials (i.e., explosives), for example. However, in the detailed database we built for this analysis, all information on organizational affiliation and the source of the citation is included. The database is structured with the entries in Table C.6 numbered in consecutive order (e.g., the 140-foot Towing Basin is Facility Number 1, the 24-inch and 360-inch Cavitation Channels are Facility Number 2, and the Submarine Fluid Dynamics Facility is Facility Number 31. This structure makes it a simple matter to add or remove facilities as requirements change, and the detail is sufficient for informed analysis.

Table C.5

Most-Staffed NAVSEA Job Titles Under 15 RAND Occupational Clusters (bold type)

Admin, Personnel, Supply Specialists
- Secretary Series
- Production Control Series
- General Business and Industry Series
- Miscellaneous Admin
- Miscellaneous Clerk and Assistant Series
- Equipment Specialist Series
- Management and Program Clerical and Assistance Series
- Accounting Technician Series
- Office Automation Clerical and Assistance Series
- Supply Clerical and Technician Series
- Inventory Management Series
- Materials Handling
- Procurement Clerical and Technician Series
- Mail and File Series

Aircraft, Automotive, and Electrical Maintenance Specialists
- Electrician
- Marine Machinery Mechanic
- General Facilities and Equipment Series
- ? General Maintenance and Operations Work
- Heavy Mobile Equipment Mechanic
- ? General Industrial Equipment Maintenance
- Air Conditioning Equipment Mechanic
- Production Machinery Mechanic

Computer Systems Specialists
- Computer Specialist Series
- Computer Science Series

Construction and Engineering Operators
- Pipefitting
- Rigging
- Painting
- Insulating
- Shipwright
- Crane Operating
- Fabric Working
- Wood Crafting
- Plastic Fabricating

Emergency Management and Laboratory Specialists
- Physical Science Technician Series

Finance and Accounting Managers
- Budget Analysis Series
- Accounting Series
- Financial Administration and Program Series

Functional Specialty Managers
- Management and Program Analysis Series
- Logistics Management Series
- Contracting Series
- Administrative Officer Series
- Security Administration Series
- Supply Program Management Series
- Personnel Management Series

Health, Education and Welfare Workers
- Training Instruction Series
- General Attorney Series
- Library Technician Series
- Education and Training Technician Series
- Technical Information Services Series
- Librarian Series
- Patent Attorney Series

Law Enforcement Specialists
- Police Series
- Security Clerical and Assistance Series
- General Inspection, Investigation, and Compliance Series

Life Scientists
- Health Physics Series
- General Biological Science Series

Machinists, Technicians, and Cargo Specialists
- Welding
- Shipfitting
- Machining
- Sheet Metal Mechanic
- ? General Metal Work
- Boilermaking
- Toolmaking

Table C.5—Cont'd.

Ordnance Specialists • Ordnance Equipment Mechanic • Explosives Operating **Precision Equipment Repairers** • Electronics Technician Series • Quality Assurance Series • Electronics Mechanic • Electronic Industrial Controls Mechanic **Public Information Managers and Journalists** • Technical Writing and Editing Series • Public Affairs Series • Visual Information Series • Editorial Assistance Series • General Arts and Information Series	**Scientists and Engineers** • Electronics Engineering Series • Mechanical Engineering Series • Engineering Technician • General Engineering • Nuclear Engineering Series • Naval Architecture Series • Electrical Engineering Series • Mathematics Series • Physics Series • Computer Engineering Series • Engineering and Architecture Student Trainee • Chemical Engineering Series

RAND*MR1303-TC.5 b*

? indicates a discrepancy between the job title provided by the NAVSEA staff and conventional OPM Job Titles. The closest related OPM Job Title was adopted.

INTERACTIONS WITH PRODUCTS

Corporate-level decisions are not only based on product-market interactions but depend on the characteristics of product-activity interactions evaluated at the planning time horizon. In the commercial world, such interactions involve all aspects of the activity, including associated processes and organized resources (technologies, facilities, people) and the extent to which these aspects must change to at least maintain the current product position in the marketplace.

Our method of analysis associates processes, technologies, personnel, and facilities with all the products in turn. These valuations are calculated according to how the characteristics of the components of one list, or database, interact with those of another, magnifying or diminishing a given measure, or observable.

In this section, we assess interactions of products with each of the components of the Activity portion of the Market-Product-Activity Model, presenting a separate scoring system for each component. For each interaction set, we then present the measures of these interactions, which will facilitate management decisions on actions to be taken.

Table C.6

NAVSEA Facilities

- 140-foot Towing Basin
- 24-inch and 36-inch Cavitation Channels
- Anechoic flow facility
- Circulating Water Channel
- Data and Image Processing Systems
- David Taylor Model Basin Complex
- Deep Submergence Pressure Tanks
- Dynamic Control System Simulator
- Explosives Test Pond
- Hydrodynamic/Hydroacoustic Technical Center
- Low Observable Materials Lab
- Maneuvering and Seakeeping Basin
- Marine Coatings and Corrosion Control Facility
- Marine Composites Lab
- Radio-controlled Model Facility
- Rotating Arm Basin
- Shipboard Environmental Protection Facility
- Simulation, Planning and Analysis Research
- Structural Evaluation Lab
- Acoustics Materials Lab
- Advanced Electrical Machining
- Advanced Shipboard Auxiliary Machinery
- Deep Ocean Pressure Simulation Facility
- Electric Power Tech Lab
- Fire Research and Air Contamination Facility
- Machinery Systems Silencing Lab
- Magnetic Fields Lab
- Metallic Materials and Processing Facility
- Pulsed Power Facility
- Shipboard Environmental Protection Facility
- Submarine Fluid Dynamics Facility
- Technology and Development Facility
- Steam Propulsion Test Facility
- Gas Turbine Development Facility
- Propulsion and Auxiliary Diesel Engine
- Materials and Processing Facilities
- Cargo and Weapons System Facility

- Large Cavitation Channel
- Shock Trials Instrumentation
- Carr Inlet Test Facility
- Southeast Alaska Facility
- Combatant Craft Engineering Detachment
- *Lauren* and *Athena* Research Vessels/Ship
- Research Vessel *Hayes*
- South Florida Test Facility
- 100-Meter Underground Firing Range
- Electrochemical Power Systems Facility
- Electron Linear Accelerator Facility
- Electron K Mfg Productivity Center
- Failure/Material Analysis Facility
- Glendora Lake Testing Facility
- High-Energy Battery Evaluation Facility
- Hydroacoustic Test Facility
- Microwave Components Specialized Power
- Mines Countermeasure Software Support
- Pyrotechnics Development and Evaluation
- Weapons Development and Test Facility
- Aegis Computer Center
- Anechoic Test Facility
- Chem-Bio Eng Facility
- Compartmented Laboratory
- EM Pulse Facility
- EM Vulnerability Assessment Facility
- Explosives Experimental Area
- General-purpose labs
- Hypervelocity Wind Tunnel
- Nuclear Weapons Radiation Effects Complex
- Phalanx Instrumented Test Facility
- Potomac River Test Range
- Pulsed Power Test Facility
- Search and Track Sensor Rest Facility
- Strategic Systems Development
- Surface Warfare Analysis Facility (and White Oak)
- Warhead Res. Test Facility
- Countermeasures Evaluator
- Diving and Life Support Systems

- Electro-Optics Laboratory
- Expeditionary Warfare Modeling
- Fleet Diving Support Complex
- Hydrospace Laboratory
- Gulf Test Range
- Heliport Complex with Equipment
- Magnetic Detection and Classification Range
- Mine Exploitation Complex
- Mines and Mine equipment and systems
- Ocean simulation to 2,250-foot depth
- Pier Space, Boats
- Special Warfare Mission Equipment
- Specialized Environmental Testing
- Specialized Mine Warfare
- Transducers and Sonar Modeling for MCM
- Underwater Weapons Systems Laboratory
- Explosives Chemical/Physical Characterizations
- Composite propellant and plastic bonded
- Energetic chemicals pilot plant
- Energetic chemicals synthesis laboratory
- Energetic materials f&C labs
- Energetics environmental evaluation facility
- Energetics non-destructive test analysis facility
- Energetics performance evaluation facility
- Explosive test chambers (bombproofs)
- Explosives and propellant aging facilities
- Explosive Safety and Ordnance Environmental Support
- Extruded Products Facility
- Functional Ground Test Facility
- Joint services cartridge and propellant
- Multibase propellant processing facility
- Nitramine gun and high-energy propellant
- Ordnance device development
- Ordnance Test and Evaluation Facilities

RAND*MR1303-TC.6a*

Table C.6—Cont'd.

- Pyrotechnic materials facility
- Rocket motor and warhead process
- Rocket motor case braiding facility
- Solid energetic material continuous
- Solventless double base propellant facility
- Surface warfare engineering analysis
- Tomahawk functional ground test facility
- Weapons Product Development
- Weapons device development and prototype
- Self-Defense Test Ship (SDTS)
- Surface Warfare Engineering Facility
- Software program generation and life-cycle
- Surface Warfare Engineer Facility (SWEF)
- Integrated Combat Systems Test Facilities
- Underway Replenishment (UNREP) Test Site
- Acoustic Test Facility (ATF)
- Combat Systems Facility
- CV ASW Module Laboratory
- Hardware Environmental Test Facility
- Hyperbaric Chamber
- Industrial Waste Treatment Facility
- Target MK 30 IMAS, and Range Tracking
- Navy Mine Depot
- Material, Chemical and Failure Analysis
- Mechanical and Electronic Repair
- Fleet Operational Readiness Accuracy Check
- Hawaiian Area Tracking System
- Hawaiian Island Underwater Range
- Surface Ship Radiated Noise Measurement

- Nanoose Range
- Dabob Bay Range
- Quinault Range
- Post-operational Analysis Critique
- Range Information Display Center
- Range Launch, Recovery, and Target
- Rapid Prototyping and Fabrication
- Shipboard Electronic Systems
- Fleet Operational Readiness Accuracy Check
- San Clemente Island Underwater Range
- Surface Ship Radiated Noise Measurement
- Torpedo Explosive Operating Complex
- Torpedo Storage Magazines
- Transducer Automated Test Facility
- Undersea Weapon Evaluation Facility
- Undersea Weapons Repair
- Underwater Noise Analysis Facility
- Weapon Acceptance and Operational
- Acoustic Systems Engineering
- AUTEC
- Dodge Pond Acoustic Measurement Facility
- Heavyweight Primary Battery Electric
- Heavyweight/Lightweight Tactical Torpedo
- Land Based Evaluation Facility
- Submarine Antenna Test Complex
- Land-Based Integrated Test Site
- Sea-water tow tank (3000 feet long)
- Submarine Launcher System Test
- Propulsion Test Facility
- UUV, Target, Torpedo R&D Facility

- Narragansett Bay Shallow Water Test Facility
- Littoral Undersea Warfare Complex
- Shipboard Electronic Evaluations
- Sonar Complex
- Submarine Combat Systems Complex
- EHF SATCOM Development Terminal
- Emsort Development and Support Facility
- Imagery Archive and Video Editing Facility
- Periscope Engineering RDT&E Facility
- Periscope Regional Maintenance Facility
- Photonics Mast Land Based Test Site
- Special Mission Electro-Optic Sensor Support
- Trident Periscope Facility periscope complex
- Undersea Warfare Analysis Laboratory
- Weapons Analysis Facility (WAF)
- Advanced materials laboratory (WDFC)
- Anechoic chamber (64,000 cu ft) (WDFC)
- Anechoic wind tunnel (WDFC)
- Deep Depth Propulsion Test Facility (WDFC)
- High Energy Chamber (WDFC)
- Propulsion Noise Test Facility (WDFC)
- Reverberant Acoustic Tank (WDFC)
- Torpedo Life Cycle Support Facility (WDFC)
- UUV, Target, Torpedo R&D Facility
- Distributed Engineering Plant

RAND*MR1303-TC.6b*

The total score for a product divided by the total score for all products results in a certain percentage. The range of all the percentages can be divided into four (and sometimes more) parts corresponding to the four ranks of High, Medium, Low, and Very Low. The result aggregates the component into one bin of four bins corresponding to the rank assigned to one of the four parts of the range of percentages. This information can be exported to EXCEL for further plotting.

This section begins with examples of how the product-market observables were calculated, then assesses product-activity interactions, which include product-process interactions, product-technology interactions, product-facility interactions, and product-personnel interactions.

Product-Market Observables

Corporate-level decisions on which products and associated activities will be considered of higher or lower importance will depend on the characteristics of product-market interactions evaluated at the planning time horizon. In the commercial world, these interactions involve positioning a product with respect to current or emerging customer needs and preferences and positioning the product with respect to competing products. In Chapter Three, we adopted five measures, or observables, of product-market interactions that facilitate management decisions on actions to be taken that may affect organizational structure. Before we produced the histograms and portfolio-analysis charts, we prepared spreadsheets listing all the products on the left side and the markets and observables and other measures across the top. A page from this spreadsheet is shown in Table C.7, at the end of the observable definitions. We provide definitions of the observables below, along with sample calculations for the first product in the Test, Evaluate, Assess product group: USW Operational Range Assessment Systems.

- Specific Product Importance: The importance of a product to a specific market, where *importance* measures the extent to which the product satisfies customer needs and preferences in that market. We use the rating system developed earlier in this appendix:

    6 = Market Defining. An essential product in the market. The market would not exist or function at all without this product. The product is an essential definer of the market.

    3 = Important. A major contributor to the market. The market depends on this product, but the product does not define the market.

    1 = Support. Contributes to the market, but not a major contributor.

    0 = Not Important. Does not contribute to the market.

- Relative Product Importance: The specific importance of a product summed across all markets to which it contributes. Here, the values in the three markets are added: $3 + 3 + 1 = 7$. We see in Table C.7 that this product is given a 3 in the ASU and ASW markets, but only a 1 in the DEF market. The corresponding products were then distributed into the bins in Figure 3.8. As we can see from the other products in this product group, USW

Operational Range Assessment Systems is the next-to-lowest product in relative importance.

- Market Breadth: The total number of markets to which a product contributes. The cells showing values were added. For the first product, there are values in 3 markets, again indicating this product to have the next-to-lowest market breadth for products in its group.

- Relative Product-Importance Growth: The importance of a product in markets growing in emphasis, calculated by multiplying the emphasis-growth factor of a specific market by the specific product importance of a given product and summing the results across all markets. The market-emphasis-growth factor is the strategy-weighted factor discussed in Chapter Three, which assigns 3 to those markets in the High category; 2 to markets in the Medium category; 1 to markets in the Low category; and 0 to markets in the Very Low category. For the first product in the table, that sum is as follows:

$(0\times0) + (2\times0) + (1\times3) + (2\times3) + (1\times0) + (1\times0) + (3\times0) + (2\times0) + (0\times0) + (0\times0) + (0\times0) + (3\times0) + (0\times0) + (2\times0) + (3\times1) = 12.$

At a glance, we see that the importance for this product is lower than all but that for Aircraft Modeling and Simulation.

- Market-Breadth Growth: The breadth of products in markets growing in emphasis, calculated by summing the market-emphasis-growth factor for each of the markets to which the product contributes. The first product contributes to ASU (1), ASW (2), and DEF (3): $1 + 2 + 3 = 6$.

Table C.7 presents these observables for the Test, Evaluate, Assess product group.

As we see in the next subsections, the dimensions of importance, breadth, and market-emphasis growth of the products in the marketplace can continue to be used as weighting factors for importance and breadth of the processes and organized resources, which are the activities that support the products.

Product-Process Interactions

To evaluate the products in light of the processes they encompass, the research team took the basic processes associated with main task 4, "Execute Agency's Mission" (Table C.3) as shown in Table C.8, which has direct relevance for evaluating how products are actually produced. The other main tasks have more to do with how resources are acquired to accomplish the production or were for internal planning purposes. As discussed in Chapter Three, the supporting

Table C.7
Section of Product–Market Observables Rating Sheet

Major Product Groups and Products, with Specific Product-Importance Score by Market	NAVSEA Market (and Market-Emphasis-Growth Factor[a])															Relative Product Importance	Market Breadth	Market-Breadth Growth	Relative Product-Importance Growth
	AAW (0)	AMW (2)	ASU (1)	ASW (2)	CCC (1)	IW (1)	INT (3)	OPA (2)	OMW (0)	MOB (0)	MOS-NCO (0)	ACQ (3)	NSW (0)	STW (2)	DEF (3)				
Test, evaluate, assess																			
USW Operational Range Assessment Systems	0	0	3	3	0	0	0	0	0	0	0	0	0	0	1	7	3	6	12
USW Analysis	0	0	3	3	0	0	0	0	0	0	1	1	3	0	3	14	6	6	21
Missile Simulators, Trainers, and Test/Diagnostic Equipment	3	1	0	0	0	0	0	3	0	0	0	0	0	0	3	10	4	7	17
Weapon and Combat System Assessment Systems	3	3	3	3	0	0	0	0	3	0	1	0	3	3	3	25	9	10	30
Readiness Analysis	3	3	3	1	1	0	0	0	3	3	1	1	3	3	3	29	11	13	33
Navy Metrology Systems	1	1	1	1	1	0	0	3	1	1	1	0	1	1	1	15	12	13	17
MIW Simulation Software	0	1	0	1	0	0	0	0	6	0	1	1	1	0	3	14	7	10	16
Coastal Warfare Analysis	1	3	1	1	0	0	0	0	3	3	1	1	6	1	3	24	11	13	23
Aircraft Modeling and Simulation	0	0	0	0	0	0	0	0	0	0	0	0	0	0	0	0	0	0	0
Theater Warfare Analysis	3	3	3	3	0	0	0	0	3	3	1	1	3	3	3	29	11	13	30
Bullets																			

(Continues to include all product groups and products)

a See Figure 3.5 for market-emphasis-growth scores.

RANDMR1303-TC.7

activities, such as strategic planning, resource acquisition, and human-resource management, are not in the activities database.

Given the items in Table C.8 as the major categories by which to evaluate the embedded processes for the product, the basic question becomes a matter of *product-process change:*

Will the supporting processes be different in 2007 from what they are today?

To measure this interaction, the research team evaluated the processes embedded in NAVSEA products on the basis of our site visits, our own expertise, and the documentation we had obtained during our site visits. The team judged some of the products to be provided by world-class organizations— organizations that had a good business model and that could handle the changes in the future—requiring no adjustment of the processes. Therefore, although the products may change, the embedded processes are robust. For these products, the answer to the above question was, No, the processes would not be different and would get a zero in the ranking system: 0 for not different, 1 for different. This example illustrates the way the research team assessed the stability of the processes: focusing on the processes themselves, not on inputs (raw resources) and outputs (design prototype products).

Each of the 108 products was rated according to the aggregate of information just described, with binary scoring across the nine processes listed in Table C.8. The results of this rating were summed across all processes, resulting in a maximum of 9 and a minimum of 0. If the team was in doubt about the relevance of a process to a product, we used the detailed processes shown in Table 3.9 for clarification. We arranged the binary results in a spreadsheet, a portion of which is shown in Table C.8. As with relative product-importance growth in Table C.7, the product USW Operational Range Assessment Systems shows a similarly Low gross process-change score of 2.

Note that Navy Metrology Systems, which is similar to USW Operational Range Assessment Systems in having Low relative product importance in Table C.7, has a High gross process-change score of 7 in Table C.8. We will keep an eye on this product as well as the first product through the analyses in the following subsections to see if other dimensions change.

Some of the products in the complete spreadsheet, such as Torpedoes and Ballistic Missile Systems, show no process changes across the board. These products were shown by the analysis to be supported by robust processes that would endure through the coming decade or beyond. This is not to say that other parts of the environment, such as technology or strategic need, are not changing, only that the processes embedded in these products can handle the change.

Table C.8

Portion of Product-Process Rating Sheet

Product, by Product Group	Designate office of responsibility	Provide operational information support	Identify and market customer requirements	Develop and manage technology	Design products and/or services	Market and sell	Produce and deliver products/services	Invoice and service customer	Evaluate program against objectives	Gross process-change score	Adjusted process-change score
Test, evaluate, assess											
USW Operational Range Assessment Systems	0	0	1	0	0	1	0	0	0	2	1
USW Analysis	0	1	0	0	0	1	0	0	0	2	1
Missile Simulators, Trainers, and Test/Diagnostic Equipment	0	0	0	0	1	0	0	0	0	1	1
Weapon and Combat System Assessment Systems	0	0	1	0	1	0	0	0	0	2	1
Readiness Analysis	0	1	0	1	0	1	0	1	0	4	2
Navy Metrology Systems	1	0	1	1	1	1	0	1	1	7	3
OMW Simulation Software	0	0	1	1	0	0	0	0	0	2	1
Coastal Warfare Analysis	0	1	0	0	0	1	0	0	0	2	1
Aircraft Modeling and Simulation	1	0	1	1	1	1	0	0	0	5	2
Theater Warfare Analysis	1	1	0	0	0	0	0	0	0	2	1
Bullets											

(Continues to include all product groups and products)

NOTE: High   = 7–9
       Medium   = 4–6
       Low   = 1–3
       Very low = 0

RAND*MR1303-TC.8*

Because the processes do not span a wide numerical range, the research team decided to bin the results according to the system shown in Table 3.10. The hard-zero products were placed in a separate bin. All other results were binned uniformly across the remainder of the range. The product-process interaction analysis—the final results of this process—is shown in Figure 3.13.

Product-Technology Interactions

A process involves technology, people, and facilities. One of our sources, *Shipbuilding Technology and Education* (NRC, 1996, p. 25), mentions several areas of ship-building technologies in addition to shipyard production-process technologies: business-process technologies, system technologies, and technologies for new materials and products—rather a broad spectrum. It goes on to define technology as "a practical application of knowledge (or capability thus provided) or a manner of accomplishing a task, especially using technical processes, methods, or knowledge." Using the extensive NSB-NRC technology survey (1997a, especially Table 6.1, p. 44) as the source of changing technologies relevant to the Navy, the research team assessed the impact of technology change on NAVSEA products. In this group of interactions, there are two measures: product-technology change and technology relative importance.

Product-Technology Change. The primary measure of product-technology interaction, *product-technology change,* is defined by the following question:

> Is this changing technology embedded in the product?

That is, "To what extent will the technologies embedded in a given product be different in 2007 from what they are today?" Some anticipated technologies will have matured by then; others will still be developing.

The list of technologies is already known to be changing from that in the NSB-NRC study; moreover, it is already known to be of relevance to naval equipment. All NAVSEA products were reviewed for each of the approximately 100 technologies. The above question was asked and a product was given a 1 for a Yes answer or a 0 for a No answer, with a maximum possible score of 100 and a minimum of 0 when scores for the products are summed across all technologies. These assessments were supplemented with information gathered on the site visits and with additional technology discussions available from ONI documents (1998). The results of this analysis are shown in Figure C.17.

The total scores were sorted into four bins ranging from High to Very Low. The product-technology change peaks at the Very Low end of the range, with a gradual decrease in number of products moving toward higher technology change. This is not to say that the technologies embedded in those products in the Very Low category are not changing at all, but that there are fewer changing technologies in those products than in the products at the High end of the range.

The more complex a product is, the more different technologies it will involve. Thus, many of the products with complex systems are in the High technology-change bin. The analysis indicates that three products—Unmanned Undersea Vehicles, Surface Combat Systems, and SOF Sensor Systems—involve a high number of the changing technologies listed in Table C.4 and discussed in the Strategic Imperatives section of Chapter Two. Therefore, these products will be

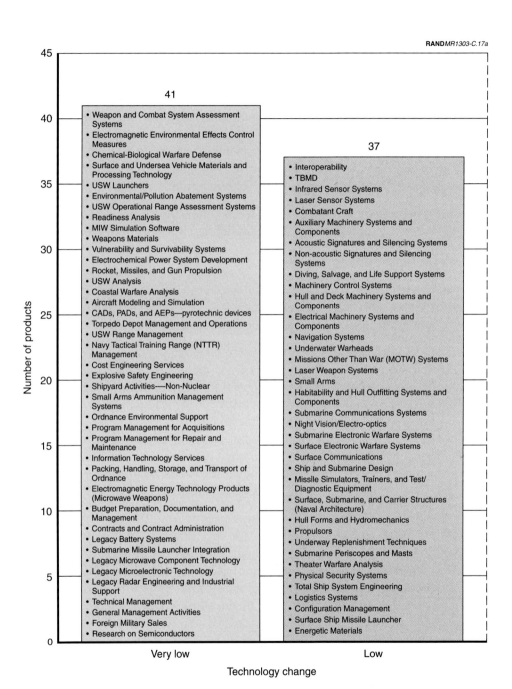

Figure C.17—Number of Products Falling into Each of Four Bins Based on
Product–Technology-Change Evaluation Category. The Very Low category
indicates that the technology embedded in a given product will not be
much different in 2007 from what it is now.

RAND_MR1303-C.17b_

Technology change is the extent to
which embedded technologies for a
given product will be different in 2007

23

- Torpedoes
- Ballistic Missile Systems
- Submarine Defensive Systems
- Surface USW Systems
- Tomahawk Systems
- General Missile Systems
- Submarine Combat Systems
- Fire Control Systems
- Surface Defensive Systems
- Mine Countermeasure Systems
- USW Deployed Systems
- Torpedo Countermeasures
- Surface Weapons
- Precision Guided Munitions
- Sonar Systems
- Mine Systems
- Tactical Control System Software
- Navy Metrology Systems
- Sonar Imaging Systems
- Radar Systems
- Marine Corps Vehicle Systems and
  Components
- Decision Support Systems
- Propulsion Machinery Systems and
  Components

7

- Unmanned Undersea Vehicles
- Small Manned Underwater Vehicles
- SOF Mobility, Life Support and Mission Support
  Equipment and Systems
- SOF Sensor Systems
- Gun Weapon Systems
- Surface Combat Systems
- Carrier Combat Systems

Medium   High

Technology change

Figure C.17—Cont'd.

most affected by changes in technology. In making resource-allocation decisions on these products, a manager would want to follow these products' rankings in the following analyses and in relation to the overall environment for specific products. An example of how such rankings can guide decisions is provided in the next subsection.

Technology Relative Importance. In addition to using the technologies to look at new aspects of products, we can also use the products to take a new look at technologies. In particular, we can ask, "To what extent are changing technologies being used on relatively important products? The resulting list of technologies will be ranged by their relative importance, which is measured by their use on important products. The scoring is then aggregated for all NAVSEA products across all markets. This measure is similar to that of a product's specific importance across all markets—a product's relative importance.

In this portfolio-analysis approach, questions relating to resource allocation for all of NAVSEA can be addressed. However, for detailed questions regarding a specific technology, the role of that technology and the role of the products it supports in the markets of interest need to be considered as well.

The relative importance of a technology is calculated by multiplying the relative product importance score of each product (Figure 3.8) by the technology-utilization score for the technology[4] for that product and summing across all products. The resulting score expresses the importance of the technology relative to products of importance to NAVSEA (see Figure 3.8).

The final scores, arranged from High to Very Low, revealed a discontinuity in the High group, which caused us to designate the highest part of that bin as Very High, with the other scores in the usual four bins. To gain a better understanding of the technology-relative-importance measure, the research team split out the Very High relative importance technologies (see Table C.9) and distributed the rest in the histogram bins (see Figure C.18).

Most of the Very High relative importance technologies come from the technology cluster associated with Enterprise Processes, indicating the very broad-based importance these technologies have for NAVSEA products. In any resource-allocation decisions, these technologies and their associated processes, facilities, and personnel should be given special priority. Moreover, such broad basing can figure in the structuring of the organization, leading to competitive advantage if NAVSEA can share technologies across segments, as

---

[4]The data for the technology-utilization score are not shown in the report. They are similar in format to those in Table C.10 (Portion of Product-Facility Rating Sheet) in that the expected use by a product is shown for each technology.

Table C.9

Very High Relative Importance Technologies

- Systems engineering
- Modeling and simulation
- Simulation-based system design and acquisition
- Rapid prototyping
- Functional low-cost computing
- Microelectronics
- Agile manufacturing
- Cognitive process modeling
- Specialty materials—superconductive, organic coatings, adhesives, energetic materials
- Data storage

RAND*MR1303-TC.9*

was suggested in Chapter Three for the High market-breadth product groups of Engineering Services and Communications Systems and Capabilities.

From High to Very Low, the distribution of the remaining technologies is flat, indicating a fairly uniform mix of Low and High relative importance technologies in the aggregate for NAVSEA products. In resource decisions at the NAVSEA corporate level, the technologies in the High and Medium categories should certainly be treated with some priority. Decisions regarding the other categories need to be supplemented by reference to more-specific information on products and markets, beginning with the 2-D charts in the Product-Market Interactions section of Chapter Three.

Process and Technology Change Environment

We can use the results of the analysis on technology and process change to learn about the stability of the products in relation to their *environment,* which is defined by the embedded processes and technologies. Because most NAVSEA products are high technology, the other environmental variables, such as facilities and personnel, should track with the technology-change variable. A two-dimensional view of the process- and technology-change environment is displayed in Figure C.19 (which combines Figures C.17 and 3.13), which lists the products with characteristics of each intersecting bin.

The products in the upper-right-hand quadrant of the plot have embedded technologies and processes undergoing rapid change, an environment that can

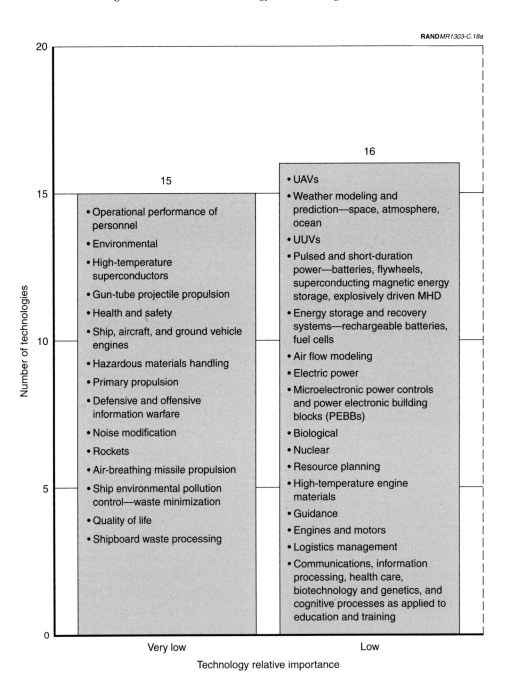

RAND*MR1303-C.18a*

Figure C.18—Binned Technology Relative Importance Scores, After Very High Relative Importance Technologies Have Been Separated Out (see Table C.9). The total number of technologies in a category is centered over the top of each histogram bar.

RAND*MR1303-C.18b*

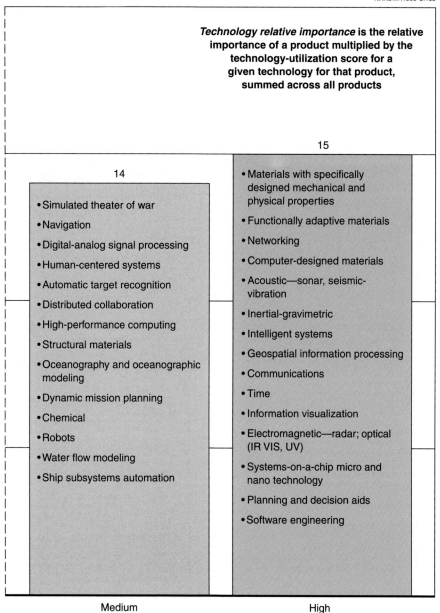

Technology relative importance **is the relative importance of a product multiplied by the technology-utilization score for a given technology for that product, summed across all products**

15

14

- Simulated theater of war
- Navigation
- Digital-analog signal processing
- Human-centered systems
- Automatic target recognition
- Distributed collaboration
- High-performance computing
- Structural materials
- Oceanography and oceanographic modeling
- Dynamic mission planning
- Chemical
- Robots
- Water flow modeling
- Ship subsystems automation

- Materials with specifically designed mechanical and physical properties
- Functionally adaptive materials
- Networking
- Computer-designed materials
- Acoustic—sonar, seismic-vibration
- Inertial-gravimetric
- Intelligent systems
- Geospatial information processing
- Communications
- Time
- Information visualization
- Electromagnetic—radar; optical (IR VIS, UV)
- Systems-on-a-chip micro and nano technology
- Planning and decision aids
- Software engineering

Medium   High

Technology relative importance

Figure C.18—Cont'd.

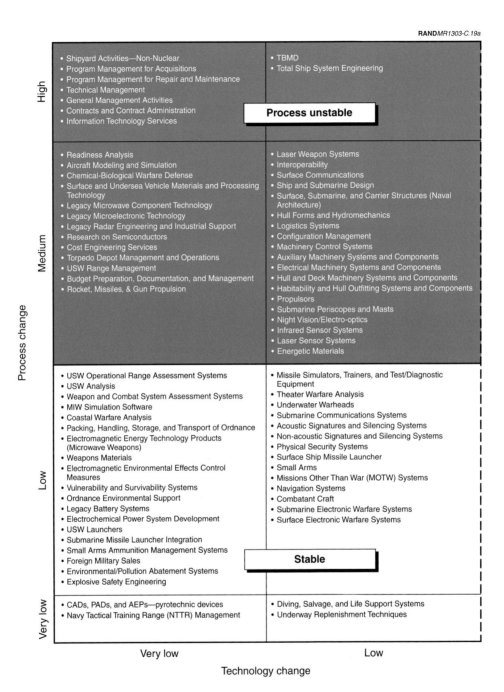

Figure C.19—Process Change Plotted Against Technology Change for All NAVSEA Products, Overlaid with Stability Levels Indicating Need for More (Unstable) or Less (Stable) Managerial Attention. This figure combines Figures C.17 and 3.13.

RANDMR1303-C.19b

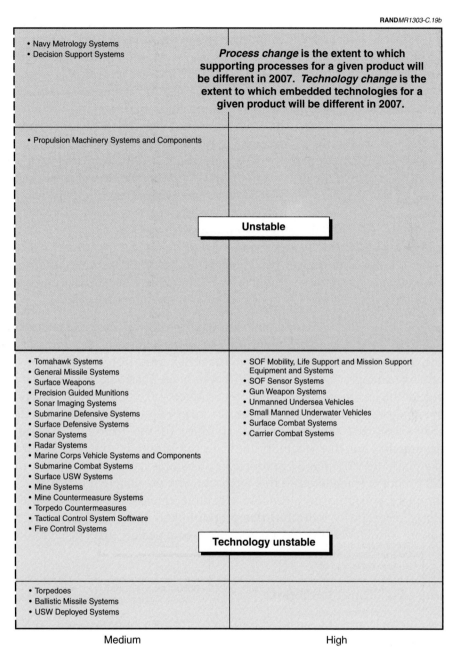

Figure C.19—Cont'd.

be characterized as Unstable. To make resource-allocation decisions, a manager would want additional information on the product, such as that on its importance and breadth in Figure 3.10. If, on the one hand, the product is categorized as Very High in importance and breadth in Figure 3.10, a signal for investment, then it should receive more managerial attention to ensure its continued success in the marketplace. If, on the other hand, a product is of relatively low importance and low breadth, then the decision to invest resources in upgrading its processes and technologies would be contra-indicated. NAVSEA appears to have only three products in this Unstable category. As noted in the discussion of Figure 3.10 in relation to Figure C.19, in Chapter Three, Decision Support Systems has High relative importance and breadth, indicating that a decision to invest in this product would be appropriate. However, the other two products, Navy Metrology Systems and Propulsion Machinery Systems and Components, are in the "Maintain; consider relative importance risk" category, indicating that even though they have Medium breadth, these products have Low relative importance and hence lower priority than Decision Support Systems for investment decisions.

Products that are in an environment with relatively low process and technology change can be considered Stable (see the lower-left-hand quadrant of the chart), not requiring substantial managerial attention for process and technology change. Note that the grid is only an observation on the rate of change of the environment in which the products are embedded. At this point in the analysis, decisions with respect to investment or divestment of these products will not depend on the stability of the products' operating environments, nor does stability indicate the products' importance in the marketplace. NAVSEA has 37 products in this Stable category—fully one-third of the products considered in this analysis. The off-diagonal quadrants, the Technology Unstable and Process Unstable quadrants, have 27 and 41 products, respectively, indicating that proportionally more NAVSEA managerial attention should be directed toward process redesign than to technology development.

Product-Facilities Interactions

Just as the measures of the NAVSEA markets' interactions with the NAVSEA products can be used to understand the role and significance of the processes and technologies embedded in them, so too can these interactions be used to understand the role of the NAVSEA facilities and their relative importance. The NAVSEA facilities are the second of the three components of the Organized Resources part of the Activity portion of our Market-Product-Activity Model.

As discussed earlier in this appendix, no single list of NAVSEA facilities was available for analysis. The research team built a facilities list up from the Laboratory Managers Research Council Reports from 1995 to the present (NLCCG, 1994), from the DoD RDT&E facility descriptions (DoD, 1997a), and from input obtained during the many site visits to NAVSEA field activities. For simplicity, the research team used the abbreviated facility titles in Table C.6 in the further analysis. The detailed, computerized database is designed for easy changes as additional details become available. Shipyard facilities could be added easily to complete the database.

Two measures of product-facilities interactions are discussed in the following subsections: facility utilization by products and facility relative importance.

Facility Utilization by Products. To answer the question,

> Will the facility be used by a given product during its life-cycle development and service in the planning time horizon, 2007?

the research team viewed the list of facilities against the NAVSEA products, giving the answer Yes a 1 and No a 0. We assembled a spreadsheet of the answers, placing the abbreviated list of facilities along the left-hand side of the spreadsheet and the name of each product at the head of each column across the sheet. A portion of the spreadsheet and answers is presented in Table C.10.

The data for the facility-utilization metric are built from the sums of facility use down a given product. Because there are some 150 facilities in the current database, the maximum for a product that is a heavy user of facilities could be 150; the minimum for a product could be 0. After summing down all facilities, we noted that some products make broad use of facilities and that some NAVSEA products use no facilities. In this analysis of facilities, the research team treated these extreme cases as distinct from the overall range of facility utilization exhibited by the remaining products. The 27 Very High facility-use products[5] and the 18 zero facility-use products are listed in Table C.11.

The zero facility-use products are easiest to understand because they are related to services, such as Budget Preparation and Technical Management, which do not require specialized facilities. Information on some zero facility-use products, such as Research on Semiconductors or Aircraft Modeling and Simulation, which certainly require special facilities, was not available to the research team from the extensive resources used. Many of the Very High facility-use products are easy to understand as well. Products such as Sonar Systems and Energetic Materials require specialized facilities; Mine Systems,

---

[5]One of our reviewers, Elliot Axelband, suggested that this measure would be more significant if weighted by the cost of these facilities—for example, the annual operating cost plus depreciation.

Table C.10
Portion of Product-Facility Rating Sheet

Abbreviated Facility Master List 2000	Facility Number	Submarine Combat Systems	Surface USW Systems	Torpedo Depot Management & Operations	Sonar Systems	Torpedoes	USW Ranges	USW Operational Assessment Systems	USW Launchers	Unmanned Undersea Vehicles	Submarine Communication Systems	USW Analysis	Submarine Defensive Systems	Submarine Missile Launcher Integration	Sonar Imaging Systems	Budget Preparation, Documentation, & Management
Relative Product Importance		40	25	8	38	17	3	7	41	21	36	14	17	17	25	12
140-foot Towing Basin	1	0	0	0	0	0	0	0	0	1	0	0	0	0	0	0
24-inch and 36-inch Cavitation Channels	2	0	1	0	0	0	0	0	0	0	0	0	0	0	0	0
Anechoic flow facility	3	0	1	0	0	0	0	0	0	1	0	0	0	0	0	0
Circulating Water Channel	4	0	0	0	0	0	0	0	0	1	0	0	0	0	0	0
Data and Image Processing System	5	1	0	0	1	1	0	0	0	0	0	0	0	0	1	0
David Taylor Model Basin Complex	6	0	0	0	0	0	0	0	0	1	0	0	0	0	0	0
Deep Submergence Pressure Tanks	7	0	1	1	1	0	0	0	0	0	0	0	0	0	0	0
Dynamic Control System Simulator	8	0	0	0	0	0	0	0	0	1	0	0	0	0	0	0
Explosive Test Pond	9	0	1	0	0	1	0	0	0	0	0	0	0	0	0	0
Hydrodynamic/Hydroacoustic Technical Center	10	0	1	0	1	0	0	0	0	1	0	0	0	0	0	0
Low Observable Materials Lab.	11	1	0	1	0	0	0	0	0	1	0	0	0	0	0	0

RAND*MR1303-TC.10a*

Table C.10—Cont'd.

Product Name and Relative Product Importance

Abbreviated Facility Master List 2000	Facility Number	Submarine Combat Systems (40)	Surface USW Systems (25)	Torpedo Depot Management & Operations (8)	Sonar Systems (38)	Torpedoes (17)	USW Ranges (3)	USW Operational Assessment Systems (7)	USW Launchers (41)	Unmanned Undersea Vehicles (21)	Submarine Communication Systems (36)	USW Analysis (14)	Submarine Defensive Systems (17)	Submarine Missile Launcher Integration (17)	Sonar Imaging Systems (25)	Budget Preparation, Documentation, & Management (12)
Maneuvering and Seakeeping Basin	12	0	0	0	0	0	0	0	0	0	0	0	0	0	0	0
Marine Coatings and Corrosion Control Facility	13	0	0	0	0	0	0	0	0	1	0	0	0	0	0	0
Marine Composites Lab.	14	0	0	0	0	0	0	0	0	1	0	0	0	0	0	0
Radio-controlled Model Facility	15	0	0	0	0	0	0	0	0	1	0	0	0	0	0	0
Rotating Arm Basin	16	0	0	0	0	0	0	0	0	1	0	0	0	0	0	0
Shipboard Environmental Protection Facility	17	0	0	0	0	0	0	0	0	0	0	0	0	0	0	0
Simulation, Planning and Analysis Research	18	0	0	0	1	0	0	1	0	0	0	0	0	0	0	0
Structural Evaluation Lab	19	0	0	0	0	0	0	0	0	1	0	0	0	0	0	0
Acoustics Materials Lab.	20	0	1	0	1	0	0	0	0	1	0	0	0	0	0	0
Advanced Electrical Machining	21	0	1	0	1	1	0	0	0	1	0	0	0	0	0	0
Advanced Shipboard Auxiliary Machinery	22	0	1	0	1	0	0	0	0	1	0	0	0	0	0	0

Table C.10—Cont'd.

Abbreviated Facility Master List 2000	Facility Number	Submarine Combat Systems	Surface USW Systems	Torpedo Depot Management & Operations	Sonar Systems	Torpedoes	USW Ranges	USW Operational Assessment Systems	USW Launchers	Unmanned Undersea Vehicles	Submarine Communication Systems	USW Analysis	Submarine Defensive Systems	Submarine Missile Launcher Integration	Sonar Imaging Systems	Budget Preparation, Documentation, & Management
(Product Name and Relative Product Importance)		40	25	8	38	17	3	7	41	21	36	14	17	17	25	12
Deep Ocean Pressure Simulation Facility	23	0	1	0	0	0	0	0	0	0	0	0	0	0	0	0
Electric Power Tech. Lab.	24	0	1	1	0	1	1	0	0	1	0	0	0	0	0	0
Fire Research and Air Contamination Facility	25	0	0	0	0	0	0	0	0	1	0	0	0	0	0	0
Machinery Systems Silencing Lab	26	0	1	1	1	1	0	0	0	1	0	0	0	0	0	0
Magnetic Fields Lab.	27	0	1	0	0	1	0	0	0	1	1	0	0	0	0	0
Metallic Materials and Processing Facility	28	0	0	0	0	1	0	0	0	1	0	0	0	0	0	0
Pulsed Power Facility	29	0	0	0	0	0	0	0	0	0	0	0	0	0	0	0
Shipboard Environmental Protection Facility	30	0	0	0	0	0	0	0	0	0	0	0	0	0	0	0
Submarine Fluid Dynamics Facility	31	0	0	0	0	0	0	0	0	1	0	0	0	0	0	0

RANDMR1303-TC.10c

Table C.11

Very High Facility-Use and Zero Facility-Use Products

Very High facility-use products (27)	Zero facility-use products (18)
• Submarine Combat Systems • Surface USW Systems • Torpedoes • Sonar Systems • Unmanned Undersea Vehicles • Small Manned Underwater Vehicles • Navy Tactical Training Range (NTTR) Management • Navigation Systems • Interoperability • USW Operational Assessment Systems • Acoustic Signatures and Silencing Systems • USW Ranges • Mine Systems • Energetic Materials • Hull Forms and Hydromechanics • Gun Weapon Systems • Small Arms • Weapons Materials • Rocket, Missiles, and Gun Propulsion • Ship and Submarine Design • USW Analysis • Underwater Warheads • Readiness Analysis • Mine Countermeasure Systems • USW Deployed Systems • Submarine Periscopes and Masts • Missile Simulators, Trainers, and Test/ Diagnostic Equipment	• Budget Preparation, Documentation, and Management • Program Management for Acquisition • General Management Activities • Contracts and Contract Administration • Technical Management • Information Technology Services • Aircraft Modeling and Simulation • Missions Other Than War (MOTW) Systems • Research on Semiconductors • Small Arms Ammunition Management Systems • Physical Security Systems • Security Systems • Total Ship System Engineering • Logistics Systems • Cost Engineering Services • Foreign Military Sales • Configuration Management • Program Management for Repair and Maintenance

RAND*MR1303-TC.11*

Hull Forms, USW Ranges, and Mine Countermeasures require large facilities for their development.

The remaining products are easier to interpret. We calculated the total number of facilities used by a given product from the database and binned the totals as shown in Figure C.20 for the 63 products that remained after the Very High facility-use and zero facility-use products were subtracted. Peaks occur at both ends of the range, indicating that those products in the High category truly belong with the Very High facility-use products, given the assumptions of the RAND Product-Rating System section of this appendix. The remaining products have a Gaussian distribution, gradually rising to a peak in the Very

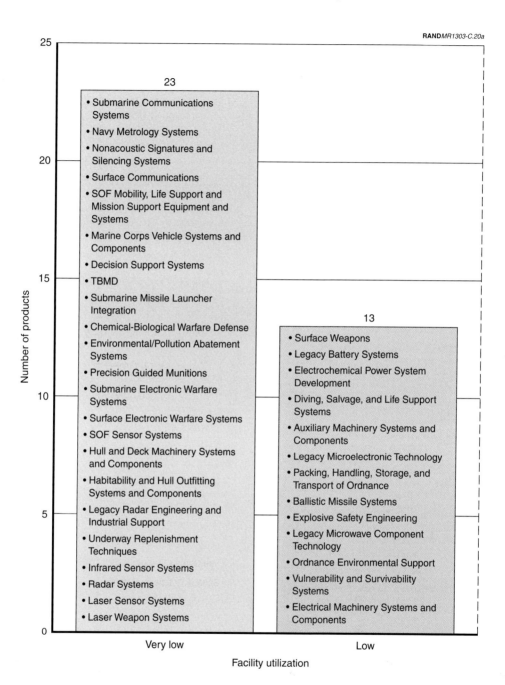

Figure C.20—Binning of Products According to Facility Utilization, by Product

RAND*MR1303-C.20b*

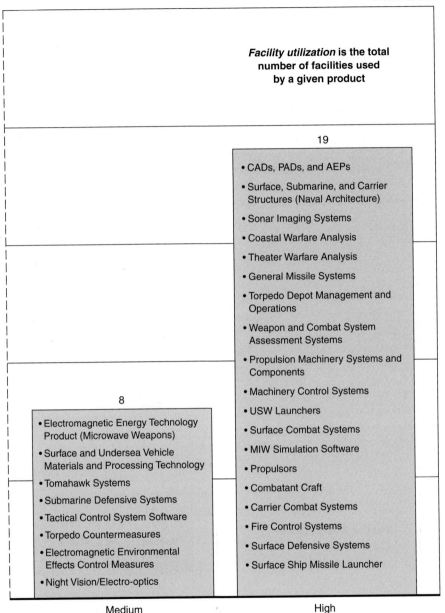

Facility utilization is the total
number of facilities used
by a given product

19

- CADs, PADs, and AEPs
- Surface, Submarine, and Carrier Structures (Naval Architecture)
- Sonar Imaging Systems
- Coastal Warfare Analysis
- Theater Warfare Analysis
- General Missile Systems
- Torpedo Depot Management and Operations
- Weapon and Combat System Assessment Systems
- Propulsion Machinery Systems and Components
- Machinery Control Systems
- USW Launchers
- Surface Combat Systems
- MIW Simulation Software
- Propulsors
- Combatant Craft
- Carrier Combat Systems
- Fire Control Systems
- Surface Defensive Systems
- Surface Ship Missile Launcher

8

- Electromagnetic Energy Technology Product (Microwave Weapons)
- Surface and Undersea Vehicle Materials and Processing Technology
- Tomahawk Systems
- Submarine Defensive Systems
- Tactical Control System Software
- Torpedo Countermeasures
- Electromagnetic Environmental Effects Control Measures
- Night Vision/Electro-optics

Medium   High

Facility utilization

Figure C.20—Cont'd.

Low category. Almost half of the NAVSEA products make broad use of facilities (19 products in the High facility-use category and 27 in the Very High facility-use category). From a portfolio perspective, the NAVSEA product portfolio appears to lean heavily toward products that are very facility-dependent; therefore, decisions regarding facility expansions will enhance the NAVSEA product portfolio, whereas facility closures will adversely affect the portfolio.

Facility Relative Importance. The overall relative importance of facilities to products is derived similarly to the product relative-importance growth and is a function of relative product importance. It is each product's relative importance multiplied by whether that product uses the facility, summed across all products. In this way, the market importance of a product can be related to facility importance. For example, for Facility Number 26 in the section of the Product-Facility Rating Sheet shown in Table C.10, the facility relative importance would be

$$(25{\times}1) + (38{\times}1) + (17{\times}1) + (21{\times}1) = 101$$

for the four of 15 products using that facility. The resulting sum is for product relative importance for all products using that facility. The final data set showed seven Very High relative importance facilities and three zero relative importance facilities (see Table C.12). All others are in a range between these two extremes.

It is not surprising that the Self-Defense Test Ship or the Distributed Engineering Plant is in the Very High relative importance facilities group. These facilities are in frequent and widespread use by many products of High relative importance. Therefore, in making resource-allocation decisions and upgrade initiatives, they should be given special consideration.

The only way a facility could be rated at zero relative importance is if it supported no NAVSEA products. We were unable to link the three facilities in

Table C.12

Very High and Zero Relative Importance Facilities

Very High relative importance facilities (7)	Zero relative importance facilities (3)
• Distributed Engineering Plant • Combat Systems Facility • Target MK 30 IMAS, and Range Tracking • CV ASW Module Laboratory • Software Program Generation and Life-Cycle • Self-Defense Test Ship (SDTS) • AUTEC	• Electron Linear Accelerator Facility • Failure/Material Analysis Facility • Nuclear Weapons Radiation Effects Complex

RAND*MR1303-TC.12*

this category to any products that arose either initially from a detailed study of NAVSEA activities or from future product requirements. This suggests that these facilities should be studied in more detail to determine relevance and contribution to the NAVSEA facility portfolio.

The range of relative importance for the remaining facilities, in Figure C.21, appears to be biased toward the Low end. Overall, it is almost flat, indicating a good mix of facility relative importances at NAVSEA. In the aggregate, no portfolio of facilities for a technology-intensive organization should be peaked at the High end. General-use facilities are usually built to handle such a distribution. However, as discussed for facility utilization, some high-technology products require specialized facilities—some so specialized that they can serve only one or two products. In this aggregated portfolio analysis, such facilities would be rated Very Low in relative importance, although essential, similarly to niche products or products for which niche analysis is required. As with the technologies in the Unstable environment portion of Figure C.20, detailed judgments on specific facilities need to examine their individual contributions to products and markets (for example, by referring to product importance and breadth markets, Figure 3.10).

Product-Personnel Interactions

The final component of the Activity portion of the NAVSEA model, and the most important category of the organized resources to be analyzed, is the interactions between products and personnel. This category is important because it is the people who will be formulating and redesigning technologies and processes, operating the specialized equipment those technologies enable, performing engineering tasks and solving problems, and being educated to run operations in 2007—all involving the products that are the focus of Chapter Three.

As with the other components of the Activity portion, the initial analysis of personnel is to identify which of the 15 occupational clusters (Figure C.16) and 100 job titles (Table C.5) presented earlier in this appendix will be important in 2007 and how these categories interact with the market characteristics of the products assessed at the planning time horizon of 2007. This combination of occupational clusters and job titles accounts for 99 percent of NAVSEA personnel.

For completeness, job titles associated with Navy nuclear reactors have not been excluded from the listing of such titles in the clusters. However, by

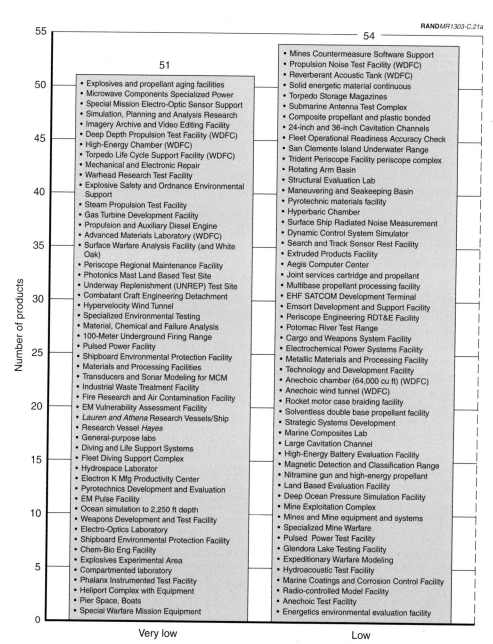

Figure C.21—Binned Facility Relative Importance, After Facilities with Very High Relative Importance and Zero Relative Importance Have Been Removed (see Table C.12)

RAND*MR1303-C.21b*

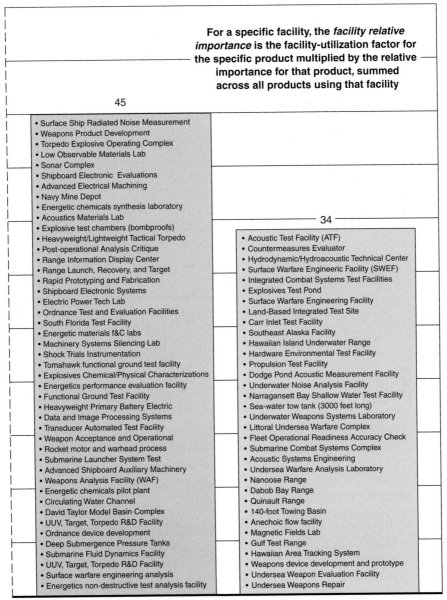

For a specific facility, the *facility relative importance* is the facility-utilization factor for the specific product multiplied by the relative importance for that product, summed across all products using that facility

45

- Surface Ship Radiated Noise Measurement
- Weapons Product Development
- Torpedo Explosive Operating Complex
- Low Observable Materials Lab
- Sonar Complex
- Shipboard Electronic Evaluations
- Advanced Electrical Machining
- Navy Mine Depot
- Energetic chemicals synthesis laboratory
- Acoustics Materials Lab
- Explosive test chambers (bombproofs)
- Heavyweight/Lightweight Tactical Torpedo
- Post-operational Analysis Critique
- Range Information Display Center
- Range Launch, Recovery, and Target
- Rapid Prototyping and Fabrication
- Shipboard Electronic Systems
- Electric Power Tech Lab
- Ordnance Test and Evaluation Facilities
- South Florida Test Facility
- Energetic materials f&C labs
- Machinery Systems Silencing Lab
- Shock Trials Instrumentation
- Tomahawk functional ground test facility
- Explosives Chemical/Physical Characterizations
- Energetics performance evaluation facility
- Functional Ground Test Facility
- Heavyweight Primary Battery Electric
- Data and Image Processing Systems
- Transducer Automated Test Facility
- Weapon Acceptance and Operational
- Rocket motor and warhead process
- Submarine Launcher System Test
- Advanced Shipboard Auxiliary Machinery
- Weapons Analysis Facility (WAF)
- Energetic chemicals pilot plant
- Circulating Water Channel
- David Taylor Model Basin Complex
- UUV, Target, Torpedo R&D Facility
- Ordnance device development
- Deep Submergence Pressure Tanks
- Submarine Fluid Dynamics Facility
- UUV, Target, Torpedo R&D Facility
- Surface warfare engineering analysis
- Energetics non-destructive test analysis facility

34

- Acoustic Test Facility (ATF)
- Countermeasures Evaluator
- Hydrodynamic/Hydroacoustic Technical Center
- Surface Warfare Engineeric Facility (SWEF)
- Integrated Combat Systems Test Facilities
- Explosives Test Pond
- Surface Warfare Engineering Facility
- Land-Based Integrated Test Site
- Carr Inlet Test Facility
- Southeast Alaska Facility
- Hawaiian Island Underwater Range
- Hardware Environmental Test Facility
- Propulsion Test Facility
- Dodge Pond Acoustic Measurement Facility
- Underwater Noise Analysis Facility
- Narragansett Bay Shallow Water Test Facility
- Sea-water tow tank (3000 feet long)
- Underwater Weapons Systems Laboratory
- Littoral Undersea Warfare Complex
- Fleet Operational Readiness Accuracy Check
- Submarine Combat Systems Complex
- Acoustic Systems Engineering
- Undersea Warfare Analysis Laboratory
- Nanoose Range
- Dabob Bay Range
- Quinault Range
- 140-foot Towing Basin
- Anechoic flow facility
- Magnetic Fields Lab
- Gulf Test Range
- Hawaiian Area Tracking System
- Weapons device development and prototype
- Undersea Weapon Evaluation Facility
- Undersea Weapons Repair

Medium   High

Facility relative importance

Figure C.21—Cont'd.

specific request, the analysis does not include products that need these job titles. No statement as to their importance is made or implied in this work.[6]

To facilitate the analysis and make comparisons more revealing, the research team related each of the job titles to each of the NAVSEA products by whether that job title would have no involvement (N); would be in the foreground of a product, i.e., would contribute directly (D); or would be in the background of a product, i.e., would contribute indirectly (I) to the product. These distinctions ensure that the latter two labor categories receive unbiased attention in the analysis.

For example, individuals from the Naval Architecture Series job title will be designing the structure of future ships or ship upgrades, thereby contributing directly to the Ship and Submarine Design product. Individuals from the Management and Program Analysis Series will oversee the design process, thereby contributing indirectly. Similarly, individuals from the Contracting Series prepare proposals and contracts with vendors, thereby contributing directly to the Contracts and Contract Administration product, whereas individuals from the General Engineering Series could answer questions about a related project or provide specifications, thereby contributing indirectly.

The results of this direct-versus-indirect labor assignment are reflected in the overall labor mix in the NAVSEA occupational clusters, in Figure C.22. Because the NAVSEA product mix is focused more on specific products such as systems than on services such as Cost Engineering Services and Contract Support, those occupational clusters emphasizing service or support positions will be mostly indirect; those occupational clusters emphasizing more product-oriented positions will be mostly direct. Separately summing all the direct-labor contributions to the products and all the indirect-labor contributions and calculating the percentages of each contribution in the clusters yields the breakdown in the figure.[7]

The expectation that the Scientists and Engineers cluster would be largely direct and that the Admin, Personnel, Supply Specialists cluster would be largely indirect is borne out in the figure. The 100-percent direct-labor clusters— Construction and Engineering Operators, and Machinists, Technicians, and Cargo Specialists—are also consistent with expectations, revealing the research team's consistency of judgment in making labor assignments.

---

[6]The Nuclear Propulsion Organization (SEA 08) was excluded from the scope of this study at the request of the COMNAVSEA.

[7]One small occupational cluster was excluded from the assessment, because its only product involvement was a direct contribution to one product, which caused a misleading conclusion to be drawn about it.

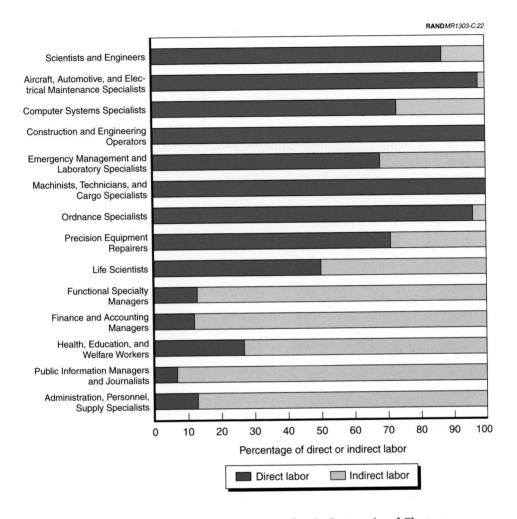

Figure C.22—Mix of Direct and Indirect Labor in Occupational Clusters

From a portfolio perspective, understanding which occupational clusters and job titles are involved with relatively important products is an important input to high-level management decisions for staffing NAVSEA as a whole. The measure of the interaction between product and personnel is the *personnel relative importance,* which derives priorities for staffing distributions for 2007 from the extent of involvement of various occupational clusters and job titles with High relative importance products.

Personnel Relative Importance. Personnel relative importance is calculated as the *job title utilization score*—whether a specific job title contributes to a product—separately for the direct and indirect labor utilization for a given job title. Each result was multiplied by the relative product importance for a given product. Utilization was calculated separately for both direct and indirect labor, then multiplied by product relative importance and summed across all products. The results for all job titles in an occupational cluster were then summed to enable comparison with the labor-mix results in Figure C.22. For the direct-labor category, the results are shown in Figure C.23.

Discontinuities in the direct-labor cluster relative importance scores suggested three categories—Low, Medium, and High—displayed in the figure against the total number of clusters in each of those categories. Out of the 14 occupational clusters, the five in the High relative importance direct-labor category include, not surprisingly, Scientists and Engineers, Construction and Engineering Operators, and Precision Equipment Repairers. The Low category includes most of the support occupational clusters. It could be argued that there is a correlation between the binning of support products for management, documentation, and physical security in the Very low bar of Figure 3.8 for relative product importance and the definitions of *direct labor* and *indirect labor* at the beginning of this subsection.

We repeated this process with the indirect-labor cluster relative importance scores. Their discontinuities also suggested three categories—Low, Medium,

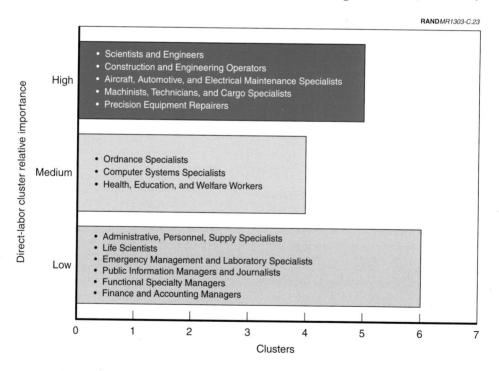

Figure C.23—Direct-Labor Occupational Cluster Relative Importance

and High—and we plotted the ranked clusters against number of clusters in a category, in Figure C.24. The total number of clusters is 12 rather than 14, because the two 100-percent direct-labor clusters could not be included.

Among the five High relative-importance indirect-labor clusters are Functional Specialty Managers, Finance and Accounting Managers, and Admin, Personnel, Supply Specialists. All clusters in the Low category are direct-labor. The Medium relative-importance category includes Scientists and Engineers and Precision Equipment Repairers, which are in the High category in Figure C.23.

Computer System Specialists, a cluster that is shown to be 75-percent direct-billable in the labor-mix analysis of Figure C.22, scores in the Medium category for both direct and indirect labor. To score at the Medium level for both direct and indirect indicates that the products to which this cluster contributes indirectly must be of High relative importance to outweigh the initial labor-mix score. Also from the labor-mix perspective, the Life Scientists, which clusters 50-50 in direct and indirect labor, scores Low in the direct-labor relative-importance category and Medium in the indirect-labor relative-importance category. This inequality indicates that, overall, the products to which this cluster contributes indirectly must be of higher relative importance than those to which it contributes directly.

RANDMR1303-C.24

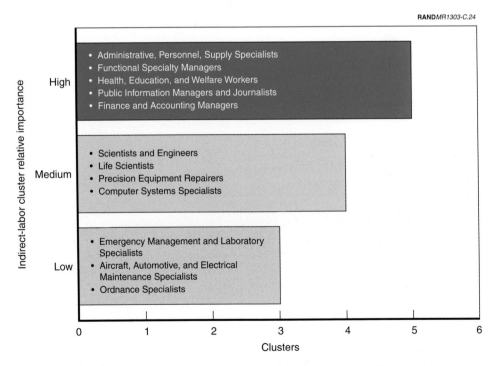

Figure C.24—Indirect-Labor Occupational Cluster Relative Importance

We now backtrack from occupational clusters to job titles, to see how the product relative importance scores intersect with the job titles themselves, considering that the relative importance scores for the clusters were built from the individual relative importance scores for the job titles in a cluster. From the portfolio perspective of corporate NAVSEA, a more-detailed examination of the interaction of product relative importance with personnel at the job-title level can have utility for human resources (HR) decisions and manpower planning for the planning time horizon of 2007. We demonstrate by considering the rank-ordering of job titles in the top five direct-labor occupational clusters, in Table C.13.

This rank-ordered list suggests that, in HR and staffing decisions regarding the Scientists and Engineers cluster, Electrical, Computer, and Mechanical

Table C.13

Job Title Relative Importance for the Top Five Direct-Labor Occupational Clusters

Scientists and Engineers
- Electrical Engineering Series
- Naval Architecture Series
- Electronics Engineering Series
- Computer Engineering Series
- Engineering Technician
- Mechanical Engineering Series
- Physics Series
- Mathematics Series
- General Engineering
- Nuclear Engineering Series
- Chemical Engineering Series
- Engineering and Architecture Student Trainee

Construction and Engineering Operators
- Crane Operating
- Rigging
- Pipefitting
- Plastic Fabricating
- Painting
- Insulating
- Shipwright
- Fabric Working
- Wood Crafting

Aircraft, Automotive, and Electrical Maintanence Specialists
- Electrician
- Air Conditioning Equipment Mechanic
- Marine Machinery Mechanic
- Heavy Mobile Equipment Mechanic
- ? General Maintenance and Operations Work
- ? General Industrial Equipment Maintenance
- General Facilities and Equipment Series
- Production Machinery Mechanic

Machinists, Technicians, and Cargo Specialists
- Shipfitting
- Welding
- Machining
- Toolmaking
- ? General Metal Work
- Sheet Metal Mechanic
- Boilermaking

Precision Equipment Repairers
- Electronic Industrial Controls Mechanic
- Electronics Mechanic
- Electronics Technician Series
- Quality Assurance Series

RAND*MR1303-TC.13*

? indicates a discrepancy between the job title provided by the NAVSEA staff and conventional OPM Job Titles. The closest related OPM Job Title was adopted.

Engineers, as well as Naval Architects, would be given higher consideration than Chemical Engineers. Similarly for the Machinists, Technicians, and Cargo Specialists cluster, Shipfitting, Welding, and Machining would be given higher consideration than Boilermakers or Sheet Metal Mechanics. From the portfolio perspective for corporate NAVSEA, this type of staffing input can affect sizing decisions across all of NAVSEA. Of course, for detailed HR and staffing decisions on specific products and markets, more-detailed consideration would also have to be given to product relative importance, breadth, and emphasis growth for a specific market and to the strategic vision of organizational needs.

We performed the same rank-ordering of job titles for the indirect-labor clusters. The rank-ordered job titles for the top five indirect-labor occupational clusters, in Table C.14, suggest that, in HR and staffing decisions, the Management and Program Analysis Series in the Functional Specialty Managers cluster would be given more consideration than the Logistics Management Series. Likewise in the Health, Education, and Welfare Workers cluster,

Table C.14

Job Title Relative Importance for the Top Five Indirect-Labor Occupational Clusters

Admin, Personnel, Supply Specialists
- Mail and File Series
- Secretary Series
- Office Automation Clerical and Assistance Series
- Management and Program Clerical and Assistance Series
- Procurement Clerical and Technician Series
- Supply Clerical and Technician Series
- Accounting Technician Series
- Equipment Specialist Series
- Materials Handling
- Inventory Management Series
- Production Control Series
- Miscellaneous Clerk and Assistant Series
- Miscellaneous Admin
- General Business and Industry Series

Functional Specialty Managers
- Administrative Officer Series
- Personnel Management Series
- Management and Program Analysis Series
- Contracting Series
- Security Administration Series
- Supply Program Management Series
- Logistics Management Series

Health, Education and Welfare Workers
- Patent Attorney Series
- Training Instruction Series
- Librarian Series
- Technical Information Services Series
- Library Technician Series
- Education and Training Technician Series
- General Attorney Series

Public Information Managers and Journalists
- Technical Writing and Editing Series
- Visual Information Series
- Editorial Assistance Series
- General Arts and Information Series
- Public Affairs Series

Finance and Accounting Managers
- Budget Analysis Series
- Accounting Series
- Financial Administration and Program Series

decisions regarding the Patent Attorney Series would be given more consideration than would the General Attorney Series. The Patent Attorney Series is related more directly to technology and to products that are more corporate-central, as discussed at the end of Chapter Three.

Job titles that are associated with products that are changing either in process or in technology will require different human-resources decisions from those for job titles associated with products that will not be very different in process or technology in 2007 from what they are today. To assess for personnel intersections with relatively important products and their growth characteristics and with technology or process change, managers can project the product-market characteristics for technologies and facilities onto the interactions of personnel and products, similarly to what was done for those products in the Unstable environment in the 2-D process-technology change chart.

"An Acquisition Concept for 'Cradle to Grave' Partnerships with Industry," Tiger Team White Paper, October 16, 1998.

Adamy, David L., *EW 101: A First Course in Electronic Warfare*, Artech House Radar Library, Norwood, Mass.: Artech House, 2001.

Alberts, David, John J. Garstka, and Frederick P. Stein, *Network-Centric Warfare: Developing and Leveraging Information Superiority*, Washington, D.C.: Department of Defense C4ISR Cooperative Research Program (CCRP), 1999.

Alexander, Yonah, and Michael S. Swetnam, eds., *Cyber Terrorism and Information Warfare*, Terrorism: Documents of International and Local Control, Second Series, Vols. 5–8, Dobbs Ferry, N.Y.: Oceana Publications, 1999.

American Productivity & Quality Center's (APQC's) International Benchmarking Clearinghouse, *Process Classification Framework*, 2000.

"An Approach for Efficiently Managing DoD R&D Portfolios," *Acquisition Quarterly*, Vol. 5, No. 4, Fall 1998, pp. 339–356.

Baldwin, Laura H., Frank Camm, Edward G. Keating, and Ellen M. Pint, *Incentives to Undertake Sourcing Studies in the Air Force*, Santa Monica, Calif.: RAND, DB-240-AF, 1998.

Birkler, John, *Aircraft Carrier Industrial Base*, Santa Monica, Calif.: RAND, CT-142, April 1997.

Birkler, John, et al., *The U.S. Aircraft Carrier Industrial Base: Force Structure, Cost, Schedule, and Technology Issues for CVN 77*, Santa Monica, Calif.: RAND, MR-948-NAVY/OSD, 1998.

——, *The U.S. Submarine Production Base: An Analysis of Cost, Schedule, and Risk for Selected Force Structures*, Santa Monica, Calif.: RAND, MR-456-OSD, 1994.

————, *The U.S. Submarine Production Base: An Analysis of Cost, Schedule, and Risk for Selected Force Structures: Executive Summary*, Santa Monica, Calif.: RAND, MR-456/1-OSD, 1994.

Birkler, John, Joseph Large, Giles Smith, and Fred Timson, *Reconstituting a Production Capability: Past Experience, Restart Criteria, and Suggested Policies*, Santa Monica, Calif.: RAND, MR-273-ACQ, 1993.

Birkler, John, C. Richard Neu, and Glenn Kent, *Gaining New Military Capability: An Experiment in Concept Development*, Santa Monica, Calif.: RAND, MR-912-OSD, 1998.

Birkler, John, Giles Smith, Glenn A. Kent, and Robert V. Johnson, *An Acquisition Strategy, Process, and Organization for Innovative Systems*, Santa Monica, Calif.: RAND, MR-1098-OSD, 2000.

Blatstein, Ira (Naval Surface Warfare Center [NSWC]), "A Tradition of Excellence," NSWC Strategic Initiatives briefing, October 19, 1998.

Bowman, ADM Frank L., "Submarines in the New World Order," *Undersea Warfare*, Spring 1999, pp. 2–8.

Bracken, Paul, John Birkler, and Anna Slomovic, *Shaping and Integrating the Next Military: Organization Options for Defense Acquisition and Technology*, Santa Monica, Calif.: RAND, DB-177-OSD, 1996.

Brock-Mack, Judith, *An Analysis of NAVSEA Downsizing*, Thesis, Monterey, Calif.: Naval Postgraduate School, September 1994.

Brown, Peter, NAVSEA Executive Director, "Framing NAVSEA's Business Plan," briefing, November 1998.

Bryson, John M., *Strategic Planning for Public and Nonprofit Organizations: A Guide to Strengthening and Sustaining Organizational Achievement*, rev. ed., San Francisco, Calif.: Jossey-Bass Publishers, 1995.

Buchanan, H. Lee II, Assistant Secretary of the Navy (RD&A), "Inspired Efforts, Directed at the Future," *Sea Power*, April 2000, p. 61.

Builder, Carl, "The American Military Enterprise in the Information Age," in Zalmay Khalilzad, John P. White, Andrew W. Marshall, eds., *Strategic Appraisal: The Changing Role of Information in Warfare*, Santa Monica, Calif.: RAND, MR-1016-AF, 1999, pp. 19–44.

Campen, Alan D., and Douglas H. Dearth, eds., *Cyberwar 3.0: Human Factors in Information Operations and Future Conflict*, Fairfax, Va.: AFCEA International Press, 2000.

Carlisle, Rodney P., *Management of the U.S. Navy Research and Development Centers During the Cold War Era: A Survey Guide to Reports*, Washington,

D.C.: a joint publication of the Navy Laboratory/Center Coordinating Group and the Naval Historical Center, Department of the Navy, 1996.

Cebrowski, VADM A. K., "21st Century War College/21st Century Warfare/21st Century Navy," briefing, March 1999.

————, "Sea, Space, Cyberspace: Borderless Domains," text of 26 February 1999 address, www.nwc.navy.mil/pre/speeches/borderless.html.

Cebrowski, Vice Admiral (U.S. Navy) Arthur K., and John J. Garstka, "Network-Centric Warfare: Its Origin and Future," *Naval Institute Proceedings,* January 1998.

Center for Naval Analyses, *Analysis of the Navy's Commercial Activities Program,* Arlington, Va.: CNA, CRM 92-226, July 1993.

————, *Avoiding a Hollow Force: An Examination of Naval Readiness,* Alexandria, Va.: CNA, CRM-95-238, April 1996.

Chandler, Alfred D., *Strategy and Structure: Chapters in the History of the American Industrial Enterprise,* Cambridge, Mass.: MIT Press, 1962.

Chang, Ike, et al., *Use of Public-Private Partnerships to Meet Future Army Needs,* Santa Monica, Calif.: RAND, MR-997-A, 1999.

Cohen, William S., Secretary of Defense, *Report of the Quadrennial Defense Review,* Washington, D.C., May 1997.

————, *Actions to Accelerate the Movement to the New Workforce Vision: Executive Summary,* Report to Congress, Washington, D.C., April 1998.

"The Cooperative Engagement Capability," *Johns Hopkins APL Technical Digest,* Vol. 16, No. 4, 1995, pp. 377–396.

Cote, Owen R., "Innovation in the Submarine Force: Ensuring Undersea Supremacy," *Undersea Warfare,* Spring 1999, pp. 14–16.

Dardia, Michael, *Defense Cutbacks: Effects on California's Communities, Firms, and Workers—Executive Summary,* Santa Monica, Calif.: RAND, MR-689-OSD, 1996.

Dardia, Michael, et al., *The Effect of Military Base Closures on Local Communities: A Short-Term Perspective,* Santa Monica, Calif.: RAND, MR-667-OSD, 1996.

Davis, Paul K., et al., *Strategic Issues and Options for the Quadrennial Defense Review,* Santa Monica, Calif.: RAND, DB-201-OSD, 1997.

Davis, Paul K., James H. Bigelow, and Jimmie McEver, *Analytical Methods for Studies and Experiments on "Transforming the Force,"* Santa Monica, Calif.: RAND, DB-278-OSD, 1999.

Defense Intelligence Agency, *Future Technology Impact on Global Security Trends by 2025,* Washington, D.C. (not available for public release), December 1999.

Defense Management Review, *Report to Congress,* July 19, 1989.

Defense Systems Management College Press, *Systems Engineering Fundamentals* (Supplementary Text), Fort Belvoir, Va., December 1999.

Denning, Dorothy E., *Information Warfare and Security,* New York: ACM Press, 1999.

Department of Defense, *In-House RDT&E Activities Report FY94–FY98,* 1997b, http://www.ihreport.com.

―――, *In-House Research, Development, Test & Evaluation (RTD&E) Activities Report,* FY97, Foreword and Sections on "Naval Surface Warfare Center" and "Naval Undersea Warfare Center," 1997a, http://www.ihreport.com.

―――, *Vision 21: Defense Laboratories and Test and Evaluation Center Infrastructure Requirement,* Report to the President and Congress, Washington, D.C., 1996.

Department of the Navy, "Changing the Way It Does Business—Acquisition Reform Change Elements," June 22, 1999, www.acq-ref.navy.mil/implmanc.html.

―――, *2000 Posture Statement,* at http://www.chinfo.navy.mil/navpalib/policy/fromsea/pos00/pos00-fw.html.

―――, *Forward . . . from the Sea,* Washington, D.C., 1994.

Department of the Navy, Chief of Naval Operations, *Establishment and Disestablishment of Certain Shore Activities,* Washington, D.C.: Department of the Navy, OPNAV Notice 5450, June 17, 1974.

―――, *Notional Intervals, Durations, Maintenance Cycles, and Repair Mandates for Depot Level Maintenance Availabilities of U.S. Navy Ships,* Washington, D.C.: OPNAV NOTICE 4700, March 1, 1996.

Dertouzos, James, et al., *Facilitating Effective Reform in Army Acquisition,* Santa Monica, Calif.: RAND, DB-233-A, 1998.

Dewar, James A., Carl H. Builder, William M. Hix, and Morlie H. Levin, *Assumption-Based Planning: A Planning Tool for Very Uncertain Times,* Santa Monica, Calif.: RAND, MR-114-A, 1993.

"Downsizing and Budget Cutting: Alternative Strategies," *Navy Comptroller,* January 1993.

Duncan, Andrew, et al., *Trouble Spots: The World Atlas of Strategic Information*, Stroud, Glouchestershire, United Kingdom: Sutton Publishing, 2000.

"ERP Selection," *APICS—The Performance Advantage*, www.apics.org/magazine/June99/ERPTravis.html.

"ERP Software Improves Productivity and Customer Service," *APICS—The Performance Advantage*," http://www.apics.org/magazine/June99/Solutions.html.

"Evolution and Revolution As Organizations Grow," *Harvard Business Review*, July–August 1972.

Fink, Daniel J. (Committee Chairman), National Research Council, *Assessment of Technology Development in NASA's Office of Space Science*, Washington, D.C.: National Academy Press, Space Studies Board, National Research Council, 1998.

Forno, Richard, and Ronald Baklarz, *The Art of Information Warfare: Insight into the Knowledge Warrior Philosophy*, 1999.

Friel, John, Arthur Huber, Daniel Jones, John Pinder, and Darius Sankey, "The Utility for the Air Force Laboratory System of Commercial and Other Government Laboratory Management Practices," Santa Monica, Calif.: unpublished RAND research.

Gaffney, RADM Paul, and Fred E. Saalfeld, "Science and Technology from an Investment Point of View," *Program Manager*, September–October, 1999, pp. 12–17.

Galbraith, Jay R., *Designing Organizations: An Executive Briefing on Strategy, Structure, and Progress*, San Francisco, Calif.: Jossey-Bass Publishers, 1995.

Galbraith, Jay R., and Edward E. Lawler III and Associates, *Organizing for the Future: The New Logic for Managing Complex Organizations*, San Francisco, Calif.: Jossey-Bass Publishers, 1993.

Gansler, Jacques S., *Defense Conversion: Transforming the Arsenal of Democracy*, Cambridge, Mass.: The MIT Press, 1998.

General Accounting Office (GAO), *Best Practices: Elements Critical to Reducing Successfully Unneeded RDT&E Infrastructure*, Washington, D.C.: GAO/NSIAD/RCED-98-23, January 1998.

————, *Defense Acquisition Infrastructure: Changes in RDT&E Laboratories and Centers*, Washington, D.C.: GAO/ASIAD-96-221 BR, September 1996a.

————, *Executive Guide—Effectively Implementing the Government Performance and Results Act ("Reinventing Government")*, Washington, D.C.: GAO/GGD-96-118, June 1996b.

————, *Navy Ship Maintenance: Allocation of Ship Maintenance Work in the Norfolk, Virginia, Area*, Washington, D.C.: GAO/NSIAD-99-54, February 24, 1999.

Giambastiani, VADM E. P., "Flag Pilot," *Undersea Warfare*, Spring 1999, p. 1.

Goldwater-Nichols Department of Defense Reorganization Act and National Security Decision Directive (NSDD) 219, P.L. 99-433, enacted in 1986.

Greiner, Larry E., "Evolution and Revolution As Organizations Grow: A Company's Past Has Clues for Management That Are Critical to Future Success," *Harvard Business Review*, July–August 1972, pp. 37–46.

Hamel, Gary, and C. K. Prahalad, "Competing for the Future," *The Harvard Business Review*, July–August 1994, pp. 122–128.

Haney, Patrick, *Ship Availability Planning and Engineering Center (SHAPEC) Review*, briefing to the NAVSEA 04 SUPSHIP/Naval Shipyard Joint Board of Directors, October 5, 1999.

Hax, Arnoldo, and Nicolas S. Majluf, *The Strategy Concept and Process: A Pragmatic Approach*, 2nd ed., Upper Saddle River, N.J.: Prentice-Hall, 1996.

Held, Bruce, "Statutory Innovations in Real-Estate Public-Private Partnerships," RAND briefing, March 1997.

Horn, Kenneth P., Elliot I. Axelband, Ike Yi Chang, Paul S. Steinberg, Carolyn Wong, and Howell Yee, *Performing Collaborative Research with Nontraditional Military Suppliers*, Santa Monica, Calif.: RAND, MR-830-A, 1997.

Horn, Kenneth P., et al., "Generating Revenue to Help Offset Declining Infrastructure and R&D Budgets," Santa Monica, Calif.: unpublished RAND research.

————, "Maintaining Adequate Army Capability in Science and Technology," Santa Monica, Calif.: unpublished RAND research.

Horn, Kenneth P., Ike Chang, Bruce Held, Elliot Axelband, Jamie Studebaker, Carolyn Wong, and Paul Steinberg, "Collaborating and Partnering with Industry," Santa Monica, Calif.: unpublished RAND research.

Hynes, Michael, Sheila N. Kirby, and Jennifer Sloan, *A Casebook of Alternative Governance Structures and Organizational Forms*, Santa Monica, Calif.: RAND, MR-1103-OSD, 1999.

Inter-Agency Benchmarking & Best Practices Council, *Government Process Classification Scheme*, October 1996.

Jackson, John H., and Cyril P. Morgan, *Organization Theory: A Macro Perspective for Management*, Englewood Cliffs, N.J.: Prentice-Hall, Inc., 1978.

Johnson, Robert S., "The Changing Nature of the U.S. Navy Design Process," *Naval Engineer's Journal*, April 1980, pp. 88–113.

Joint Chiefs of Staff, *Joint Strategy Review 1999 Report*, Washington, D.C. (not available for public release), 1999.

———, *Joint Vision 2020*, Washington, D.C.: Director for Strategic Plans and Policy, J5, Strategic Division, U.S. Government Printing Office, June 2000.

———, *National Military Strategy: Shape, Respond, Prepare Now—A Military Strategy for a New Era*, 1997, at http://www.dtic.mil/jcs/nms.

Joint Staff, *Mobility Requirement Study 2025*, Washington, D.C. (not available to the public), n.d.

Joint Staff J-6, "The Emerging Joint Strategy for Information Superiority," information briefing at www.dtic.mil/JCS/J6.

Jones, Vernon Dale, *Downsizing the Federal Government: The Management of Public Sector Workforce Reductions*, Armonk, N.Y.: M.E. Sharpe, 1998.

Kalmach, E. L., Commander Puget Sound Naval Shipyard, "Data Request to Support RAND CVN 77 Study," Puget Sound, Wash., October 1996.

Kast, Fremont E., and James E. Rosenzweig, *Organization and Management: A Systems Approach*, New York: McGraw-Hill Book Company, 1970.

Katz, Daniel, and Robert L. Kahn. *The Social Psychology of Organizations*, 2nd ed., New York: John Wiley & Sons, 1978.

Khalilzad, Zalmay, et al., eds., *Strategic Appraisal: The Changing Role of Information in Warfare*, Santa Monica, Calif.: RAND, MR-1016-AF, 1999.

Kilman, Ralph H., Louis R. Pondy, and Dennis P. Slevin, eds., *The Management of Organization Design: Strategies and Implementation, Vols. I and II*, New York: Elsevier North-Holland, Inc., 1976.

Lange, Ed, "ERP's Future Focus," *APICS—The Performance Advantage*," Vol. 9, No. 6, June 1999, http://www.apics.org/magazine/June99/ERPLange.html.

Leonard, Robert S., Jeffrey A. Drezner, and Geoffrey Sommer, *The Arsenal Ship Acquisition Process Experience: Contrasting and Common Impressions from the Contractor Teams and Joint Program Office*, Santa Monica, Calif.: RAND, MR-1030-DARPA, 1999.

Levine, Arnold, and Jeff Luck, *The New Management Paradigm: A Review of Principles and Practices*, Santa Monica, Calif.: RAND, MR-458-AF, 1994.

Levy, Dina G., Harry Thie, Al Robbert, Scott Naftel, Charles Cannon, Rudolph H. Ehrenberg, and Matthew Gershwin, *Characterizing the Future Defense Workforce*, Santa Monica, Calif.: RAND, MR-1304-OSD, 2001.

Likert, Rensis, *The Human Organization: Its Management and Value*, New York: McGraw-Hill Book Company, 1967.

Lorell, Mark, Julia Lowell, Hugh Levaux, and Michael Kennedy, "Enhanced Air Force Use of the Commercial Industrial Base: Initial Findings," Santa Monica, Calif.: unpublished RAND research.

Malley, VADM Kenneth C. (former Commander, NAVSEA), "Strategic Challenge: Restructuring the NAVSEA Corporation (SAS Special Report)," *Sea Power*, April 1992, pp. 85–88.

Marine Board Commission on Engineering and Technical Systems, National Research Council Committee on National Needs in Maritime Technology, *Shipbuilding Technology and Education*, Washington, D.C.: National Academy Press, 1996.

McIntosh, Malcolm K., and John B. Prescott, *Report to the Minister for Defence on the Collins Class Submarine and Related Matters*, Canberra ACT, Australia: Report of the Collins Class Submarine Project Review Team, June 1999.

Miles, Raymond E., and Charles C. Snow, in collaboration with Henry J. Coleman, Jr., *Organizational Strategy, Structure, and Process*, New York: McGraw-Hill Book Company, 1978.

Mintzberg, Henry, "Managing Government, Governing Management," *Harvard Business Review*, May–June 1996, pp. 75–83.

———, *Structure in Fives: Designing Effective Organizations*, Englewood Cliffs, N.J.: Prentice-Hall, 1993.

Moe, Ronald C., "Let's Rediscover Government, Not Reinvent It," *Government Executive*, June 1993.

———, "The Reinventing Government Exercise: Misinterpreting the Problem, Misjudging the Consequences," *Public Administration Review*, March/April 1994.

Nanos, George P., Jr., "The Naval Sea Systems Command: Preparing for the 21st Century," *Almanac of Sea Power*, January 1999, pp. 78–84.

National Aeronautic and Space Administration (NASA) Federal Laboratory Review (response to Presidential Directive), February 1995, www.hq.nasa.gov/office/ fed-lab.

National Defense Panel, *Transforming Defense: National Security in the 21st Century*, Arlington, Va.: Report of the National Defense Panel, December 1997.

National Research Council, *Shipbuilding Technology and Education*, Washington, D.C.: National Academy Press, 1996.

National Research Council, Aeronautics and Space Engineering Board, and Space Studies Board, Joint Committee on Technology for Space Science and Application, *Reducing the Costs of Space Science Research Missions: Proceedings of a Workshop,* Washington, D.C., 1997.

National Research Council, Computer Science and Telecommunications Board, *Realizing the Potential of C4I: Fundamental Challenges*, Washington, D.C.: National Academy Press, 1999.

Naval Sea Systems Command, *Core Equities—Red Team Review*, Arlington, Va., February 11–12, 1999a.

Naval Sea Systems Command, *NAVSEA Outlease Program*, enclosing "Outlease Procedures Revised August 1997" and "Outlease Timeline," Arlington, Va., September 1997.

Naval Sea Systems Command, "Report of the Engineering Capabilities Working Group," Arlington, Va., March 11, 1994.

Naval Sea Systems Command, "Framing NAVSEA's Business Plan . . . Background and the Core Equities Contribution," briefing for the "Red" Team, Arlington, Va., February 11, 1999b.

Naval Sea Systems Command, Naval Shipyard Business Unit, *Corporate FY00 Business Plan*, Arlington, Va., n.d.

Naval Sea Systems Command/Naval Surface Warfare Center, "Overview Presentation for RAND," Arlington, Va., April 1998.

Naval Sea Systems Command/Naval Surface Warfare Center, Port Hueneme Command, "RAND Study Group Visit," Port Hueneme, Calif., September 20–21, 1999c.

Naval Sea Systems Command/Naval Surface Warfare Center, Port Hueneme Command, "The Next Underway Replenishment System," Port Hueneme, Calif., September 1999d.

Naval Sea Systems Command/Naval Surface Warfare Center, "Battle Force Information Center Overview," presentation by CAPT (Sel.) Barney J. Cramp, Port Hueneme, Calif., September 20, 1999e.

Naval Sea Systems Command/Naval Undersea Warfare Center, *NUWC Business Process Re-Engineering (BPR) Savings*, Newport, R.I., October 14, 1998.

Naval Sea Systems Command/Naval Undersea Warfare Center, *NUWC Core Equities FY98*, Newport, R.I., January 26, 1999f.

Naval Sea Systems Command, Navy Technical Liaison Program, "The Direct Line to the Technology Front Lines," Arlington, Va., briefing, May 1998.

Naval Studies Board, Committee on Technology for Future Naval Forces, and National Research Council, Commission on Physical Sciences, Mathematics, and Applications (NSB–NRC), *Technology for the United States Navy and Marine Corps, 2000–2035: Becoming a 21st-Century Force, Vol. 1: Overview*, Washington, D.C.: National Academy Press, 1997a.

————, *Technology for the United States Navy and Marine Corps, 2000–2035: Becoming a 21st Century Force, Vol. 2: Technology*, Washington, D.C.: National Academy Press, 1997b.

————, *Technology for the United States Navy and Marine Corps, 2000–2035: Becoming a 21st Century Force, Vol. 4: Human Resources*, Washington, D.C.: National Academy Press, 1997c.

Naval Studies Board and National Research Council, *Network-Centric Naval Forces (Overview): A Transition Strategy for Enhancing Operational Capabilities*, Washington, D.C., National Academy Press, 1999.

————, *Recapitalizing the Navy*, Washington, D.C., 1998.

Naval Surface Warfare Center, NAVSEA, *NSWC Model for Identifying and Quantifying Core Technical Capabilities of the Naval Surface Warfare Center*, Arlington, Va., May 1998.

————, *Technical Capability Narratives by Division*, Arlington, Va., 1999.

Naval Undersea Warfare Center, *Program for the Visit of RAND to the NUWC Division Keyport and NUWC Division Newport*, Newport, R.I., September 2 and 3, 1999 (2 volumes).

Navy Laboratory–Center Coordinating Group (NLCCG), *Management Briefs for NUWC, NSWC, NRL*, Arlington, Va., as of 30 September 1994.

"Navy Labs Could Be in for Changes As Pentagon Looks to Cut R&D Costs," *Inside the Navy*, September 7, 1988.

Normann, Richard, and Rafael Ramírez, "From Value Chain to Value Constellation: Designing Interactive Strategy," *Harvard Business Review*, July–August 1993, Reprint No. 93408.

Nye, Joseph S., *Bound to Lead: The Changing Nature of American Power*, New York: Basic Books, 1990.

Office of the Assistant Secretary of Defense (Force Management Policy), *Rewarding, Organizing and Managing People in the 21st Century: Time for a Strategic Approach, Executive Report*, Washington, D.C.: Report of the Eighth Quadrennial Review of Military Compensation, June 1997.

Office of Naval Intelligence (ONI) , *World Wide Threats to U.S. Navy and Marine Forces 1997–2017* (Vols. I and II), Washington, D.C., ONI-1200-00 (not available to the public), January 1998.

Office of the Secretary of Defense (OSD), *A Report to the United States Congress by the Secretary of Defense: Report on Allied Contributions to the Common Defense*, Washington, D.C., March 1999.

"Operating Agreement Between the Commander, Naval Sea Systems Command, and NAVSEA's Affiliated Program Executive Officers (PEOs)," Arlington, Va., April 1997.

Ostroff, Frank, *The Horizontal Organization: What the Organization of the Future Actually Looks Like and How It Delivers Value to Customers*, New York: Oxford University Press, 1999.

Peters, John, *Futures Intelligence: Assessing Intelligence Support to Three Army Long-Range Planning Communities*, Santa Monica, Calif.: RAND, MR-995-A, 1998.

Petz, Mike, "Alteration Management Planning Office," RAND briefing, Santa Monica, Calif., October 1999.

Pfeffer, Jeffrey, *The Human Equation: Building Profits by Putting People First*, Boston, Mass.: Harvard Business School Press, 1998.

Pint, Ellen M., and Laura H. Baldwin, *Strategic Sourcing: Theory and Evidence from Economics and Business Management*, Santa Monica, Calif.: RAND, MR-865-AF, 1997.

Porter, Michael E., *The Competitive Advantage of Nations*, New York: The Free Press, 1990.

Porter, Michael E., and Victor E. Millar, "How Information Gives You Competitive Advantage," *Harvard Business Review*, July–August 1985, Reprint No. 85414.

Portsmouth Naval Shipyard, *SSN-688 Class Corporate Planning Initiatives*, Portsmouth, N.H., 2000.

Prahalad, C. K., and Gary Hamel, "The Core Competence of the Corporation," *Harvard Business Review*, May–June 1999.

Presidential Directive on Laboratory Reform, September 1995, see http:// clinton3.nara.gov/WH/EOP/OSTP/NSTC/html/pdd5.html, visited August 15, 2002.

Presidential Request for Review of All DoD, DOE, NASA Labs, Washington, D.C., PDD/NSTC-1, May 1995.

Quinn, James, *Intelligent Enterprise: A Knowledge and Service Based Paradigm for Industry*, New York: The Free Press, 1992.

Rattray, Gregory J., *Strategic Warfare in Cyperspace*, Cambridge, Mass.: MIT Press, 2001.

Rayport, Jeffrey F., and John J. Sviokla, "Exploiting the Virtual Value Chain," *Harvard Business Review*, November–December 1995, Reprint No. 95610.

Robbert, Albert, et al., *Outsourcing of DoD Commercial Activities: Impacts on Civil Service Employees*, Santa Monica, Calif.: RAND, MR-866-AF, 1997.

Rock, Milton L., and Robert H. Rock, eds., with James Kristie, *Corporate Restructuring: A Guide to Creating the Premium-Valued Company*, New York: McGraw-Hill Publishing Company, 1990.

SAM Project Team, "Hewlett-Packard Knows What It Takes and What It Costs," *As Easy As ABC*, Issue 21, Summer 1995.

Sapolsky, Harvey M., *The Polaris System Development: Bureaucratic and Programmatic Success in Government*, Cambridge, Mass.: Harvard University Press, 1972.

Sarsfield, Liam, *The Applications of Best Practices to Unmanned Spacecraft Development: An Exploration of Success and Failure in Recent Missions*, Santa Monica, Calif.: RAND, DB-319-NRO, 2000.

Saunders, Kenneth V., Bruno W. Augenstein, Paul Bracken, et al., *Priority-Setting and Strategic Sourcing in the Naval Research, Development, and Technology Infrastructure*, Santa Monica, Calif.: RAND, MR-588-NAVY/OSD, 1995.

Schank, John, John Birkler, Michael Mattock, and Gordon Lee, "Modeling the Navy's Ship Industrial Base: Where We Are, Where We Want to Be," Santa Monica, Calif.: unpublished RAND research.

Scheib, CDR Timothy, "Welcome to the Norfolk Naval Shipyard," briefing to the RAND NAVSEA Study Team, Norfolk, Va., November 23, 1999.

Schleher, D. Curtis, *Electronic Warfare in the Information Age*, Norwood, Mass.: Artech House, 1999.

Schoeni, Robert, *Life After Cutbacks: Tracking California's Aerospace Workers*, Santa Monica, Calif.: RAND, MR-688-OSD, 1996.

Schwartau, Winn, *Information Warfare: Chaos on the Electronic Superhighway*, New York: Thunder's Mouth Press, 1996.

Sethi, Vikram, and William R. King, *Organizational Transformation Through Business Process Reengineering: Applying the Lessons Learned*, Upper Saddle River, N.J.: Prentice Hall, 1998.

Sharp, Walter G., Sr., *Cyberspace and the Use of Force*, Aegis Research Corporation, 1999.

Simon, Jeffrey, *NATO–Warsaw Pact Force Mobilization*, Washington, D.C.: The National Defense University Press, 1988.

Sirmalis, John (Naval Surface Warfare Center [NSWC], Acting Commander and Technical Director), "We Are Undersea Warfare," briefing, Newport, R.I., October 19, 1998.

Spaceport Florida, "Industry-Government Partnership: From Polaris to Lunar Prospector and Beyond," Navy Change Through Ex-Change Conference briefing, Miami, Fla., May 4, 1998.

Spaceport Florida Authority, "Dual Use Launch Complex 46," October 12, 1998, www.spaceport.com/Florida/lc46.html.

"Strategy and the Art of Reinventing Value," in "Perspectives," *Harvard Business Review*, September–October 1993, Reprint No. 93508.

Thaler, David, "Strategies-to-Tasks: A Framework for Linking Means and Ends," Santa Monica, Calif.: unpublished RAND research.

Thomas' Register of American Manufacturers, New York: Thomas, 1997.

Tighe, Carla, et al., *Implementing A-76 Competitions*, Arlington, Va.: Center for Naval Analyses, CRM 96-24, 1996.

——, *Outsourcing Opportunities for the Navy*, Arlington, Va.: Center for Naval Analyses, CRM 95-224, 1996.

U.S. Department of Commerce, *Standard Industrial Classification System*, 1997, www.census.gov/epcd/www/sic.html.

U.S. Marine Corps, *Operational Maneuver from the Sea*, 1997, www.usmc.mil.

U.S. Naval Institute, Periscope Database, at http://www.periscope.ucg.com.

Vann, John M. (John Vann Associates Management Consulting), "Government Uses of Activity-Based Costing," *As Easy As ABC*, Issue 29, Summer 1997.

Venkatesan, Ravi, "Strategic Sourcing: To Make or Not to Make," *Harvard Business Review*, November–December 1992, pp. 98–107.

Vernez, Georges, *California's Shrinking Defense Contractors: Effects on Small Suppliers*, Santa Monica, Calif.: RAND, MR-687-OSD, 1996.

Vivar, Jonathan H., and James Reay, *Defense Working Capital Fund: The Application of the Government Corporation and Other Organizational Concepts to the Defense Working Capital Fund (DWCF)*, McLean, Va.: Logistics Management Institute, DR901T1, 1999 (unpublished).

Walters, Jeff, Pat Rattan, Steve Smith, and Doublas Webster (American Management Systems), "ABC at NASA's Lewis Research Center," *As Easy As ABC*, Issue 23, Fall 1996.

Waltz, Edward, *Information Warfare Principles and Operations*, Norwood, Mass.: Artech House, 1998.

Ware, Willis H., *The Cyber-Posture of the National Information Infrastructure*, Santa Monica, Calif.: RAND, MR-976-OSTP, 1998.

Wathen, LT Jason, "COMSUBPAC Future Ideas Initiative," *Undersea Warfare*, Spring 1999, pp. 9–11.

The White House, *A National Security Strategy of Engagement and Enlargement*, Washington, D.C.: U.S. Government Printing Office, 1995.

Why Submarines? N87 and NAVSEA, Arlington, Va., internal report, June 10, 1999.

Wier, Cathie, and the SAM Project Team, "Hewlett-Packard: Asking the Right Questions—Getting the Right Answers," *As Easy As ABC*, Issue 22, Fall 1995, http://www.abctech.com/library/Issue22/22_hp.htm.

Wong, Carolyn, *An Analysis of Army Collaborative Research Opportunities for the Army*, Santa Monica, Calif.: RAND, MR-675-A, 1998.

Wong, Carolyn, Paul Steinberg, Kenneth Horn, et al., "An Approach for Efficiently Managing DOD Research and Development Portfolios," *Acquisition Review*, Fall 1998, Vol. 5, No. 4, pp. 339–356 (Reprinted by RAND, Santa Monica, Calif., RP-791, 1998).

Wright, E. A., "The Bureau of Ships: A Study in Organization," *A.S.N.E. Journal*, February 1959, pp. 7–22.